WE'LL MEET AGAIN

THE OXFORD MUSIC / MEDIA SERIES
Daniel Goldmark, Series Editor

oxford
music/media series

We'll Meet Again: Musical Design in the Films of Stanley Kubrick

Kate McQuiston

OXFORD
UNIVERSITY PRESS

OXFORD
UNIVERSITY PRESS

Oxford University Press is a department of the University of Oxford.
It furthers the University's objective of excellence in research, scholarship,
and education by publishing worldwide.

Oxford   New York
Auckland   Cape Town   Dar es Salaam   Hong Kong   Karachi
Kuala Lumpur   Madrid   Melbourne   Mexico City   Nairobi
New Delhi   Shanghai   Taipei   Toronto

With offices in
Argentina   Austria   Brazil   Chile   Czech Republic   France   Greece
Guatemala   Hungary   Italy   Japan   Poland   Portugal   Singapore
South Korea   Switzerland   Thailand   Turkey   Ukraine   Vietnam

Oxford is a registered trademark of Oxford University Press
in the UK and certain other countries.

Published in the United States of America by
Oxford University Press
198 Madison Avenue, New York, NY 10016

Library of Congress Cataloging-in-Publication Data
McQuiston, Kate.
We'll meet again : musical design in the films of Stanley Kubrick / Kate McQuiston.
pages cm
Includes bibliographical references and index.
ISBN 978-0-19-976765-6 (hardcover : alk. paper) — ISBN 978-0-19-976766-3 (pbk. : alk. paper)
1. Motion picture music—History and criticism.   2. Kubrick, Stanley—Criticism and interpretation.
I. Title.
ML2075.M37 2013
781.5′42—dc23
2013006822

This volume is published with the generous support of the AMS 75 PAYS Endowment of the American
Musicological Society, funded in part by the National Endowment for the Humanities and the Andrew W.
Mellon Foundation.

9 8 7 6 5 4 3 2 1
Printed in the United States of America
on acid-free paper

To my parents,
Henry and Nancy

Contents

Illustrations

Table

Acknowledgments

THIS BOOK OWES greatly to support and encouragement from many sectors. First, I thank the Research Council at the University of Hawaiʻi at Mānoa for a generous grant to conduct research at the Stanley Kubrick Archive, and the Department of Music at Columbia University for supporting my research at the Nelson Riddle Archive. Many thanks to the Kubrick family for establishing the archive and sharing Mr. Kubrick's materials, and especially Jan Harlan, who gave generously of his time and insight. I thank the fine staff at the Stanley Kubrick Archive: Sarah Mahurter, Richard Daniels, Karen Stuckey, and especially Wendy Russell, whose expertise and professionalism made my visits to the archive a real pleasure. I owe much to my research assistant in London, Sam MacAuliffe, whose patience and keen thinking expedited the process of searching the archive for musical clues. I thank Keith Pawlak, curator at the Nelson Riddle Archive at the University of Arizona, for generously giving his time and sharing his knowledge. For their expert help in preparing examples, I am grateful to Caitlin Daly and Jennifer Sutton.

Elaine Sisman, Walter Frisch, Leeman Perkins, and Royal Brown helped this project in the early stages with countless astute insights and guidance. I am grateful to the students of my film-music classes at the University of Hawaiʻi at Mānoa for inspiring me with their thoughtful and enthusiastic discussions. I also owe a great debt to those scholars and commentators represented in the notes and bibliography in this book, without whom this book would not be possible. Special thanks to Krin Gabbard and Christine Leja for reading substantial parts of the manuscript and offering suggestions that improved my thinking and writing throughout this project.

Permission to use digital images of items in the Stanley Kubrick Archive was kindly granted by Jan Harlan. Yale University Press granted permission to use David Levy's translation of Friedrich von Schiller's poem "An die Freude."

For encouragement, suggestions, and thought-provoking conversation, I owe thanks to Jack Sullivan, Julia Heimerdinger, William Rosar, James Wierzbicki, Paul Chihara, and to my colleagues in the Music Department at the University of Hawai'i at Mānoa. I am also grateful to Christine Gengaro for sharing with me her thoughts and her work on music in Kubrick. For expert guidance through the process of composing the manuscript, and for responding cheerfully and helpfully to my many questions, I am very grateful to Norman Hirschy at Oxford University Press, and to series editor Daniel Goldmark for his input and good advice. Thanks also to Christi Stanforth for her keen eye and good ideas during the editing process.

For their encouragement, many thanks to Paul Palcko, John Smalley, Jacob Lieberman, and Lisa Murphy, and my family: Henry and Nancy McQuiston, Bruce McQuiston, and Patricia and Michael Arizin. For giving so freely and often of his support and strength throughout the writing process, I thank my husband, Bryson Jhung.

INTRODUCTION

STANLEY KUBRICK'S OEUVRE traverses a variety of film genres and subjects and is rife with difficult themes and unsympathetic characters. Famous for his painstaking attention to detail, Kubrick stands alongside other distinctive directors of his generation who brought a high level of craftsmanship and artistry to their work. Kubrick's filmmaking has long been admired and studied for its narrative and thematic aspects and visual impact; however, another central element of his style is the unique, often startling encounters between music and the moving image and the use of classical music. A musicological approach to Kubrick's oeuvre is both urgently needed and long overdue in an understanding of these films, whose most compelling features are, I argue, musically conceived and expressed. For Kubrick, a director who habitually compared filmmaking with music and devoted his characteristic scrutiny to music in his work, music is primary and generative to the films' themes, designs, and meanings.

This study is concerned with showing music to be both a consistent, vital force in Kubrick's imagination and an aesthetic foundation for the creation and reception of many of Kubrick's films—and famous moments within them—beginning with *Killer's Kiss* (1955) and ending with *Eyes Wide Shut* (1999). To this end, it provides historical context for music and film-music tropes and film-music analysis, and it draws on recent archival research, including my own in the Stanley Kubrick Archive at the University of the Arts, London, in 2008.

Though it is clear Kubrick knew of music's efficacy in engaging the audience and intensifying the audience's experience—both during and after the experience of watching and listening—commentary on the remarkable musical moments in his films has nevertheless remained marginal, or subsumed within a discussion of visual or thematic elements. In this study, music will be primary in order to privilege the point of audition rather than the point of view. *We'll Meet Again* is organized according to the musical features and techniques that play important roles across Kubrick's films; the book synthesizes these to reveal music-centered conceptions of narrative and corresponding modes of audience experience.

A study of the archive documents with regard to music brings to light not only the attention and time Kubrick devoted to this aspect of his work, but also the collaborative nature of his working process, including his reliance on experts in a variety of fields who would help shape his decisions—facts that strongly suggest an alternative to long-held notions of the director as an isolated creative genius. That Kubrick made all final decisions and made diverse cinematic forces speak with unanimity could create the impression of the singular mastermind, but it would be more accurate to say he marshaled his forces: ideas, images, snippets of music, and the input of his production team. He was an auteur with many good helpers.

The first part maps out the major areas of sonic interest in Kubrick's work, their components, and their impact. Chapter 1 shows how Kubrick distinguishes the soundscape—for example, with speech, voice types, silence and unspoken words, music, and types of sounds—to substantiate his characters and character relationships within their respective settings, to shape audience response to characters, and to construct original aesthetic positions that amplify and embody his larger themes and interests.

Chapter 2 explores the deployment of musical works and styles as settings within and across his films. Music marks various dramatic climates and tracks the progress of characters. The impact of a second major technique, the traversal of the conventional divide between diegetic and nondiegetic music and the related use of voice-over narration, is also explored in this chapter in two case studies: *Lolita* and *A Clockwork Orange*.

Part 2 illuminates ways in which formal and temporal qualities of music—whether inherent or newly derived by virtue of Kubrick's particular use of it—render palpable several otherwise invisible themes and aesthetics. Gradation and symmetry animate the invisible forces in *The Shining*, the subject of chapter 3, in a way Kubrick preferred over other means in much of the film. Music's temporal aspects are uniquely qualified here to suggest states of consciousness and the supernatural and to constitute a register in which continuum is a dominant shape.

Chapter 4 explores numerous steps and facets in Kubrick's working process regarding music in *Barry Lyndon*, with special attention to the slow movement of Franz Schubert's Piano Trio in E-flat, op. 100, a work which Kubrick's producer Jan Harlan recomposed and had re-recorded for the film. Schubert's piece is also considered with relation to its status as a late-style work, a tack that views late style as both an articulation of the composer's cognizance of mortality and an answer to it. This strategy emphasizes the role of Schubert's music in the estrangement and ultimate destruction of the central characters.

Chapter 5 addresses the most cohesive instances of recurring music and image or narrative born in Kubrick's films that exhibit a process I call inscription. Inscription pairs recurring music with action and dialogue in close moment-to-moment relationships; the meaning of both the drama and the music emerges over the course of the film that uses this technique, each appearance of the music a new piece of the puzzle. Inscription is significant for engaging the audience in a game of recognition and ongoing interpretation that would result in a greater sense of investment and involvement. Kubrick would rely on similar mechanisms, though sometimes in isolated moments, in employing existing familiar works from the concert hall.

Part 3 of this book situates Kubrick's use of existing music with respect to music-historical concerns, contemporary reception history, and cinematic tradition. In addition to investigating ways in which musical works shape the films, I draw attention to ways the films have contributed to contemporary trends in understanding the musical works. Chapter 6 brings together historical contexts and connotations for musical works, trends in critical response, and archival evidence of Kubrick's working process relating to *2001: A Space Odyssey*. This chapter discusses this landmark film and its famous adoption of existing music from the concert hall, a choice that represented new aesthetic possibilities for filmmakers and audiences and that continues to generate discourse about creativity, originality, and legality as much as it continues to influence contemporary multimedia.

Chapter 7 takes on the shifting musical dialectics of *A Clockwork Orange* and its implications for interpreting Beethoven and his problematic Ninth Symphony in the twentieth and twenty-first centuries. The film voices the trope of Beethoven violence and at the same time casts doubt on the stability of musical value in an effective parallel construction of the film's central questions about free will, government control, and criminality.

In chapter 8, the films of Max Ophüls provide a framework for understanding prominent stylistic and thematic trends in Kubrick's work. Kubrick's use of waltzes owes in particular to Ophüls, whom Kubrick admired, and speaks to the waltz's broader legacy in cinema as an ambiguous and even dangerous music. Waltzes in both *Paths of Glory* and *Eyes Wide Shut* serve as both homage and answer to Ophüls and draw on the waltz's paradoxes of freedom and restriction, and permission and punishment that lie at the heart of its social history. *Eyes Wide Shut,* Kubrick's most assiduous engagement with Ophüls's world, reveals Kubrick's own preoccupation with those ideals and mores that persist from the late nineteenth century. Kubrick's final film articulates distinctive solutions in Ophülsian terms, including costumes, dancing, waltzes, and traversals of the diegetic border.

The Anatomy of the Kubrick Soundscape

1

LANGUAGE, LYRICS, VOICE, AND SOUND

TO SET THE stage for a discussion of music in Stanley Kubrick's films, this chapter undertakes an exploration of Kubrick's broader aural topography. Examining the entirety of audible sound yields a sense of a filmmaker's tastes for certain sounds, sound qualities, and designs. Furthermore, it is the junctures—and, conversely, gaps—between music, sound, language, and silence that in Kubrick's films prove powerful sites for developing characters, measuring their emotional states and relationships, shaping audience identification, and generating comedy and prompting emotional reactions. Kubrick shapes sound elements with an almost musical sensitivity to affect the audience's response and to set up a dynamic topology in which music is one part—I argue, the most important part. This chapter shows how the sonic and linguistic trends in the films, however, manifest trends in his aural aesthetic and resonate with his broader thematic interests and with broader trends in his methods.

Kubrick's approach to aural elements reflects his particular engagement of the audience in an active, investigative way, as his remark to William Kloman vividly suggests. Kubrick's broad tendency toward fragmentation and suggestion rather than continuity and explication extends to all component parts, including the visual, narrative, and sonic. The different elements of film bear usefully upon each other in analysis, and all must be considered in relation to a larger whole (for example, a song in the context of a particular scene in a longer drama, with attention to a wide range of visual, sonic, and narrative details). Particularly in Kubrick, however, it is the partial, obscure, fragmentary, or misfitting nature of cinematic elements that prompts an imaginative, creative response on the part of the audience. This might help explain why interpretations of his films, especially *2001: A Space Odyssey*, vary so greatly.

The audible soundscape offers a great range of possibilities for shades of meaning by way of volume, placement of sound in the diegesis (i.e., the world of the characters), lyrics sung or implied by their tune, the connotations of a broad musical style, an actor's distinctive voice and delivery, and associations suggested within the film or from a sound's contexts in the real world. Most intriguing are the juxtapositions of these sounds, subtle variations upon them, and conspicuously missing elements, all of which constitute sites of strong audience response.

Language itself is an important theme in Kubrick's films—especially its failure, an idea dramatized in the collisions and misses between the sonic, linguistic, and visual in the sharply contrasting *Dr. Strangelove or: How I Learned to Stop Worrying and Love the Bomb* and *Eyes Wide Shut*. Despite the director's seeming distrust of language across his films, he nevertheless ensured that their foreign-language versions did not omit anything essential by having them re-translated into English, a testament to his concern about linguistic clarity and meaning.[2]

In addition to spoken words, "language" also includes unspoken, omitted, printed, and written words, which have their own force in cinema, particularly in *2001*, *The Shining*, and *Eyes Wide Shut*.[3] Though related and often simultaneous, Kubrick considered aspects of language and voice both separately and in combination.

Actors and Voices

Kubrick has acknowledged in interviews the importance of actors who, after all, speak and sometimes sing words, and a thoroughgoing interest with words—spoken and otherwise—pervades his films. Kubrick's famous assertion that *2001* is a non-verbal experience is a poignant reminder of this film's—and several of his others'—visual impact and laconic stretches. Though Kubrick's work favors the subjective, symbolic, and metaphorical over the expository and declamatory mechanisms of the classic Hollywood style, words take on a symbolic vitality in his films, in large part due to his actors; Kubrick observes:

> Writers tend to approach the creation of drama too much in terms of words, failing to realize that the greatest force they have is the mood and feeling they can produce in the audience through the actor. They tend to see the actor grudgingly as someone likely to ruin what they have written rather than seeing that the actor is in every sense their medium.[4]

Here Kubrick readily admits his reliance on the talents actors bring to a film, a fact that is apparent on watching the films but is sometimes forgotten because of the persistent misconception of Kubrick as an autonomous entity rather than the collaborative craftsman he was. His identification of actors as a medium reflects his pragmatic attitude, which would result in the honing of compelling performances, and spontaneous problem solving during production, such as asking Malcolm McDowell to sing a song for his role as Alex—he chose "Singin' in the Rain"—in *A Clockwork Orange*. Kubrick's working process during production (and preproduction and postproduction) attended to all media, including the visual, linguistic, cinematic, and musical, and even the people themselves.

Acting performances can be as memorable for their sheer sound as for their words. Douglas Rain's even, edgeless elocution for the voice of HAL in *2001* and the rapid-fire inanities of *Dr. Strangelove*'s colorful cast are ready examples. The diatribes of Sergeant Hartman (R. Lee Ermey) in *Full Metal Jacket* (see Figure 1.1), which Sidney Pollack calls "operatic,"[5] and Alex's strange words and delectable, measured, and sometimes theatrical delivery in *A Clockwork Orange* stand out among the vocal performances in the films and are frequently imitated and referenced in popular culture.

Kubrick's preference of broad themes over individual characters in his films comes out most clearly in some of his early work, particularly *The Killing* and *Dr. Strangelove*, in which the dictates of pulp fiction and satire alike benefit from caricature and an emphasis on character *types* onscreen—both lend to the crafting of memorable voices and vocal performances. For Kubrick, words were perhaps a function more of actors than of scripts.

Words are playful in *Lolita*, *A Clockwork Orange*, and *Full Metal Jacket*. They comically fail in *Dr. Strangelove*. They have the ability to conceal even as they purport

FIGURE 1.1 R. Lee Ermey's vocal performances make an impact with tone and words in *Full Metal Jacket*. Warner Bros. Pictures, 1987.

FIGURE 1.2 Bill's conversation with Ziegler in *Eyes Wide Shut* is a
lengthy display of the distrust of language that permeates Kubrick's
films. Warner Bros. Pictures, 1999.

to communicate, in the double entendres of *Lolita* and throughout *Eyes Wide Shut*.
This final film goes the furthest, in its restrained way, in showing that sound and
meaning cannot be trusted to coincide and that the gaps between words and meaning constitute a rich site of response on the part of the listener. Taking such an
approach to words in cinema risks the clarity of the plot, and its success is difficult
to ensure, as divided responses to the film attest; despite all its words and the lack
of remarkable action, the final dialogue between Ziegler (Sidney Pollack) and Bill
(Tom Cruise) fails to disclose much about what Bill has seen and what has happened
to the other characters (see Figure 1.2). The failure of this cinematic dialogue to elucidate meaning is precisely the point.[6]

The failure of communication in moments of great pressure is a thematic pillar
in Kubrick's work, and these moments often come with a feeling of comeuppance
or karmic fulfillment. Fay (Coleen Gray) is unable to hail a taxi at the airport at the
end of *The Killing*, and Bill fails in kind while attempting to evade the stalker in
Eyes Wide Shut. Tortured by the violence onscreen as a result of the Ludovico treatment, Alex's entreaties for the doctors to stop is patiently heard, then unheeded.
Dr. Strangelove is an extended exercise in ineffectual communication whose conse-
quence is nothing less than the destruction of the world.

Even when sound and word deliver facts, like the replayed words of the racetrack
commentator and radio report about the heist in *The Killing*, they do not guarantee
the robbers' success. Kubrick takes advantage of the nonlinear timeline of the story
in this virtuosic early film to get the most out of spoken words. Though the commentator's words are clear, they are fast and excited. Upon multiple repetitions, the

FIGURE 1.3 The exaggerated, expressionistic qualities of more extreme characters include idiosyncrasies of speech. Nicky slurs his words through clenched teeth in *The Killing*. MGM, 1956.

effect becomes oneiric yet overwhelming; the spectator knows what he will say and can hear the sounds of the words as such—a procession of incessant, punchy syllables. To amplify the effect, the commentator repeats phrases in real time as well, such as the announcement about Red Lightning's spill in the seventh race, and Nicky (Timothy Carey) repeats the words "Red Lightning," in conversation with the parking lot attendant (see Figure 1.3). That Kubrick replays Maurice's line "Hey! How about some service, you stupid looking Irish pig?" participates in the strategic repetition of *The Killing* but also speaks to Kubrick's taste for colorful insults—both in *The Killing* and throughout his films. Charlotte reads aloud Humbert's demeaning assessments of her in *Lolita*, insults fly in the War Room in *Dr. Strangelove*, and Alex lobs oddly poetic jabs at Billy Boy and his gang. Bullingdon's (Leon Vitali) litany of damning complaints about Redmond (Ryan O'Neal), addressed to his mother in the music-room confrontation in *Barry Lyndon* are doubly insulting for their declaration in front of an important audience and for not being addressed to Redmond himself, who is present. Even HAL's matter-of-fact assessment of "human error" reads unmistakably as a slight against his human companions. At the top of the heap, Hartman's role in *Full Metal Jacket* is a veritable tapestry of insults. Consistent with other elements of Kubrick's filmmaking, these insults mix amusement with discomfort.

Kubrick attends to the sounds of spoken words as much as to the words themselves—indeed, if the audience were to fail to perceive his words as insulting, Bullingdon's crisp, measured, superior-toned elocution would do the job. Kubrick's encouragement to his actors to improvise their lines likely contributed to such charged performances. Regarding script memorization, Kubrick offered a musical comparison: "It's like a concert musician. He can't be reading the music…He could play it just as well just reading from the page, but he is not going to give it what he has got. The problem that I have had sometimes is the actors don't spend enough time the night before learning [the script]."[7] Kubrick's attention to voices extended to the foreign-language dubbed releases of his films, as evidenced in a letter from François Truffaut, in which he suggests French actors with suitable vocal qualities for Kubrick's films.[8]

The Killing's rich array of voices includes George Peatty (Elisha Cook Jr.) and his wife Sherry (Marie Windsor); George's voice is pleading and whispery, while Sherry's is a weary, sarcastic drone. Kubrick cast Kola Kwariani, wrestler and chess player, for the role of Maurice, a heavy hired by Johnny to start a fight; physically, Kwariani suits the role, but it is his cryptic and almost unintelligible philosophical statements, couched in a remarkable thick accent and low melodious voice, that memorably define his character. Timothy Carey's fuzzy, lock-jawed enunciation and flashing teeth capture his edgy eccentricity.

Each character in this film has a vocal signature, and Johnny's (Sterling Hayden) is a fast-talking monotone. The ultimate moment of defeat in *The Killing* therefore comes not in the flurry of dollars on the airplane runway, but in Johnny's uncertain and muttered final line—barely inflected as a question, and barely audible: "Ehh, what's the difference?" Character interplay along the lines of vocality attains a polished, taut sheen and even faster pace in *Dr. Strangelove*.

For *Dr. Strangelove*, the array of voices in their defining moments include President Muffley's (Peter Sellers) attempts to placate Prime Minister Kissov over the phone, attempts made more hilarious by the grave silence of those sitting with Muffley at the table. Vocal virtuosity plays out in belabored points of conversation between the ensemble cast: the blustering bravado of Buck Turgidson (George C. Scott), the absurd counterpoint between the nervous Colonel Mandrake (Sellers) and the stern-faced, conspiracy-addled General Ripper (Sterling Hayden), and Mandrake's fumbling attempts to place a call to the president, foiled further by Colonel Bat Guano (Keenan Wynn), who represents another sideline into communications failure. There is also the cackling drawl of Major Kong (Slim Pickens) and his screams as he famously rides the bomb to its target, and the peculiar German caricature, Dr. Strangelove (Sellers again), who seems unable to refrain from accenting certain words as he says them, not unlike the writer Mr. Alexander in the later scenes of *A Clockwork Orange*. Sellers's Dr. Strangelove also has an antecedent in his role of Dr. Zempf in *Lolita*.

Miss Scott (Tracy Reed), Turgidson's secretary and girlfriend, takes a call for Turgidson in a scene made all the more silly by her relation of highly detailed and lengthy pieces of information from the caller and her translation back to the caller of Turgidson's responses as she stands all the while in a bikini, as though posing for a photo shoot. Turgidson's growl "Bull! Tell him to do it himself!" becomes Miss Scott's placatory, smooth "Freddy, the General asks if you could possibly try again yourself."

In *Lolita*, a domestic comedy of errors of Humbert's life with Charlotte plays out in the duet of James Mason's dulcet tones and the shrill vivacity of Shelley Winters. Lolita, perhaps as part of Kubrick's efforts to not sexualize her for the censors' sake, seems vocally unmarked by comparison. Vocal inflection was carefully crafted and directed in Humbert's voice-overs in *Lolita*, as evidenced in the notes taken during recording sessions. The twenty-seven pages of transcriptions of James Mason's narration (much of it not in the film or in any screenplay or script for the film that I have been able to find) include notes, interspersed between the takes, calling for various adjustments, many geared toward maintaining the audience's sympathy for Humbert. Regarding Mason's reading of an introductory poem written by Humbert in a sanatorium, for example, notes read, "Stanley interrupts asking for it to be read more apologetically." Comments on other pages include "should be more cynical" (with regard to the line "The wedding was a quiet affair"), "slower," "more awesome and astonished," and—of particular importance for *Lolita*, "more innuendo."[9]

The question of voice would be perhaps most important for HAL, a character represented almost exclusively by voice. Would-be HALs included Alistaire Cooke and Martin Balsam, who read for the part but was deemed too emotional. Kubrick set assistant Benn Reyes to the task of finding the right actor, and expressly not a narrator, to supply the voice. He wrote, "I would describe the quality as being sincere, intelligent, disarming, the intelligent friend next door, the Winston Hibler/ Walt Disney approach. The voice is neither patronizing, nor is it intimidating, nor is it pompous, overly dramatic, or actorish. Despite this, it is interesting. Enough said, see what you can do."[10] Even Kubrick's US lawyer, Louis Blau, was among those making suggestions, which included Richard Basehart, Jose Ferrer, Van Heflin, Walter Pigeon, and Jason Robards.[11] In Douglas Rain, who had experience both as an actor and a narrator, Kubrick found what he was looking for: "I have found a narrator...I think he's perfect, he's got just the right amount of the Winston Hibler, the intelligent friend next door quality, with a great deal of sincerity, and yet, I think, an arresting quality."[12]

Kubrick's most intense explorations of spoken language come in *A Clockwork Orange* and *Full Metal Jacket*, which, although its dialogue is as dynamic and immaculately delivered as in the other films, walks a frightening line between caricature and realism. Patrick Magee's performance as Mr. Alexander, the writer, reads primarily through the madness of his facial expressions, and stilted, uneven speech that threatens to become a strained shout, as when he asks Alex, "*FOOD*...alright?" Both Hartman in *Full Metal Jacket* and Alex in *A Clockwork Orange* are virtuosic speakers—Hartman in his rapid-fire pace and abusive yet comical lines, and Alex with his confident, lilting dialect and strange words. The strangeness of the language in both cases leaves the spectator at a bit of a distance, which might be welcome considering the characters' violent antagonism.

In crucial moments, subtleties of tone stand out in bold relief; the deadly realization that HAL has no intention of opening the pod bay doors creeps over the audience through his chillingly calm tones.[13] Lord Bullingdon's formal speech and chiseled enunciation stands out against the brutal, fumbling business of the last duel with Barry. In other moments, the voice is remarkable for blending in. Murray Melvin's vocal performance as Reverend Runt in *Barry Lyndon* is a fine example; his oration for Bryan's funeral procession has a musical quality, not only because Handel's music accompanies the scene in measured step, but also because he draws the sound of each syllable out on steady tones, in a nearly musical manner, and the declamation has a musiclike sense of measure.

Voices at the Extremes

Just as important as the sound of voices are places where vocal sound is missing. Marianne Stone stands out memorably as Clare Quilty's (Peter Sellers) antithetical silent, dark partner in several scenes in *Lolita*. The masked, robed figures at the orgy in *Eyes Wide Shut* and the unspeaking man who hands Bill an envelope through the bars of the mansion gates are rendered powerful for not speaking. The missing components of communication point to the unknown and, in the case of *Eyes Wide Shut*, enact and exaggerate the film's theme of the muddled dead ends and other inhibitors of human understanding.

Perhaps the most powerful symbol of communication in Kubrick is the telephone, however, it fails to guarantee clear communication, and induces anxiety by reminding the speaker of the physical remoteness of the person on the other end of the line.[14] The telephone is a locus of crucial yet fumbling and halting conversations in *Dr. Strangelove*—especially since the audience infers much of the dialogue and its comedic effects. Anxiety dominates telephony in *Lolita*. Humbert lies on the bed in the foreground as Charlotte talks to Lolita (Sue Lyon), who is calling from summer camp. The telephone is, like Charlotte herself, another rude intervention between him and Lolita; by the time Charlotte hands him the phone to speak with Lolita, he is too late and hears only a dial tone. The telephone continues to threaten Humbert, for example when he sees Lolita talking to an unknown person on the other end of the line. The telephone is a strong symbol of Lolita's independence and relationships with invisible others who threaten to take her away from Humbert. The telephone persecutes Humbert again when Quilty calls in the middle of the night to make vague threats. Only the call to Humbert (by a watching neighbor?) about Charlotte's death seems to work in his favor, yet even this caller's words are initially doubted and his identity unknown.

The telephone and other devices of personal announcement are powerful forces in curtailing character interactions in *Eyes Wide Shut*. A call comes as Alice (Nicole Kidman) finishes telling Bill of her desire for another man, preempting further conversation, and taking him away to visit the daughter of a deceased patient. Bill and Marion's conversation is likewise cut short by Carl's appearance, announced by the doorbell. Nick's phone rings, bringing him the address and password for his party, interrupting his conversation with Bill but opening the door to Bill's adventures. Bill's phone rings when he is with Domino, interrupting yet again. When Bill tries to telephone Marion, Carl answers instead.

Eyes Wide Shut trades in inscrutability through seemingly plain language. Phrases, even when they are clearly spoken and repeated, gain nothing in clarity. The theme of failed communication carries through the film's many scenes in which Bill's actions are interrupted by sounds of telephones, a doorbell, even a shouting voice. This series of intrusions articulates the chain of Freudian substitutions and denials of various characters in place of Bill's wife, Alice. Sound becomes the primary tool that carves Freudian lack into the story, and the uncanny timing and persistent participation of everyday sounds creates the impression that forces are somehow stacked against Bill.

Since the invention of the telephone, films have attested to the importance of telephony in the cinematic imagination, showing it to have an irresistible and often dangerous magic. Several of Alfred Hitchcock's films depend on the telephone for crucial scenes, as do more recent films including *The Matrix* and *Inception*, the latter bringing back the romance of the rotary dial in a sort of dream machine. In both *Inception* and *The Matrix*, the telephone is a portal to a parallel reality. David Lynch captures telephonic anxiety concisely in *Lost Highway* in the scene Fred (Bill Pullman) meets the Mystery Man (Robert Blake) at Andy's party. The Mystery Man tells Fred that he is at his house right now and offers Fred a telephone to call his house to prove it. The Mystery Man's voice indeed answers, an acousmatic double of the man who stands in front of Fred. And beyond the sheer startle of a telephone ringing, phones have played important roles in horror films such as *The Ring* and the *Scream* franchise.

The stillness of the human characters—and of course of the aspatiality of HAL in *2001*—plays into a portrayal of HAL's perceptive, cognitive, and emotional capacity—in other words, the nature of his apparent consciousness. Though he may be the most emotional and human-behaving character onboard the *Discovery*, the impossibility of interpreting HAL's dialogue with certainty, and his invisibility beyond a red light in a dark circle, renders him fairly inscrutable, and he takes on the disturbing air of a too-quiet genius. When he finally acts, his murder of the hibernating astronauts plays out in changes on the vital signs monitors, accompanied by different sounds, and words that appear in illuminated display. That we see nothing else happening poignantly renders HAL's elusive nature; at the same time, Kubrick displaces the locus of action to the words of the status monitors. Kubrick would again stoke dread with the unheeded warnings of stillness and virtual silence on the part of Private Pyle (Vincent D'Onofrio) in *Full Metal Jacket*, and he would introduce speech by Dr. Strangelove late in the eponymous drama with particular flair, as though playing the winning card at the critical moment.

At the other extreme, sonic overlay comes sparingly in moments of high tension and conflict. Vocally noisy moments in *Lolita* articulate the film's psychological temperature. Lolita's and Humbert's screaming fight comes at a moment of high tension and conflict. Charlotte forces out a greeting over the music to Quilty at the dance, in stark contrast to the absolute silence of Vivian Darkbloom (Marianne Stone), who literally retreats out of the frame (see Figure 1.4). If HAL was fashioned as a voice of knowledge (if not reason) for much of *2001*, his recitation of old speeches and singing of songs sound out his demise. Likewise, the babbling of Quilty, the sheer volume of Charlotte, and the verbal assaults of Hartman suggest the ills of excess.

FIGURE 1.4 Charlotte Haze and the silent Vivian Darkbloom are vocal opposites in *Lolita*. Charlotte overloads the soundtrack with her voice in her most desperate moments. MGM, 1962.

As important as voice and acting are in Kubrick, the dialogue generally resists quotability—his images and even his uses of music have been quoted far more often. The memorability of the lines "You can't fight in here! This is the War Room!" and "Mein Führer, I can walk!" rests in irony in the first case, and Sellers's grotesque, idiosyncratic performance in the second. But memorable though they may be, they are tough to slip into everyday conversation or to adopt as catch phrases. On the other hand, lines like "Go ahead, make my day" have doubtless enhanced countless mock confrontations. There is nothing in Kubrick quite like "I'm mad as hell and I'm not going to take this anymore," "Hasta la vista, baby," "You talkin' to me?" or "I coulda been a contender." What these lines all have in common, in addition to their circulation in popular culture, are their roots in the strong identities of the characters that speak them. Kubrick's relative lack of such lines is perfectly in keeping with his tendency to sublimate characters—even a character as intense as Hartman—in the service of the larger themes and dramatic mechanisms.

Douglas Rain's placid "I'm sorry Dave, I'm afraid I can't do that," "My mind is going. I can feel it," and his entreaties for Dave to stop are stunning in effect, but Dave's request to open the pod bay doors is probably the most quoted line from *2001*, and its remarkability greatly depends on its context. The dialogue in *A Clockwork Orange*, almost all of which originated in Anthony Burgess's novel, is too foreign and difficult for English speakers for it to become absorbed into pop culture, rendering the film's linguistic landscape distinctive, especially in Malcolm McDowell's delivery, but beyond the reach of ready quotation.[15]

R. Lee Ermey's lines for the part of Sergeant Hartman in *Full Metal Jacket*, many of which Ermey invented and improvised based on his experiences as a staff sergeant in the US Marine Corps, are quoted often by fans of the film but are too expletive-laden or elaborately obscene for mainstream absorption. Ermey, however, has continued to use and develop the character type he played in *Full Metal Jacket*, and previously (though more gently) in *The Boys in Company C* for many hard-edged military and other authority roles in a variety of films and other contexts, such as the voice of the Sergeant in Pixar's *Toy Story* films, Colonel Hapablap in an episode of *The Simpsons*, and voice work in video games, and his popular recordings for answering machines. His turn in *Full Metal Jacket* is largely responsible for his audible presence in popular culture.

It is probably Papillon Soo Soo's lines in the same film that have gotten the most actual air play; her prostitute's enticements to the young marines, "Me so horny" and "Me love you long time," were taken from the film and sampled repeatedly by 2 Live Crew for their controversial 1989 hit "Me So Horny," which itself spawned several parodies. Soo Soo's lines were also spoken by the character Eric Cartman of television's animated pop-culture repository *South Park* in a context that pays more explicit homage to *Full Metal Jacket*; as a result of head trauma, Cartman believes he is a Vietnamese prostitute.[16]

Prompted to recall a favorite line from a Kubrick film, a spectator may point to "All work and no play make Jack a dull boy," an invention of the film which is never spoken. For Kubrick, written words leave a strong mark, perhaps all the stronger for going unsaid. The experiential differences between hearing dialogue and seeing text become especially apparent when one mode replaces the other. In the case of written text, which can assume a factual gravity in comparison to spoken words, meaning arises without the help of vocal inflection or volume, but visual characteristics of the text figure importantly in meaning and impact.

Words in the Mise en Scène

Text in Kubrick falls in line with cinematic conventions, for example by appearing in opening and closing credits, announcing the sections in epic films, and supplying intertitles that name time and place in *2001*; Kubrick was familiar with the use of text in conjunction with images because of his background in photojournalism. Kubrick well understood the power of the caption and, in the case of his films, the way in which words in the mise en scène can assume an especially uncanny guise by acting like captions *within* the world of the film. In this duality, these visible words somewhat resemble diegetic music; they operate for the benefit of the spectator in supplying a believable part of the scenery and atmosphere, yet never seem genuinely incidental. Amplifying the instructive "to-be-read-ness" of captions, the text in the screen evokes a feeling of urgency and import by reminding the viewer of the now absent hand that wrote or left it. Spoken dialogue is of its moment, whereas we may wonder about the origin of a written message and how long it has been there, seemingly waiting to be seen. The message on a sign, "Watch your step," is a realistic object in the stairway leading from the dance hall in *Killer's Kiss*, but it comments too on the dangers the characters face (see Figure 1.5).

The scrolling disclaimer about the unlikelihood of the events depicted in the film at the start of *Dr. Strangelove* has an ominous gravity nonetheless. The absence of sound leaves the viewer with no sense of inflection or tone, yet it hangs over Kubrick's film like a dubious promise. The film's later shot of Mandrake's doodles and puzzling over the three-letter recall code typify Kubrick's interest in written items—some of the writing appears to be in Kubrick's hand, as do the handwritten addresses in *The Killing*.[17] Finally, there is the stubborn light on the word "CLOSED" on the bomb door indicator in *Dr. Strangelove* and the words "EXPLOSIVE BOLTS," which would prefigure a similar crisis with the same words in *2001*. These words take on a

FIGURE 1.5 Visible words in the mise en scène carry multiple meanings, usually warnings. Gloria notices the men, but not the sign or the danger, in *Killer's Kiss*. MGM, 1955.

poetic vitality in *2001* because of the distortion of the letters on the round space pod—it looks as though a force were pushing from inside, adding a kinetic dimension to the violence implied in the message. The curve of the pod and fisheye lens are the material reasons for this effect, but a physical, visceral threat nonetheless animates the words as they appear here. In case the audience does not catch it the first time, Kubrick does all he can to compel them to read the message when the door and its letters slide past the eye and into place.

The audience detects HAL's murder of the hibernating astronauts only in the signs that report status: "COMPUTER MALFUNCTION," "LIFE FUNCTIONS CRITICAL," "LIFE FUNCTIONS TERMINATED." These appear with the flat factuality of any other update on systems operations (reflecting HAL's perspective on human life); the last of these gleams rhythmically in the quiet of the spaceship. The alarming appearance and meaning of these words, and several words seen in *The Shining* leap into the viewer's mind like a sudden, psychic intrusion. The words' dominance of the frame especially drive this impression home, as though HAL and the forces of the Overlook Hotel were willing their messages of death into the minds of anyone unfortunate enough to see them. As for the intertitles in *The Shining*, Michel Chion notes their propulsion toward the crux of this drama of few words in which every word matters.[18]

Printed words and the act of writing continue exerting strong forces and exuding a sense of the uncanny in *Eyes Wide Shut*. Nick's decisive act of writing the password, "FIDELIO," clears the way for Bill to enter the mansion, but it also foretells Bill's salvation by Mandy by connection to the plot of Beethoven's opera, in which Florestan is saved by his wife, Leonore, who has disguised herself as a prison guard to infiltrate the prison and set him free. The relevance of this denouement to Kubrick's film is clear, but so is the opera's preoccupation with extolling the virtue of a faithful wife, a tenet seemingly threatened by Alice's capacity for fantasy and extramarital desire, though it remains unfulfilled.

When the spectator sees written words that are unseen by characters, the effect is amplified. After Bill's bizarre adventures in *Eyes Wide Shut*, he reads the inner pages of a newspaper in a café while the cover page, which has escaped his attention, displays, "LUCKY TO BE ALIVE." By showing this to the audience, Kubrick fosters the suspicion of ruse or conspiracy with which Bill has struggled for much of the story. Even the too-large letters of the headline seem to announce their artificiality. Bill's failure to immediately perceive the words—and especially the fact that the audience must wait for him to find them—acts out in miniature his general failure to comprehend despite such things as the long, painstaking conversation he has with Ziegler (Sidney Pollack).

In his novel *The Shining*, Stephen King makes expressive and imaginative use of italics and parentheses, capital letters, and even excessive punctuation alongside his more conventional prose. In Kubrick's treatment, visible words assume a connection to the supernatural forces that lurk in the Overlook Hotel: Jack's (Jack Nicholson) typewriter; Danny scrawling "REDRUM" with Wendy's lipstick. In an early scene important for establishing the role of visible words, Dick Hallorann (Scatman Crothers) leads Wendy and Danny (Shelley Duvall and Danny Lloyd) past many signs in capital letters that, as Michel Chion has observed in similar cases, seem to "shout out their silent message to be read."[19] Inordinately huge lettering emanates warning on the sliding door to the kitchen, which the characters do not see: "FIRE EXIT MUST BE KEPT CLEAR." In the course of his study of adaptation in *The Shining*, Greg Jenkins offers an observation that helps explain why the visible words take on an extra charge: "The minimalist give-and-take of the film…comes to nurture a terrible apprehension that much is going unsaid; the want of words speaks as loudly as the words themselves, and creates suspense."[20] I would add that the words also contribute greatly to the impression that their settings have a sense of consciousness.

Who Is the Listener?

Though the analyses and interpretations in this book reflect a listener knowledgeable about music and music history, audience members (and the readers of this book) represent a great range of listening behaviors and aptitudes. An attentive film audience is influenced by music in film on some level, even if unconsciously. Music guides and shapes emotional responses and influences the listener's physiological responses, for example by increasing tension and anxiety with dissonant chords and an accelerating tempo. While some audience members will consider music's role to be "mood music" and nothing more, others will find the music beautiful or powerful or evocative of a time and place. A number of musical conventions are well in place in Western narrative film to inform an understanding of character, gravity, setting, and genre. Audiences who are familiar with these musical conventions and styles bring, to varying degrees, previously formed associations and knowledge to bear upon the experience of hearing music in a new context. The same applies in the case of a particular piece of music that a filmmaker borrows for a film; the audience is apt to understand the music's new context in light of old ones.

This book writes from the perspective of an attentive and knowledgeable listener—this is the listener I believe gets the most out of Kubrick's films in the same way those who have attended to visual symbolism, matters of history in relation to Kubrick's plots, accuracy of detail, adaptation, and other aspects, have revealed new insights into Kubrick's films and how they work. Some of the musical moments this book describes might register with audiences on first viewing, such as Ligeti's commanding music in *Eyes Wide Shut* or the potentially familiar popular tunes from the '60s in *Full Metal Jacket*. But many moments discussed in these pages are the type that emerge after many viewings and listenings and involve attention to local detail and large-scale design, immediate contexts, and more distant ones.

Kubrick had in mind a repeat audience for his films—a fact that points to music's importance as a site of experience not just upon first encounter, but over time. As the audience gains familiarity with a film, they likely begin to notice music more. They may recognize the effects of sonic characteristics on the mood or pace of a scene. They may distinguish pieces of music from each other, even if they cannot identify them by name, and notice when they return. They may notice whether music is diegetic or nondiegetic. This study considers all of these aspects and includes broader historical and contextual considerations. Kubrick's great care in musical matters and his ideal of a repeat audience practically demand such a strategy.

In addition to drawing to various degrees on knowledge of movie-music conventions while taking in a film, each listener brings unique associations, conditions, and preconditions to her experience with regard to music (as to other aspects of film). Filmmakers cannot prevent listeners' subjective responses—responses that may have nothing to do with the director's intentions. Directors cannot guard against personal associations (indeed, they may hope for them), any more than they can elicit unanimous audience response. One cannot argue against the subjective association that makes a piece of music meaningful or emotionally effective in a particular way for an individual listener, nor do the interpretations in this study attempt to refute or replace these responses. Rather, this study offers context and musical description that might illuminate the reasons why and how musical characteristics tend to suggest the interpretations or responses that they do. The recurring threads of response to the *Blue Danube* in *2001: A Space Odyssey*, to take one example, call for illumination.

The analyses and commentary in these pages expose what I argue are the most resonant interpretations of the music (both original and more or less familiar) with respect to Kubrick's particular uses and settings of it and to the music's sonic and contextual aspects. While this book draws on music history, context, and detailed analyses of form and other elements to make sense of Kubrick's work, most filmgoers do not have this background. On the other hand, motivated audience members can develop listening acuity and learn about music history and form in ways that will illuminate their experiences both of Kubrick's work and film in general. Alongside the studies that look again and again at Kubrick's films, this one advocates listening again and again. The processes of learning about the music and listening again with new knowledge opens possibilities for connecting the eye, the ear, and the mind that will bring audiences a fuller understanding and experience of Kubrick's work and equip them with new strategies for listening to film.

Recognizing Songs and Styles

Aside from the broad categories of mood and signification, existing music that appears in a film can import all manner of connotations, available to the audience depending on their familiarity with it. The topics of existing music and musical familiarity in Kubrick appear throughout this study and are of particular importance in part 3 of this book. Existing musical works can bring in shared cultural ideas, and subjective memories and associations, which can potentially distract the audience (by design or accidentally) from the illusory world on the screen. The more the audience knows about a piece of music, whether a song, classical instrumental work, or any other music, the more they will have at their disposal by which to understand its role in the film. Yet even when the words or history are unknown to the listener, the style or idiom of the music still can make a great impact.

Arden Clar and Norman Gimbel's sentimental song "Once" provides a running thread and moody backdrop in *Killer's Kiss* that keeps the love story central and ties the film (along with strong visual elements) to influential forerunners, specifically Otto Preminger's *Laura* (1944) and Elia Kazan's *On the Waterfront* (1954). The song appears in instrumental arrangement by Gerald Fried on the record player in the dance hall where Gloria (Irene Kane) works, and in several different instrumental versions as underscore in many scenes. The audience is unlikely to know the words, as it apparently was never recorded with a vocalist, but the Kubrick Archive includes a letter with the lyrics, suggesting Kubrick's familiarity with them.[21] The sound of the song without the lyrics—about recollections of love and the desire to have the love again—may have been sufficiently yearning and nostalgic in Kubrick's estimation to convey the mood of a "Love Theme," as the tune is called on a spotting sheet and in the opening credits.

The song's ubiquity throughout the film—in various forms, moods, and registers—is but one clue that Kubrick may have had Preminger's *Laura* and David Raksin's title song in mind.[22] The film's debt and homage to Elia Kazan's *On the Waterfront* (1954) is much clearer, visually, narratively, and musically—particularly the resemblance of Eva Marie Saint and Irene Kane and male leads that are or were fighters. In Kazan's film, one of Leonard Bernstein's more hopeful-sounding themes transforms into the diegetic music in the bar where Terry and Edie dance. In the same way, Fried's arrangement of "Once" provides nondiegetic and diegetic music; it plays repeatedly (endlessly?) at the dance hall, adding to its stultifying atmosphere.

The ending scene of *Paths of Glory* makes a bold statement about the power of music, and specifically song. Christiane Harlan (as Susanne Christian and later married to the director) as the young German woman is made to sing a song for the French troops, and she quickly thinks of "Der treue Husar." Though the soldiers cannot understand the words she sings, the simplicity of the melody and her vulnerability gradually move them to tears, and they begin to hum the tune with her. A non-German-speaking audience is well positioned to identify with both the limits of verbal communication and song's power to transcend it, felt by the singer and the listeners in the scene. German-speaking audiences would be familiar with the song, adding to a sense of relevance and personal identification with the singer and her audience in the tavern. This scene of vulnerable, amateur singing is one of several aspects of *Paths of Glory* that pay homage to the filmmaking of Max Ophüls, which Kubrick admired (see chapter 8).

Music in film in general works with the images and drama to generate mood and meaning, for example by commenting directly on them in a way that seems to emphasize or corroborate the action, by providing ironic or contradictory meanings to the action, or by generating a sense of memory or presentiment, just to name a few. Songs too work along these lines, but lyrics, either sung or implied by their tune, inflect drama in more specific ways by virtue of language. Tom Hall's "Hello Vietnam," sung by Johnny Wright during the opening credits for *Full Metal Jacket,* is an unusually straightforward example in Kubrick in that it names the destination of most of the young men the audience sees in this succession of shots and faithfully renders a scene of preparation for leaving for Vietnam. The superficial cheer of the voices' twangy quality and harmonies work against the apprehensive looks on the boys' faces, a reminder that they do not know what awaits them.

The choice of a song whose subject matches that of a scene, however, can destroy the audience's suspension of disbelief by seeming like *too* much of a coincidence and calling attention to the film as such, especially if the song plays as source music. Kubrick's song choices evidence the same sensitivity to mood and sound as he had to actors' performances, but lyrics constitute a rich layer of semantic meaning, and in many instances the lyrics refer to dramatic elements. In *Paths of Glory*, the Frenchmen's humming along with the German tune symbolizes their desire to transcend what divides them from the music and connect with each other in a way that needs no words. The repetitive, stepwise characteristics of the song mark it as folk music and stir memories and associations—both for the soldiers in the scene as for the audience—connected to such music from each listener's past.

Kubrick clearly hopes his audience recognizes at least some specific songs he includes, and he relies upon listeners to fill in the blanks to make the films personally affecting. The first very clear instance of this comes in the pairing of "Try a Little Tenderness" (Jimmy Campbell, Reg Connelly, and Harry Woods) with the opening credits in *Dr. Strangelove*, which shows one plane refueling another in midair (see Figure 1.6). Even a listener who recognizes only the sentimental tone of the music but does not know its identity or lyrics will appreciate Kubrick's take on this activity. "Try a Little Tenderness" is a standard, which means any number of

FIGURE 1.6 An instrumental version of the familiar song "Try a Little Tenderness" helps audiences infer a tender moment at the start of *Dr. Strangelove or: How I Learned to Stop Worrying and Love the Bomb.* Columbia Pictures, 1964.

musical styles could appear here, but its Muzak-like string sheen renders it an aural would-be Viagra; the slow clunkiness of the planes, though they float, corroborates this impression. The sequence speaks volumes about Kubrick's belief in music's power not only to convey mood but to make an effective joke whose inner workings are multiple and complex. The joke has an economy of means on the surface but relies on the resources of the audience—recognition, memory, and realization of the scene's meaning with respect to the song.

An entirely different effect occurs at the end, where even if the song, "We'll Meet Again," by Ross Parker and Hughie Charles, were unknown to the spectator, the context—in other words, the juxtaposition of melodic song with images of destruc-tion—would convey the sense, or affect. It is clear that Vera Lynn's assurance of meeting again will not come to pass. Her singing is full-voiced, heartfelt, and, in this context, likely to produce a mixture of humor for the irony and twinges of discom-fort and even pain for those in the audience, perhaps especially those with personal memories associated with the song and its heyday during the Second World War. The song spoke directly to the separation and reunion of soldiers and their loved ones. For those in the audience who associate Lynn's version of the song with the anxieties and losses of World War II, concepts of war will by virtue of the song take on a frightening new dimension that rides in on the coattails of subjective, emo-tional response. Part of the power here relies on this familiarity with the song, but for young audiences, Kubrick would touch a new nerve. The effect is ironic but more important, bitter and chilling; any sense of entertainment quickly dissolves, despite Lynn's persistence during this final statement.

Kubrick knew the last scene of *Dr. Strangelove* and its song would create a sensa-tion. In a letter to Robert Ferguson of Columbia Pictures on September 23, 1963, Kubrick states his intention to use "When Johnny Comes Marching Home Again" and then includes a tantalizing description and telling question: "We are also using a version of Vera Lynn's 'We'll Meet Again' at the end of the film in a very unusual way. What specifically should we do, and who should we liaise with in order to see that these tunes are given the maximum chance of exploitation in records?"[23] Kubrick was concerned also that the song should rhyme in translation for the film's foreign-language versions too, and documents in the archive suggest that such foreign-language versions of the song were recorded. In another kind of song trans-lation, Jean-Louis Trintignant, the French voice of HAL, sings "Au clair de la lune" instead of "Daisy Bell (A Bicycle Built for Two)."[24]

Laurie Johnson's fanfare and treatment of "When Johnny Comes Marching Home Again" plays the most in *Dr. Strangelove*, as accompaniment to Major Kong's plane as it flies ever closer to its target inside Russian territory. The tune has taken on a variety of lyrics since its composition in the early nineteenth century but is best known as an American Civil War song about a soldier's heroic homecoming and celebrations after war. As in "We'll Meet Again," the song's optimistic picture of the future will not come to pass, but it serves as an apt leitmotif for Major Kong and his men, which was Kubrick's stated intention.[25]

As with "Try a Little Tenderness" and "Once," words were left out of—and, indeed, were not original to—Bob Harris's title track for *Lolita*. Sammy Cahn added very sentimental lyrics and renamed the piece "Never Before—Never Again." Adopting Cahn's words—highly similar in imagery and emotion to Clar's words for "Once," for which one could imagine a full-throated crooner's rendition—would have overwhelmed the music's innocuous, flourishy emotionalism, which prompts James Naremore to align it with "an old-fashioned woman's melodrama."[26] The instrumental version keeps the film's opening, and its image of a man painting the toenails on a feminine foot, from disclosing much about the content or tenor of the drama to come.

Nabokov's novel names several sentimental pop songs of the late 1940s and early 1950s, such as Sammy Kaye's "Laughing on the Outside," Eddie Fisher's "My Heart Cries for You," and Patti Page's "Tennessee Waltz." In Nabokov's version of the screenplay dated spring 1960, there are general references to music coming from radios, or from adjacent rooms, but in the July 1960 version, labeled "Corrected rough original draft," the music comes into sharper focus: for example, "Sounds of the television in the living room where Lolita has turned it on. A DEEP VOICE SINGS This is the girl I once adored…" Part of Nabokov's motivation for including such musical moments, aside from dramatic, could have been to promote his son Dmitri's singing career. The author's wife, Vera Nabokov, writes to Kubrick on December 4, 1960, and reminds him of this in the penultimate paragraph:

> My husband hopes you have not forgotten that he would very much like you to give our son a chance to sing the "Lolita" song. We think he is well qualified to do it since he has recently been engaged to record popular music in Italy. If you could send the music and describe as closely as possible what you would like to have, he could make a trial recording in Milan and send it to you for approval.[27]

It is *Lolita* producer James B. Harris who responds on December 21, 1960, writing, "We have not forgotten about your son and his singing. However, at this stage we are not sure how such a thing would fit in with the film. As you know, the music is the last phase of the production and will not come into being until May of next year. I therefore think it is still premature to get into this at this time."[28]

That Harris and not Kubrick responded in this unique case may suggest that Kubrick wanted to avoid any conflict over artistic differences, especially in light of

Nabokov's substantial contributions to the script and screenplay material to date. It is even possible that Kubrick avoided using the popular songs in the source novel to downplay the presence of sung music in the film and the likelihood that Nabokov would push for an opportunity for his son. It is also possible that Kubrick was not able to get the rights for the songs or was not interested in pursuing these, though he would do so in his subsequent films. Nelson Riddle's "Lolita Ya Ya," the only sung music in *Lolita*, is like shorthand for pop music; it brilliantly evokes "popular music" without the need to secure the rights of an existing song; indeed, existing songs would potentially import specific meanings that would work against this ersatz pop sound and concept. It also meant avoiding the potentially complicated question—in light of Nabokov's personal interest—of showcasing a distinctive singer.

Kubrick's sense of Riddle's "Lolita Ya Ya" is implied a letter to James B. Harris on November 8, 1963, in which he considers having the tune playing on Mandrake's radio in *Dr. Strangelove*. Kubrick describes what seems to be a rough equivalent and alternative to the song (and likely what is used in the film): "I can buy very cheap stock music here for about £20 already recorded which has, as you might imagine, a slight sound of nothing to it."[29] It is the strength of the idiom of "Lolita Ya Ya"— and perhaps its audaciously eponymous lyrics—that has given it a certain staying power and that carves a satiric perspective into the film's opening half. The addition of more semantically meaningful lyrics would compromise its agility, its replayability, and rob it of its impressionistic sense of parody. What Nelson Riddle comes up with here and with the "Shelley Winters Cha Cha" are on the surface the practical equivalent of musical props; they are not (yet) recognizable songs, but very much like them.[30] Their lack of identity in the real world freed them up to play like symbols with other elements in the film.

Kubrick attended recording sessions of Riddle's original music to make sure it would work with his dramatic concepts. Vincent LoBrutto describes Kubrick's sensitivity to musical issues:

> During the recording of a love theme composed by Nelson Riddle, Harris and Kubrick were concerned to hear that the piece had been written in a minor key. The musicians were asked to stop playing as Harris and Kubrick talked to Riddle. They wanted a straightforward romantic sound and not any form of dissonance, which might disparage Humbert in the audience's eyes.[31]

This description evidences the same kind of attention Kubrick devoted to tuning James Mason's voice-over performances, and for the very same purpose. It further reveals Kubrick's recognition of the importance of music in establishing characters.

The "Shelley Winters Cha Cha" and "Lolita Ya Ya," a rhyming set, also represent opposing musical territories in the film's soundtrack. Charlotte fails in her efforts to use music—particularly dance music—to get closer to male characters in two scenes. At the school dance, Charlotte cuts in to dance with Quilty, cutting in on the soundtrack with her loud greetings at the same time. Quilty is clearly nonplussed about the intrusion. Later, the single scene featuring the cha-cha would be part of Charlotte's effort to seduce Humbert; it is notably playing on a record that she puts on the turntable. The contrivance of her music is clearly ineffective next to the effortless and unmotivated "Lolita Ya Ya," which seems to perfume the air and is diegetic only when Lolita plays it on her radio in the garden—the moment Humbert first sees her. Charlotte's cha-cha is also interrupted by Lolita, who has come home early from the party. Lolita watches motionless, then asks, with a mixture of incredulity and mockery, "Cha cha cha?" Her question puts an end to Humbert's and Charlotte's awkward embrace, much to Charlotte's disappointment and Humbert's relief.

In both these scenes, interruption and its impact on the drama gauges relationships and power among the characters. Charlotte forces herself physically, vocally, and with the aid of music in both cases, with no real success, while Lolita is carefree, comfortable, and virtually silent in scenes with music and maintains decisive power in the story. On the heels of the cha-cha, Charlotte launches into the loudest tirade against her daughter, who has gone to bed but can presumably hear from upstairs. The more she rages, the more Humbert's responses dwindle in substance and volume until it is clear that he is not even listening. Charlotte interrupts a scene of Humbert admiring Lolita as she gyrates in her hula hoop, disrupting Humbert's reverie and "Lolita Ya Ya," which represents it. When Lolita finally seduces Humbert, she speaks to him, but in a whisper the audience is not allowed to hear; Millich the costumer's daughter in *Eyes Wide Shut* similarly whispers something to Bill that the audience never knows.

Musical idiom is especially important in *Lolita*, where pressure from censors prompted Kubrick to seek other ways of conveying meaning. In addition to standing for a pop song (before it truly became one), "Lolita Ya Ya" served the film well for what it *wasn't*. It plays in pure tone against the serious mood of John and Jean in the bathtub scene. John and Jean have come to console Humbert in the wake of Charlotte's death. The most ironic moment comes when Jean encourages him to think of Lolita, which the music indicates he clearly is already doing, though not in terms of the guardianship Jean has in mind. What's more, the bathtub scene plays like a modern descendant of the ensemble scenes of Italian comic opera in which one by one—and seemingly too many—characters appear and join in. This impression is especially salient when the doorbell rings, John matter-of-factly says, "I'll get it," and the key ascends by a half step.[32]

Kubrick deploys various guises of self-reference across the films, but he may have also hoped that using "Lolita Ya Ya" in *Dr. Strangelove* would lead to more soundtrack sales for the earlier but still recent film. In a letter to Robert Ferguson of Columbia Pictures of September 23, 1963, Kubrick expresses interest in using "Johnny Comes Marching Home Again," which "will be orchestrated by Malcolm Arnold ('Bridge on the River Kwai'), and which might prove to be a similar hit. We are going to use it in the aircraft after establishing the theme as Slim Pickens."[33] Kubrick has a clear view of both the dramatic function and lucrative potential of such a song. Kubrick's penchant for self-reference took musical form in *A Clockwork Orange*, albeit in an ironically visual way, with the soundtrack album for *2001* appearing among the records in the shop. The reference also serves as a handy if surreal double commercial for *2001* and its "original" soundtrack album.

Classical and modern concert works famously appear in *2001*, though Roger Caras, first unit publicist at the time, pressed Kubrick to use a song by citing contemporary examples of successful sales of the soundtrack from *Dr. Zhivago* and of songs from *Bridge on the River Kwai*, *The Inn of the Sixth Happiness*, *The High and the Mighty*, and *High Noon*. In spite of Caras's strong examples, Kubrick's musical choices for the film would not include any pop singles for the Billboard charts.

Evidence in the Kubrick Archive suggests that music represented a long-term area of searching and listening—a task Kubrick seems to have enjoyed. For *The Shining*, Kubrick devised ideas for music based on Stephen King's references to music in some cases, and more freely in others. Kubrick worked from a version of King's novel that quoted lyrics from a number of popular songs. This scene in the novel describes simultaneous realities at the hotel's bar. King sets up the snippets of lyrics from several songs with the sentence "The jukebox, pouring out its drinkers' melodies, each one overlapping the other in time."[34] The lyrics themselves, two to four lines in each case, come from Jimmy McHugh and Dorothy Fields's "I Can't Give You Anything but Love"; Elton John's "Daniel," which resonates with the story's Danny and images of planes; "Green Door" by Bob Davie and Marvin Moore (King presumably meant Jim Lowe's rendition, as Shakin' Stevens's postdates the novel); and Vincent Rose's "Avalon." This stylistic and anachronistic array suggests variety with a slight emphasis on the 1920s.

King's use of these songs during the scene of Jack's realization of what's happening around him evidently excited Kubrick, who wrote much in the margins on this page, including "Are the actual 'words' for this page the best way to do it?" "Surrealism? Escher? Can this be expressed?" Kubrick seems to know all the songs the sparse lyrics come from, except for "Green Door," next to which he writes, "Ref. S. King. What song is this." So much of this undated version of King's novel from which Kubrick was working remains little changed in the published version that it seems possible that the omission of the song lyrics indicates King could not obtain, or did not wish to pay for, the rights to use them. Kubrick preserved the pop music presence in *The Shining* only in the songs he chose from the 1920s and 1930s, none of which are referenced in any version of King's novel.

Inane Music

Throughout his oeuvre, Kubrick plays games with musico-stylistic relativity, juxtaposing classical works, original score, and popular music. Imagine substituting Bob Harris's title track for *Lolita* with Riddle's "Lolita Ya Ya," either during the opening credits, or at the end of the film, and the difference of meaning and tone it would create. Kubrick's ear for tone may be easiest to detect in what we might call inane music; these are songs that are remarkable for their simplistic musical setting, words, and juvenile or goofy style. These songs often come on the heels of serious music, or silence, or stand in grating contrast to the feeling of the action or a character's point of view. From Kubrick's likening of "Lolita Ya Ya" to stock music with "a slight sound of nothing to it," this song and the music on Mandrake's radio qualify as some of Kubrick's earliest inane music.

In *A Clockwork Orange*, Alex returns home to find his parents sitting with Joe, their lodger whom they treat like a son, and listening to Erika Eigen's light-hearted folk-style song "I Wanna Marry a Lighthouse Keeper." For Alex, the easy musical style adds insult to the injury of betrayal. Sharing an activity with this newcomer is all the more painful for Alex because of the fact that they are *listening to music together*—an activity highly important to Alex that he enjoys alone. Eigen's song's unabashed pop-folk style sounds trivial next to Beethoven's and Rossini's works on the soundtrack.

But Kubrick is interested in shifting perspective on musical style, so in *A Clockwork Orange*, any gravity Rossini's Overture to *La gazza ladra* attains by comparison with Eigen fades and becomes inane when defined once again in comparison to Beethoven's Ninth Symphony—particularly in light of Alex's strong reverence for Beethoven. Rossini's famous crescendos, here and in several others of his operatic overtures, have long been enjoyed for the impression they create of things building gradually until they reach a frenetic, explosive, or exultant moment, or a moment that is all of these.

The cartoon music, likely familiar to many American viewers, that drifts in the background in *The Shining* does nothing to lighten the mood of the drama; its mix of exaggerated violent and childish sounds emphasizes Danny's quiet isolation from a normal childhood and hints at the violence that lies ahead. A similar failure to lighten mood haunts the songs "Woolly Bully" and "Surfin' Bird" and the "Mickey

Mouse Club" song, all at the inane end of the musical spectrum. If anyone felt Kubrick disrespected those who died in the war—on either side—his adoption of such "regressive" music of the time may be his way of pointing out that the disrespect had already happened. This is not to say all Kubrick had to do was put the songs in uncomfortable or violent scenes. The Trashmen's lone, monotonous hit, "Surfin' Bird," for example, appears just as a young American soldier grins after shooting down two Vietnamese men. Kubrick attenuates the awkward fit of the song with disturbing images of ruined, body-strewn buildings captured in a too-slow tracking shot. The empty sophomoric threats and idle hours of Joker (Matthew Modine) and his companions are set against "Woolly Bully," a musically simplistic and repetitive tune with meaningless, rhyming lyrics. Kubrick's contexts have a way of bringing out the worst in the music of the time or making these songs seem part of a much larger American bad idea.

Kubrick hints at his concern over foreign audience reception of the songs in an interview for *Le Monde* in which he worries that non-American audiences will not fully understand the meaning of the "Mickey Mouse Club" song—something that seems for Kubrick to help convey the very wrongness at the heart of sending boys to war:

> Unfortunately in France the Mickey Mouse Club doesn't have the same meaning that it does in English, in America, but you know in America every child sits in front of his television set singing that song and what I wanted to suggest in that was that these boys are only just a few years past sitting in front of their TV set, children singing Mickey Mouse... When you realize that an 18 year old boy is only 6 or 7 years away from being a child.[35]

The novelty pop songs in *Full Metal Jacket* go a long way in establishing a particular kind of tone for the film—a psychological climate. Kubrick had considered well-known music from operas, but ultimately chose popular tunes; a note for the opening haircut scene includes "Callas, Verismo opera, late 19th century." One may speculate about whether Oliver Stone's *Platoon*, released six months before *Full Metal Jacket*, effected a change in musical direction. Emotionally moving music in the haircut scene might have fostered sympathy and pathos—something "Hello Vietnam" also accomplishes—but would have mythified the characters somewhat as well. Stone's famous use of a string orchestra arrangement of Samuel Barber's *Adagio* in his film temporarily removes the violent scenes and their significance in the drama from its setting. Kubrick spared the audience any such catharsis, distance, or ennoblement—deaths are messy, ugly moments, most of which play out amid the sounds of war; the perspective is hard and bitter. The kitschiness of the songs throughout Kubrick's film leaves a bad taste by pointing up the contradictions of American culture during the years of the United States' most intense involvement in Vietnam. What better way to convey the insanity of war than with these senseless songs? The film's most musically forthright moment comes with the closing song, the Rolling Stones' "Paint It, Black," an anthem of hopelessness and hardening.

The tone and presence of popular songs in *Eyes Wide Shut* stays subtle with low volume and logical context (the believability of "I Want a Boy for Christmas" in the coffee shop during the holiday season, for example) so that idiom takes a back seat to lyrical interpretation—a game in keeping with the play of symbols in the background of Bill's adventures.

Beginnings, Endings, and beyond the Theater

While Kubrick knew the potential for songs to become popular and lucrative in connection with the films, Kubrick's taste—sometimes regarding music suggested by others—guided the final music selections for his films. Main titles have long been a coveted spot for establishing a film's mood and genre and for showcasing music as such, whether or not selling the song is a going concern. It is Kubrick's choices for credits, however, that carry the most weight of each film's message and that reveal Kubrick's attitude about the subject matter.

For *Eyes Wide Shut*, the beginning and ending music—Shostakovich's Waltz no. 2 from his *Suite for Variety Stage Orchestra*—are the same so that the point of entry and exit are understood to be an apparently unchanged reality though the experience of the characters and their revelations balance ironically against this, much in the manner of the framing music in *Grand Hotel* (see chapter 6). Kubrick can in this way leave the audience with a sense of difference but also the insignificance of the characters in the larger scheme of the universe, by presenting the same music after significant drama has occurred. He takes a similar tack at the end of *A Clockwork Orange* in that Gene Kelly's rendition of "Singin' in the Rain," the version the audience likely knew before they came to see *A Clockwork Orange*, will appear much changed after the events of the story, though still unmistakably Kelly's in its notes, its vocal quality, and every other audible way. As a parting song from a challenging film, "Singin' in the Rain" assumes a false congeniality.

The *Blue Danube* waltzes do not frame the entirety of *2001* but do, when they appear with the closing credits, recall one delightful portion of it. It is as though Kubrick were sending the audience home with a snapshot, or a souvenir from the gift shop, rather than attempting to encapsulate the entirety of this massive cinematic undertaking in a musical finale. By placing the waltzes at the end, he takes a step back and asks the audience merely to marvel at what they have seen and heard. A snapshot literally is our parting gift at the end of *The Shining*, again, complete with the film's most congenial musical idiom. Other than "We'll Meet Again," "Midnight, the Stars and You," and "Paint It, Black," Kubrick's parting music is not top-forty material. The fact that these three songs were not contemporary for theatergoers would have diluted their potential for immediate commercial success in connection with their films. Setting the right tone in the parting music was clearly top priority for Kubrick, as was designing films that would stand the test of time. Perhaps "Paint It, Black" was close enough to the Vietnam conflict to seem contemporary in the long term, and certainly contemporaneous with the years of the conflict's bitter aftertaste; its placement over the end credits gives it a retrospective cast.

In addition to the music *in* his movie *Barry Lyndon*, Kubrick tackled music from another angle by prescribing that a record be played in the theater between portions of the film. Kubrick included a letter addressed to the film projectionist outlining a litany of tasks that entailed attention to lighting and specific instructions for playing an accompanying record (see Figure 1.7).[36] The body of the letter to the projectionist opens:

> An infinite amount of care was given to the look of "Barry Lyndon"; the photography, the sets, the costumes; and in the careful color grading and overall lab quality of the prints, and the soundtrack—all of this work is now in your hands, and your attention to sharp focus, good sound, and the careful handling of the film will make this effort worthwhile.[37]

A numbered list of details follows about changeover times for reels, running lengths of sections, aspect ratio, and lambert parameters. The item most relevant to the present subject is number 10, which reads:

> Hopefully, you have been supplied with an LP record or tape of the film score.
>
> a) Please use Side 1 for the pre-film music.
> b) During the intermission, play Side 2, starting with Band 2. You can play this for as long as you want, to the end of the record.
> c) If you play music after the film, repeat what you did on the intermission.

Curious here is the "Please" of item *a*, the imperative of item *b*, and the conditional item *c*. Kubrick was probably aware that after the film had fully ended (including all the credits), much of the audience would have already exited the theater, so the after-film music naturally gets lowest priority. His more intense call for prefilm

STANLEY KUBRICK
~ "RYAN O'NEAL ~ "MARISA BERENSON"

December 8th, 1975

Dear Projectionist:

        An infinite amount of care was given to the look of "Barry Lyndon"; the photography, the sets, the costumes; and in the careful color grading and overall lab quality of the prints, and the soundtrack – all of this work is now in your hands, and your attention to sharp focus, good sound, and the careful handling of the film will make this effort worthwhile.

        Please also note the following:

1.   REEL 3B – CHANGEOVER DOTS ERROR:

     a)   The first changeover dots at the end of Reel 3B are correct.
     b)   The last changeover dots at the end of Reel 3B are not correct. They are 1 ft. 9 frames early.
     c)   We have scribed an "X" on to the print on the correct frames for the last changeover dots.
     d)   Please use the "X" as your last changeover cue, instead of the dots.

2.   "Barry Lyndon" was photographed in 1-1:66 aspect ratio. Please be sure you project it at this ratio, and in no event at less than 1-1:75.

3.   There should be no less than 15 foot lamberts of light on the screen, and no more than 18.

4.   "Barry Lyndon" runs for three hours and four minutes (184 minutes).

5.   The first half of the film runs for one hour and forty-two minutes (102 minutes)

6.   There is an intermission 6 minutes into Reel Six.

7.   After the intermission card, there are fourteen feet of black frame, followed by an academy leader to enable you to line up Part Two.

8.   Part Two starts in Reel 6, with music, over a black screen, and after nine feet, the Part Two title fades in.

9.   Part Two runs for one hour and twenty-two minutes (82 minutes).

10.   Hopefully, you have been supplied with an LP record or a tape of the film score

     a)   Please use Side 1 for the pre-film music.
     b)   During the intermission, play Side 2, starting with Band 2. You can play this for as long as you want, to the end of the record.
     c)   If you play music after the film, repeat what you did on the intermission.

Yours sincerely,

Stanley Kubrick

FIGURE I.7 Kubrick conveys his instructions to the projectionist of *Barry Lyndon* regarding music that should play before and after the film, as well as between the two halves; sustaining a mood and extending the affect of the films was a major role for music throughout his oeuvre. Stanley Kubrick Archive, used with permission.

music and for music between the sections shows both his interest both in sustaining the feeling of the film even as the audience gets up to walk around or have a cigarette.

So concerned was Kubrick about the execution of these guidelines that he sent scouts to check the exhibition conditions at theaters. Ray Lovejoy reported from Stockholm, "The pre-performance music was identifiably Barry Lyndon—and also fed through to the foyer, where the audience mingled enjoying a last cigarette, etc., prior to taking their seats. This was repeated in concept during the intermission, there being a no smoking ban in the cinema."[38]

Sound

Despite the budget constraints in Kubrick's early feature-length films, in which Kubrick edited sound himself, sound is generally well chosen and deployed, showing the young director's sensitivity to the overall soundscape. As his career continued, he approached sound according to generic and dramatic needs and, in some cases, in tandem with music. Kubrick's concern with good sound, and his enthusiasm for Dolby in particular, inspired him to write a letter in 1975 to be sent to Mel Brooks, Mike Nichols, Irwin Allen, Roman Polanski, William Friedkin, George Lucas, and Woody Allen. It read: "If you have heard Dolby Stereo Optical Sound, and like it, would you be willing to write a short blurb for Dolby to use in a trade ad, the purpose of which is to help convince theater owners they should equip themselves to run it."[39]

In *Killer's Kiss*, Kubrick layered sound in scenes set in Rapallo's office. Rapallo (Frank Silvera) watches the boxing match on television, which itself presents a sonic double layer of the referee's words in the far background, and the television commentator's words at the same time. Music from the dance hall fills in another background layer. This use of sound parallels the conflicts to come and captures Rapallo's mounting frustration. The sounds of boats at the nearby piers in scenes at the warehouse in *Killer's Kiss* again point to the influence of Elia Kazan's *On the Waterfront*, released the year prior.

For George and Sherry's kitchen conversation in *The Killing*, a high ticking sound—more like a timer than a clock—persists conspicuously in the background to underline the fact that it is indeed the day of the robbery and heightens the sense of pressure George feels when Sherry manipulates him into admitting that the robbery will take place that day. Once the guns come out in the track locker room, Kubrick includes some exaggerated echoing locker door sounds that could themselves pass for gunshots.

Sound in *The Shining*, more than any other Kubrick film, lingers on the edges of music; music is not always evident as music but could be mistaken for sound effects, and vice versa. The ambiguity of music and sound was germane in conception, as evidenced in the track labels on several demo albums sent to Kubrick by Wendy Carlos and Rachel Elkind, who had contributed original music and synthesized classics for *A Clockwork Orange*. Sound's importance is announced in the initial scenes in the Overlook Hotel, in which characters are isolated and paired with distinctive and evocatively constructed sounds: Wendy's clattering tea trolley, Danny's bigwheel, and Jack's tennis ball and, later, his typewriter. Like the cartoons playing on the television, the lives of the main characters seem to be made of sound effects.

Carlos's and Elkind's records of music and sound effects for *The Shining* are treasures both in terms of their sheer beauty as contemporary music—little of which can be heard elsewhere, not even on Carlos's *Rediscovering Lost Scores* records (2005)—and for clues they disclose about how the soundtrack was conceptualized, particularly Carlos's and Elkind's contributions.[40] The records, numbered but not dated, trace changes and decisions in Kubrick's musical design as the soundtrack took shape and, further, support a fluid conception of soundscape rather than discrete layers of music and sound effects. Carlos sent Kubrick at least eight records of sound and music. Among the first six records, all of which bear handwritten labels, some are organized by instrumentation, like one with the label "Vocal, Piano, Mallet & Mixed Solos," and some according to purpose for the film, such as one labeled "Wind & Textures." These records reflect the starting point from which the direction for the various cues and cue types would be narrowed down, eliminated, and revised. The flexibility in the labeling applies to the tracks as well. Carlos provided description of the musical means, for example for a track called "Ghosties": "solos, soprano & alto, sighs, siren-songs, musical & very vocal-like, moves in waves (longish cue)." On the other hand are track labels that describe the effect: "Two large heavy crashes," "Vocal 'Dzzrrhhr's.'"

Notes in the margins, some clearly in Kubrick's hand, speak to identifying tracks that are sufficiently scary, that sound telepathic, or that seem suitable for a particular scene. Next to the track "Vocal Glissandi," someone has written, "Rm 237 Jack enters." Next to other cues are notes like "Ligeti like" (referring to composer György Ligeti), and next to several tracks are a bracket and the judgment "all too not scary." Kubrick seems to be looking for affect rather than effect when he hears something perhaps too realistic: "Doesn't sound telepathic, sounds like wind." In other instances, though, he obviously wants recognizable sounds, such as the heartbeat on these records that appears in several scenes.

The two records with typed labels that probably represent the end of Carlos's and Elkind's involvement still include two versions of several cues, for example,

"Thought Clusters, Danny's 1st Esp." and different tracks of "Heartbeat Passage." The most recent (highest numbered) of the records also includes the track "DC-10 @ 8AM," the sound for the airplane. It is intriguing and unusual that these are creations of the composer, not sounds borrowed from stock recordings or made by a sound specialist.[41] These details strongly suggest that a conception of sonic continuity informed Carlos's work—a conception readily evident in much of the sound and music across the film.

The heartbeat participates in several scenes where the other audible sounds seem to float free of labels like "music" or "sound effects." This fluidity and the film's paucity of dialogue prompt the spectator to hear differently, and perhaps work harder to find and even create meaning in sound as well. Greg Jenkins's writing bears this out when he describes a coyote heard in an early scene as "a grim aubade."[42] The choice of a musical term for the sound of an animal exposes the particular availability of sound and music in *The Shining* to interpretation. Carlos's expanded palette freely allowed sounds both more and less recognizable as music, an approach that reflects the overall sound of *The Shining* and its demands on the audience—more than in any other Kubrick film—to listen in a broad, imaginative way.

Alexander Walker has described Kubrick's approach to language in *2001* as "suppressing the directness of the spoken word," but in contriving other paths for his ideas, such as some taken up in the present chapter, I would contend that Kubrick comes up with a broader system of interchangeable parts that rather complicates the impulse of utterance and impacts the spectator in more subtle and engaging ways. It is this fluid region of sound, music, speech, and word that carries and shapes emotional impact and explains how music exerts a particularly strong force, depending on context, recollection within and beyond the film, sonic quality, and other local conditions.

2

DRAWING LINES AND CROSSING BORDERS

Musical Climates, the Diegetic-Nondiegetic Border,

and Voice-Over Narration

EXISTING MUSIC AND original music alike may in the context of film evoke connotations through style and generate meaning in juxtaposition; for example, the measure of the badness of a villain's theme may result from a comparison with, say, the purity and valor of the hero's. Just as lyrics specify meaning, as I show in chapter 1, instrumental music likewise carries stylistic and historical connotations that present opportunities to deepen and complicate meaning; the juxtaposition of Beethoven's and Rossini's music in *A Clockwork Orange* offers a rich example (see chapter 7). The effectiveness of the integration of music in film, and the complexity it can lend, therefore depends on some level of familiarity. But how is the audience to know which audiovisual relationships are important, or how much attention to pay to the music in each scene? I offer that we can discern foundational elements of Kubrick's musical strategies by considering the following questions: Where is the music coming from? (Is it diegetic or nondiegetic?) And how does the music relate to the whole?

Often, it is Kubrick's source material that inspires his musical selections and "location," though not always in a straightforward way, like "Hello Vietnam" at the beginning of *Full Metal Jacket*. Kubrick follows Anthony Burgess's general approach in *A Clockwork Orange* of integrating music in a prominent way into the plot (it would be difficult to omit the music and retain the substance and spirit of the story). Kubrick took inventive directions in *The Shining*, inspired by both the horror film genre and the details of King's story.

Beyond selecting music in response to source material, Kubrick further incorporates music in ways that draw attention to—and sometimes arouse suspicion of—the division between diegetic and nondiegetic music. Music often serves to animate large themes in the story or effect a particular audience response. Kubrick conjures a variety of effects and results by problematizing the line between diegetic and nondiegetic. In *Lolita*, it serves to foster sympathy for and identification with the protagonist and delineate a hierarchy of characters. In *A Clockwork Orange*, it also fosters a sense of bond with the protagonist, reinforces character hierarchy, and it enacts on the audience the same process Alex undergoes during the crucial Ludovico treatment. For *Eyes Wide Shut*, the line between diegetic and nondiegetic symbolizes the invasion of the fantastic realm into the realistic.

The question of location has implications for voice-over narration as well. When the audience hears a character's voice in the normal way and also hears that voice in voice-over narration, the effect is not simply one of potential ambiguity. Voice-over narration can endow a character with a sense of agency and therefore power in the story; *Lolita* and *A Clockwork Orange* exemplify the common use of voice-over narration for conveying the story as a character's recollection. This chapter closely inspects transition and slippage between diegetic and nondiegetic sound—in other words, moments the audience can realize that the music is now on *their* side of the screen, so to speak. In each case, this intrepid shift of sound or music intensifies a sense of the audience's connectedness to the films' respective protagonists and their worlds. These moments contribute to an illusion that the character's reach extends into the audience's world. Kubrick forges a distinctive technique in deploying characters' voices and other sound and music across the line between "here" and "there."

Getting a sense of Kubrick's approaches to music also means listening for when and how music plays and for how long, listening for recurrence, and listening to the music as such: what kind of music is it, and what is the mood? These questions drive much of the discussion in the following chapters. Even those with only a cursory acquaintance with Kubrick's films will know that music is essential and that it participates in slightly different ways each time.

Kubrick relied on actors' performances to convey mood (see chapter 1) and, in turn, relied on music played on set to help his actors feel and show the appropriate emotion. The music was therefore part of the conception of affect and would usually be replaced with a different piece of music of a matching emotional hue in the finished film. Kubrick played intense passages from Stravinsky's *Rite of Spring*, for example, to generate a high level of panic and anxiety in Danny Lloyd's final run in the hedge maze in *The Shining*, a scene accompanied by Krzysztof Penderecki's music in the film. For *Eyes Wide Shut*, Tom Cruise and Nicole Kidman listened to albums by Tracy Chapman, music that might inspire quiet, melancholy introspection.

By virtue of generating and sustaining moods, music organizes films into sections somewhat like climates in that they are distinct enough to recognize and identify, but also fluid and responsive to local currents in the drama. Musical climates help define a film's emotional landscape and navigate a film's larger themes and the progress of its characters. Regardless of whatever other musical techniques may be at work, Kubrick seems to reserve certain pieces of music to delineate broad emotional climates in his dramas and signal broad changes therein. Music can shift the psychological terrain even if the physical or geographic location does not change. So deeply did Kubrick trust in the formative and transformative power of music to govern the overall climate that he would replay scenes, or repeat aspects of the drama nearly verbatim, with different music, as in Humbert's pursuit of Quilty at the beginning and again at the end of *Lolita*, set in two different musical and emotional worlds. Likewise, in *Barry Lyndon*, Redmond relates to his son, Bryan, the story of taking the fort, but in two different musical climates. Conversely, music's return, under changing circumstances, has the power to turn Alex the antagonist into Alex the victim in *A Clockwork Orange*.

Ever trying to affect his audience and do what was possible to reach them, Kubrick could deploy music that was diegetic (sounding in the world of the characters and audible to them and to the audience), or nondiegetic (audible only to the audience), but he could also design musical moments to confuse, compromise, and even *cross* the divide between the audience's aural world and that of the characters.

The Contributions of Gerald Fried

The sound of Kubrick's early efforts is the sound of Gerald Fried, composer of original music for *Day of the Fight* (1951), *Fear and Desire* (1953), *Killer's Kiss* (1955), *The Killing* (1956), and *Paths of Glory* (1957). Fried's flexible and eclectic musical style drew upon his training at the Juilliard School and knowledge of the concert repertoire, his taste for jazz and percussion, and his work in a mambo band, all of which are evident in his original scores. Fried also attended many movies in the time he worked with Kubrick to form a sense of what worked well.

Fried's music enjoys unusual privilege in the amount of airplay it gets in *Killer's Kiss* and *The Killing*, though in the former, his efforts are mainly devoted to arrangements of Arden Clar and Norman Gimbel's song "Once," which serves as Davey (Jamie Smith) and Gloria's love theme and the dance hall music. Casting popular music—and specifically Latin pop music—as the enemy was not uncommon in Hollywood at this time; Henry Mancini's music for Orson Welles's *Touch of Evil* (1958) is an outstanding example. The connection between a Latin pop idiom and urban violence was further codified in pop culture in Jerome Robbins and Robert Wise's film adaptation of Leonard Bernstein's *West Side Story* (1961). Fried's Latin idiom in *Killer's Kiss* and *The Killing* appears most in scenes of violence, or with violent characters, like Gloria's boss, Rapallo, and his henchmen. Though Fried's stylistic diversity is typical of original film scores of the time, the score for *Killer's Kiss* nevertheless represents the first of Kubrick's films whose music falls into two types in a contrasting pair.

The excessive repetition of "Once" in *Killer's Kiss*—both as underscore and diegetic music—recalls David Raksin's "Laura" for Otto Preminger's film of the same name. As in *Laura*, "Once" appears in many forms and orchestrations throughout *Killer's Kiss*, sounding the persistent longing of the characters—Davey and Rapallo for Gloria, Gloria for Davey, and the longing of the nameless men who come to the dance hall.

Fried's taut, colorful score for *The Killing*, a more tableaux-like, varied, and quickly changing design, shifts intrepidly between dissonant, moody noir music, and original music in jazz and Latin styles. Fried exacts a splendid array of timbres, particularly from small combinations of woodwind and brass instruments, and he sets up contrasting jazz and Latin styles to help discern the film's dark locales—a bar, Val's apartment, Sherry and George's place—and gauge its jumpy temperature. Fried overlays duple and triple rhythms, for example in the main title, to generate chaotic intensity. The same music returns when Johnny walks through the crowded racetrack lobby to carry out his part of the robbery plan.

All of Fried's scores for Kubrick show a deft hand for percussion writing. For *The Killing*, he sets a march tempo and reduces the ensemble to percussion for the scene of Johnny preparing for the robbery in the locker room. The steady pace evokes the metaphoric ticking of the clock and sustains tension as the audience wonders if he will get away with it. Fried's taste for deep, resonant percussion—including bass drum, tuned timpani, and other instruments—also accompanies tense scenes in *Killer's Kiss* and *Paths of Glory*.

Fried's style stands out for its sensitivity to other colors in the orchestra as well. His choices of instrumentation and mood push toward burlesque and the operatic language of Alban Berg. His style also shares techniques with such composers as Béla Bartók, Igor Stravinsky, and Gustav Holst—especially for the characterization of George and Sherry and for violent scenes in *The Killing*. By capturing the individual dramatic moments, and in sounds that bring out earthy, seamy, and psychological aspects, Fried's musical climate for *The Killing* consists in a collage of portraits that counterbalances the film's bold narrative disarray. The lead-up to the fight scene in the mannequin warehouse in *Killer's Kiss* is similarly remarkable; Fried unleashes a variety of spectral orchestral sounds that heightens the scene's grotesque surrealism.

In *Paths of Glory*, Fried's role would be the most restrained in terms of sound qualities and, significantly, in amount of original material and air time. As in *Dr. Strangelove*, a great deal of emphasis falls on spoken word and on the broader verbal arena in which ideals clash. Fried's role is primarily arranging existing music— the *Marseillaise* for the main title, and a military march-style arrangement of the final song, "Der treue Husar." Fried crafts tense, pointillistic percussion music for the night patrol scene, culminating in a searing cymbal roll on the shot of Lejeune lying dead. Fried's percussion music here shares the sparse, moody aesthetic of the percussive elements of Vivian Kubrick's music for *Full Metal Jacket*, also deployed in scenes of ground combat. For several scenes following Lejeune's death, Kubrick trades music for the sounds of war, a shift that assails the listener with plain realism.

Halfway Points, Musical Frames, and Dialectics

As Kubrick gained more control over his films and their music, several broad musical design trends emerged, all of which depend on establishing contrasting musical climates. Existing music, and songs in particular, on one hand, and military or military-sounding music, on the other, provide two kinds of musical atmospheres in *Paths of Glory, Dr. Strangelove*, and *Full Metal Jacket*. Familiar music from the real world could drive home the realities of war by reminding members of the audience of their own memories of wartime, sparked by a familiar song. To this end, Kubrick chose well-known songs for all three films.

In these three films, music in a military idiom sounds out the unstoppable forces of man's machinations. These include the inquiry and sentencing of the wrongly accused in *Paths of Glory*, the efforts of Major Kong and his men in carrying out their orders, and the training exercises of the young recruits at Parris Island that lead to psychological breakdown, murder, and suicide. For Kubrick, military music usually sounds the ominous collectives that ruin individuals. In *Dr. Strangelove*, Laurie Johnson's arrangements of "When Johnny Comes Marching Home Again" offers a ready analogy for a military that acts on its own authority, even when there is no apparent or reasonable call for action.

A notable exception to the dooming military trope is the music in scenes in *Barry Lyndon* accompanying the protagonist's service, first with "British Grenadiers," a tune still often quoted and set with new lyrics by the British, and later with the *Hohenfriedberger March*, associated with Frederick II of Prussia. These marches, and their starkly different instrumentation—fifes and snare drums versus a band of woodwinds, brass, and larger drums—help mark Redmond's changing locations and circumstances; he escapes both into and out of military service in the course of his adventures. He is a rare Kubrick protagonist for emerging unscathed from his involvement in military service.

Johann Strauss Jr.'s *Artist's Life* waltzes in *Paths of Glory* represent the first instance of classical music in Kubrick. As the only classical work in the three war films, the waltzes stand for the corrupt and self-righteous upper echelons of the French military, and they mark the broad gulf separating Dax's (Kirk Douglas) soldiers from the society of the men who command them. The bare percussion of the scenes in the trenches and in the field contrasts starkly with the waltz of the luxurious party; these two opposing musical climates organize the elements of the film and its characters. Strauss's waltz plays with sudden loudness with a cut to the party scene; its appearance is all the more striking because it is the first music with any harmony since the start of the film, and the first music after a long musical absence during the court marshal scene. The waltzes play an important role in dramatizing Colonel Dax's conversation with General Broulard (see chapter 8).

Kubrick created more sustained and nuanced musical climates beginning with *Lolita*; in this film and almost four decades later in *Eyes Wide Shut*, a prominent, anchoring piece of music appears or disappears, respectively, about halfway through the film. In *Lolita*, two important techniques emerge for the first time. First, the film's music and drama are tied together by inscription (see chapter 5). Second, the film is broadly divided by musical means into two parts. Kubrick's division of several of his films by means of music, and in particular the addition or subtraction of striking or repetitive music, are techniques that mark distinct climates within the drama. These musical shifts can mark loss, loneliness, danger, or a change in location or emotion.

Of all the music in *Lolita*, "Lolita Ya Ya" is best known, but it is surprisingly absent in the film's second part. After so much repetition early on, the absence of the tune leaves the second part of the film flatter, lonelier, and more difficult to watch. Silence and the sounds of everyday life—now strangely portentous—fill in where the carefree song once played. Nelson Riddle's score becomes more brooding and pensive, then emotional and desperate. "Lolita Ya Ya" may have been the music signifying Humbert's fantasies of obtaining Lolita, and Humbert's distracted desire, but he is now paranoid that she will flee, or that their relationship will be discovered.

Nelson Riddle's orchestration of Bob Harris's melodramatic love theme, which literally frames the film and appears with several scenes and Riddle's own "Lolita Ya Ya" both recur and issue from two distinct locations—from a more omniscient perspective, and from Humbert's, respectively. The result is a musical double frame, with the love theme furnishing the outer frame on the story, and "Lolita Ya Ya" the local climate of the first half of the drama. Significantly, when "Lolita Ya Ya" disappears, Humbert's voice-overs nearly do as well.

The music in *Barry Lyndon* exhibits a similar design in that Handel's Sarabande frames the drama and appears throughout the film, but Schubert's late-style music plays only in the second half, in scenes of Redmond and Lady Lyndon's (Marisa Berenson) courtship, and the results of the courtship, years later. Schubert's late-style music only begins at the halfway point of the film, promising the warmth and intimacy that has so far been missing from this part of Redmond's adventures.

Though a dynamic of gradation, or continuity, characterizes the sound and music world of *The Shining* (see chapter 3), there is at the same time a dramatic and musical tipping point that hinges on the disappearance of Bartók's and Ligeti's music and the growing frequency, length, and superimposition of excerpts of Penderecki's music. While the variety of the music in the film undermines a musical frame at the outer edges, Bartók's music frames the emergence of Jack's problems with his family—tension between Jack and Wendy, the disquieting bedroom conversation between Jack and Danny—that result in chaotic violence. Again, this inner-frame music focuses the interior workings of the drama.

For all the unlikely symmetry of *A Clockwork Orange*, there is not a musical double frame; rather, the music is sorted and resorted in contrasting arrangements that are truly dialectical in nature, just as characters and their antithetical relationships are subject to inversion throughout the film. A dialectical approach to music illustrates the relativism of musical value—a main theme and metaphor for the instability of larger, humanitarian values in *A Clockwork Orange* (see chapter 7)—and its relevance to the changing experiences of the listener. The film begins in one climate, with Wendy Carlos and Rachel Elkind's electronic version of *Funeral Music for Queen Mary*, and ends with Gene Kelly's rendition of "Singin' in the Rain," not heard in the film before this moment. The point made by this musical mismatch is that Alex and the audience are not the same as they once were, and things do not sound the same because they do not *mean* the same as when the film began. This endpoint relates to the change signified with music and photograph at the end of *The Shining*, an arrival point far removed from the first shots of the family's drive up the winding road to the accompaniment of Wendy Carlos and Rachel Elkind's ominous *Dies irae*.

Vivian Kubrick's music emerges partway, then precipitates, in each of the two sections of *Full Metal Jacket* like a harbinger of death. In a film with such a striking and unequal two-part narrative structure, the musical design helps parse out dramatic weight. The outer musical frame of the film is made up of popular music, and both parts of the film begin with a popular song, but the variety of tone across the pop songs, particularly in the second part, calls for some distinction beyond the label of "pop"—indeed, Kubrick emphasizes the senselessness of war in the choice of several of these songs (see chapter 1). Musical choices and questions of tone originally took a different direction; the opening haircut scene was to have opera. As production went on, musical decisions favored a more pared-down, less sentimental approach. The scene of Joker teaching Leonard how to make the bed, for example, was at one time going to have the *Colonel Bogey March*, "to make it seem like everything will be okay."[1] Such a choice would also have imparted a sense of camaraderie. Without music, Joker helps Leonard—perhaps with some pity and concern—because it is his job, and despite his attempts, Leonard does not seem to make progress. The presence of the march would erase any reading of these feelings on Joker's part and would instead invite the audience to read the scene more optimistically and even to be entertained by it.

The protagonist and audience land in new territory in *Eyes Wide Shut* with Ligeti's *Musica ricercata*. As unexpected and arresting its first appearance is, halfway through the film, the recurrence of the piece in other settings seems even more so. Here, again, is a film with a musical double frame. Ligeti's music brings the audience as close as it can to the mysteries that entice and threaten Bill, and Shostakovich's waltz frames the entire drama at a greater distance, its sweeping, Romantic style rendering the story a modern-decadent fairy tale.

Voice-Over Narration and Ambiguous Sound

Hallmarks of Kubrick's style, music and sound included, are restraint and ambiguity. Two cites of this ambiguity are voice-over narration and the unclear or shifting status of music in the diegetic or nondiegetic register. Kubrick presents voice-over narration in several different ways; the character is visible onscreen and speaking, visible onscreen unspeaking but heard speaking at the same time, or invisible while heard speaking. These choices represent ways of empowering characters and reinforcing character hierarchy. Ambiguity of music's status as diegetic or nondiegetic, or its slippage from one to the other, is an element in Kubrick's filmmaking that likewise identifies powerful characters and prompts the audience to reframe or reassess character and drama. By engaging the audience in a game of making sense of music's source, musical ambiguity effectively opens a conduit between the world of the drama and the audience that leaves the audience more receptive to the emotional impact of the story and more invested in the characters that traverse the diegetic-nondiegetic line with spoken lines and voice-over narration.

Michel Chion's handy concept of the *acousmêtre*, a sound whose source is not seen, is most helpful here. Voice-over narration is by nature acousmatic, as are a variety of diegetic sounds that are implied, like music coming from a building nearby, or unexplained sounds that characters hear in horror movies. They carry a certain power for eluding the camera, by disorienting the audience, and denying or delaying the customary cinematic privilege of a visual counterpart. All of this creates the compulsion to wonder where the voice or sound comes from, who or what is making it, and a worry about it and what threat it might carry.

Acousmêtres proliferate in cinema—think of all the sounds of offscreen doors closing, sounds of torture from an adjacent room, eavesdroppers on a conversation, all manner of offscreen music, and sound that comes into earshot by virtue of a character's approach. Kubrick includes acousmatic sound in his films, portentously in the initial, startling bangs of Jack's tennis ball in *The Shining*, for example, and exploits the unsettling quality of the acousmatic voice of Alex in *A Clockwork Orange*, discussed below.

Most of the films include some form of voice-over narration. It was a commonplace of film noir, so it is not surprising that it appears in *Killer's Kiss* and *The Killing*, in which the words of the omniscient narrator are especially helpful in navigating the disordered drama. Voice-over narration may have held special appeal for Kubrick as a cinematic analogue to the photographer's caption. Like a caption, voice-over relates to, but retains some independence from, objects in the frame. Kubrick played with the flexible possibilities of voice-over in his work. Voice-over was also native to documentary filmmaking and was part of Kubrick's early documentaries. In *Killer's Kiss*, Davey's voice-over is intimate and more natural in tone than the strong enunciations of a newscaster and makes an immediate bid for the audience's sympathy.

Kubrick withheld voice-over in *2001*, *The Shining*, and *Eyes Wide Shut*, though it was part of the plan for both *2001*—in which HAL's part and the narration were originally one and the same—and *Eyes Wide Shut*.[2] The general, progressive abandonment of voice-over narration across Kubrick's films suggests his growing confidence in, and mastery of, nonverbal means, and concomitant interest in themes that are destroyed by verbal description, or disallow it. In some cases, Kubrick creatively sublimates spoken word into other forms, like the written words seen in *2001* and *The Shining* (see chapter 1).

Kubrick begins both *Paths of Glory* and *Dr. Strangelove* with brief establishing narration. Michael Hordern is the staid, resonant voice at a distance in *Barry Lyndon*, and the omniscient narrator of the film's major events, couched in the past tense, though notably separate from the unheard voice behind the title cards, which seems to come from a greater distance. Hordern's narration for *Barry Lyndon* would seem rather straightforward, though in places it comes after the action rather than before for the sake of recasting the tone of the drama. When Redmond leaves the German woman, for example, the narration renders the tender scene mundane by suggesting she had hosted soldiers in this way before; this recasting of the drama comes as a wry surprise, but also mocks anyone in the audience who may have viewed the scene sentimentally. In other moments, the narrator's matter-of-factness hedges on a bored cynicism, for example in the flatness of tone for descriptions of characters in love, a quality perhaps tempered by the gravity of the film's final pronouncement, in printed word, regarding the characters' ultimate equality in death.

Joker's voice-overs appear belatedly in *Full Metal Jacket*, at the ends of long sections, each retrospective of the events and indicative of changes in his character and his perspective, but in their delay they fail to provide any sense of orientation for the audience such as those in some of Kubrick's earlier films, *The Killing* most of all. Consistent with Kubrick's interest in the audience's involvement and discovery, limiting the clarity available in conventions like voice-over narration would compel the audience to make meaning for themselves.

Unusual in *Killer's Kiss* is that Davey's opening voice-over happens as the camera follows him, pacing, at the train station. Prefiguring scenes in *A Clockwork Orange* and in *Lolita*, the character is doubled in voice and image, but the voice is out of sync with the image. This makes sense because it sets up the narrating voice in the present and the image in the past, but it is still unsettling, compared to, say, hearing Davey's voice over other images. Later, it happens while he is seen having a conversation with Gloria over breakfast, though to no remarkable psychological effect. Kubrick would attenuate the uncanny effect of hearing a voice that comes asynchronously from its visible body at the beginning of *A Clockwork Orange* by making it seem not only that Alex is addressing the audience but that he is also holding the audience in his gaze.

Musical Ambiguity

Kubrick's noir films of the mid-1950s are full of musical ambiguity in terms of "where" the music is coming from. In several scenes, it is not possible to determine with certainty whether Fried's music is diegetic or nondiegetic; either seems feasible. The cinematic convention of diegetic music that happens to also function in a nondiegetic fashion serves Kubrick's sense of cruel fate in these films and helps mark areas of relative tension and rest.

The soft jazz in scenes at George and Sherry's apartment is not clearly diegetic or nondiegetic; it could be dramatically motivated by Sherry's hypersexual dominance, or realistically by an unseen radio. Likewise, the Latin music that plays when Sherry comes to Val's apartment could be diegetic or nondiegetic. The interruption of this music with Fried's more serious noir style does not clear up the question, though Fried's music seems clearly nondiegetic. When the group waits later for Johnny in Marv's apartment, the newscast is followed by what the radio announcer calls the "regularly scheduled program" and we hear Fried's Latin music, which continues to play softly through the scene until it is drowned out by gunfire. Fried's piece reaches its climax and plays at a louder volume as George dizzily surveys the dead and stumbles out the door. The music fulfills both diegetic and nondiegetic functions as source music and dramatic underscore, respectively.

The same ambiguity persists in *Killer's Kiss*. "Once" and Fried's Latin cues could feasibly be playing in a nearby apartment. When Davey looks out the window to see that policemen are in his apartment looking for him, Latin music suddenly starts playing, seemingly unmotivated by anything but the drama, but it could still be coming from a neighbor's window.

The only song played in the dance hall whose diegetic status is visibly confirmed is "Once"—the camera shows a record on a turntable as the song is heard. The Latin music in the scene in which Rapallo's men kill Albert, however, sounds diegetic and seems to belong to the dance hall as well. In one scene, a final cadence brings "Once" to a true end, and after a short silence, a fast-tempo Latin number begins. The camera does not follow Gloria back inside, so there is no visible evidence to confirm its status as diegetic. The camera cuts to Davey and the sounds of his locale farther down the street, then back to the alley near the dance hall, where Rapallo's men kill Albert; the Latin music now sounds realistic to this particular environment, reverberating in the alley as though coming from the dance hall windows.

If *2001* and *Barry Lyndon* seldom make use of diegetic-nondiegetic ambiguity, their momentary effects are poignant. A strange thing happens upon the return of the *Blue Danube*. Listeners who know and love the work will recognize that the music is resuming from an earlier point compared to where it left off the first time, creating a strange sense of disorientation. The most logical way to make sense of this atemporality in the music is to infer that the music is playing on a loop, in the manner of Muzak, or a weary ballet rehearsal accompanist; the effect asks the audience to entertain the possibility that this music could be diegetic—an idea at once preposterous and amusing. This musical choice also implies that should we check in one more time on the scene, the music would most definitely be there—as Kubrick puckishly implies by returning to the work, now in its entirety, for the closing credits.

In *Barry Lyndon*, Schubert's trio during the courtship scene has just enough reverberation to suggest diegetic status in the gaming parlor, though this impression abates as the scene goes on, and the music sounds nondiegetic by the time Michael Hordern's narration resumes. Whether originally diegetic or not in this instance, the music will return nondiegetically to recall the start of the characters' relationship.

Lolita and Its Music

Common to *Lolita* and *A Clockwork Orange* is the early establishment of the main character's voice-over and of musical ambiguity. Kubrick knew that the ingratiation of these stories' protagonists with the audience would require finesse; a permeable sound world offered a unique solution to the problem.

Among Humbert's attractive qualities are his wit, manners, good looks, and gentle way of speaking. Humbert's overall politeness and restraint rhyme those qualities in "Lolita Ya Ya" so that the song and Humbert's voice-overs conspire in a campaign for the audience's sympathy. In light of the film's racy and objectionable content, the establishment of sympathy for Humbert and the audience's investment in him was crucial. One way Kubrick effects a tight bond between Humbert and the audience, whether the audience wants this or not, is through voice-over narration. Humbert addresses the audience directly and, in many instances, conveys what he has written in his diary. This mode of address makes Humbert seem conscious of the audience and renders the audience his confidantes.

Humbert's first voice-over is conventional enough; he tells, in past-perfect tense over adventuresome, optimistic, nondiegetic music, how he came to be looking for a place to rent before his college appointment in the fall. His voice-over resumes later for a reading from his diary, about Lolita's paradoxical dreaminess and "eerie vulgarity," which concretizes Humbert's senses of superiority and cynicism. The air of secrecy upon hearing words from a diary is underlined by the lack of other sound in the soundtrack. Humbert's interest in Lolita, visually suggested up to this point only by facial expression and body language, takes on specific dimensions in his diary reading. That the audience's likely suspicions about Humbert's thoughts are here confirmed—and in amusing words and conspiratorial tone—both flatters the listener and builds the illusion of alliance with Humbert. The "strange thrill" he gets from keeping his diary is akin to the strange thrill the audience has by virtue of hearing its contents.

Humbert reads out loud Charlotte's letter confessing her love with a mixture of amusement and derision. His laughter interrupts several sentences. At the same time, the sentimental love theme playing in the underscore forebodes Humbert's demise as a result of his desire for Lolita. After Humbert and Charlotte's wedding is another diary voice-over, similar in tone to the previous diary readings, and then another voice-over shortly after, which we hear as we see Humbert, and which seems to voice his thoughts in the present moment, alone in the bedroom as Charlotte runs water for a bath. Neither of these has music, but both have the sound of water in the background; a confining, dreary rain in the first case, joined by Charlotte's running bathwater in the second. In the second voice-over, he practices lines in his head that he might later say to the police after murdering Charlotte with her gun, such as "She said it wasn't loaded." If this premeditation of murder asks too much of the audience, Humbert redeems himself when he cannot go through with it. A rather dark, dissonant sustained cue called "The Perfect Murder" had been written by Nelson

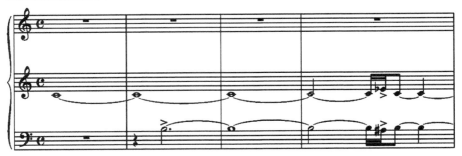

FIGURE 2.1 Nelson Riddle's cue "The Perfect Murder" was recorded but not included in *Lolita*, likely because its tone was too ominous.

Riddle (see Figure 2.1), and even recorded for the scene, but was omitted, probably because it would have made Humbert seem too evil. Also, the absence of music compels the audience to wonder just how serious his intention to murder Charlotte is.

He soon discovers Charlotte reading his diary, which will mean the end of his diary readings and a return to a much more mundane and straightforward style of voice-over narration about his move with Lolita to Beardsley College, in which he directly addresses the audience, over diegetic music: "You must now forget Ramsdale and poor Charlotte and poor Lolita and poor Humbert." By this time, the audience's sympathy and alliance are presumed. A voice-over by Humbert tells of preparations for the road trip Lolita wants, and ushers in the restless, nagging nondiegetic music that haunts the scenes of their travels. Minutes later, he notes in his final voice-over that he knows a car is following them, calling it a "designation of doom." The remaining scenes of the film play out from a slightly greater distance from Humbert; his former means of reaching the audience, including his diary readings, voice-overs, and "Lolita Ya Ya," are gone.

Toward the end of the film, the words of a typewritten letter form on the screen as Lolita writes to Humbert. Notably, the brief scene contains the sounds only of the typewriter. We do not hear Lolita's voice, or any music. It is a final, pointed reminder that "Lolita Ya Ya" was Humbert's view of the title character, and that she is, in reality, ordinary.

There are great contrasts in musical style across the score, most evident between the "Love Theme" (as it is called on the soundtrack album), Riddle's arrangement of Bob Harris's sentimental, sighing tune that opens the film, and "Lolita Ya Ya." Rounding out the soundtrack, Riddle supplies other music for dancing, for dinner background, a harpsichord theme for the quirky character Clare Quilty, and a variety of other unique cues.

Though Kubrick was concerned that Humbert seem relatable and sympathetic, as evidenced for example in his great care over James Mason's performance onscreen and in voice-over narration, Nelson Riddle's original music for the film would do a great deal more than simply foster sympathy, or simply cross from diegetic to non-diegetic. The variety and tunefulness in much of Riddle's music for *Lolita* springs from the composer's deep familiarity with popular styles and creativity in stretching them. Riddle's cues carve out parodies of popular music with a deft touch that brings out the humor and irony in scenes of Humbert's life with Charlotte and Lolita—for example, the breezy cue "Music to Eat By" plays, so simple, smooth, and cheery, as Charlotte tells Humbert that Lolita will be going to summer camp; Humbert is careful to hide his great distress, and the music makes the moment all the more sour for him.

The sheer contrast between the "Love Theme" and "Lolita Ya Ya" contributes to the humor of the latter in part with the element of surprise. The "Love Theme," dripping with piano figuration, and slow, brief, balanced phrases, conveys melodrama so strongly that the audience would not anticipate Riddle's pop send-up, even if they know the young age of the title character.

Though "Lolita Ya Ya" plays the greatest role in fostering complicity and sympathy in the audience, it is the "Love Theme" (see Figure 2.2) and its variations across the film that render Humbert's vulnerability, without which he might seem more a criminal than a man who loved and lost. The "Love Theme" is the film's most effective reminder of the sadness of Nabokov's story and the pathos of Humbert, contemptible as his actions may be. The "Love Theme" also has a special role in appearing in scenes of loss: Lolita loses her mother and asks Humbert to promise never to leave her; Lolita leaves Humbert several times in the film; and she refuses to go with him when he finally finds her again.

The "Love Theme" ties these scenes together, casts loss as a major dramatic theme, and lessens the weight of Quilty's character, who is much more consequential, if elusive, in Nabokov's novel. With respect to the dark musical frame of the "Love Theme," "Lolita Ya Ya" is some of the film's most enjoyable music—which we are invited to laugh with and at—and comes with moments of humor, if at times dark humor.

FIGURE 2.2 Bob Harris's opening theme, or "Love Theme," from *Lolita*, an aesthetic opposite to Riddle's pop-ish "Lolita Ya Ya," which points to the love and loss of the main character.

"Lolita Ya Ya" first creeps into earshot as Charlotte wraps up the tour of her house for Humbert, a prospective lodger. The music could pass for nondiegetic film music—Riddle's use of strings and gentle approach to the rhythm section raises no suspicions. There is a written indication in Riddle's handwriting above the drum part of the full score that reads "Ad lib. Rock and roll (cymbal etc.—polite, not raucous)."[3] Riddle's call for politeness reflects the need to foster outward propriety and delicacy in Humbert, even as he pursues Lolita; this music cannot be too physical or visceral. The song is the apathetic, vacuous stuff a teenager in the 1960s might listen to and, when the audience learns that it comes from Lolita's radio, seems little more than an aural prop. The lyrics of the song's chorus, "Ya Ya, Wah-o Wah-o Ya Ya…" only support this impression.

As Charlotte introduces Lolita to Humbert, she asks her to turn her music down; this is the first of several instances in which Charlotte attempts to block out the presence of her daughter, whose burgeoning sexuality threatens Charlotte's own. Softer, the music plays on as Charlotte entices Humbert to rent the room, and all the while he steals glances at the young daughter. That Charlotte, herself interested in Humbert, does not attend to the music or to Lolita establishes for this music an indication of a carefully guarded, divided attention, particularly the interest in Lolita that Humbert must keep private. After the scene in the garden, the music resumes almost immediately—after the brief intervening scene at the drive-in movie—in scenes of life in the Hazes' house, the tune's empty simplicity a perfect rhyme for Humbert's indulgent and perpetual desire.

"Lolita Ya Ya," which plays five times in the film and occupies around nine minutes of the entire soundtrack, is so sonically appealing that even when it appears in the most inappropriate and objectionable of contexts—on the heels of Charlotte's death—it becomes a springboard for humor; the "stinger" chord following the film's first news of Charlotte's death functions as the preparatory chord for "Lolita Ya Ya." This shocking elision verifies that Humbert's use of Charlotte was purely provisional: her death, musically captured in one chord, is merely a mild jolt to Humbert. The musical contrast of the sounds of rain and the stinger chord with "Lolita Ya Ya" immediately afterward equates the death of the mother with the availability of the daughter. The appearance of "Lolita Ya Ya" so soon after the car accident is both funny and disturbing—indeed, the music affords a disquieting sense of Humbert's single-mindedness, and might seem psychotic were it not for the distractingly humorous bathtub scene that follows.

Humbert sips a drink in the bathtub and receives guests who, with earnest concern, comfort him after Charlotte's death. "Lolita Ya Ya," in the nondiegetic register, conveys a buoyant irony and cordons off the audience on Humbert's side; the audience's empowering privilege of knowing what Humbert is thinking about—to the exclusion of the other characters—is couched in this ingratiating tune, so out of keeping with the visitors' distress. Kubrick couples privileged knowledge with humor in a way that nearly flatters the audience—or makes Humbert seem to—in this scene that reinforces audience sympathy; it is difficult to condemn while amused. When "Lolita Ya Ya" plays, it indicates the desire that began when he first saw Lolita in the garden. But since Humbert actually *hears* "Lolita Ya Ya" in the garden, it is possible that he recalls this music when he is thinking of her, an impression supported by his rhythmic head-bobbing at the very end of the bathtub scene, behavior that is otherwise difficult to explain.

There is no voice-over in the bathtub scene, nor during any instance of "Lolita Ya Ya," and there is no view of Humbert's face once he is driving to pick up Lolita from summer camp. The word "Narration" appears above a bar in the cue for the scene, but none made it into the film.[4] Instead, the music is the emotional locus of the scene, standing in for what Humbert cannot, or may not, put into words.

Kubrick maintained a delicate balance in *Lolita* that relied on Nelson Riddle's deft hand at pop parody, and on a permeable nondiegetic-diegetic border that would ally members of the audience with Humbert. Humbert's voice-overs and "Lolita Ya Ya" become different manifestations of Humbert's desire and private thoughts by virtue of appearing in the nondiegetic register; one might stand in for the other, especially when words might not be fitting. The choice of music over words was not purely to placate censors; Kubrick knew the potency of the audience's imagination to fill in the blanks more effectively than he could with words, and he understood that music would stimulate this imaginative mode. The payoff for ingratiating Humbert to the audience in the film's first half would be sympathy for him in the second. This rise-and-fall trajectory appears again in *A Clockwork Orange* and *Barry Lyndon*, both of which use music to demarcate and inflect nuances within the major acts.

A Clockwork Orange and Its Music

Like *Lolita*, *A Clockwork Orange* contains a thoroughgoing soundtrack strategy and ambiguity. This film's sound also depends heavily upon voice-over narration and musical recurrence to gauge the relationship between protagonist and audience. True to Anthony Burgess's novel, Kubrick's film creates a musical world that—like the rest of the dystopic setting—includes some unknown names and sounds and some very familiar ones. In the film's use of Beethoven, for example, familiarity becomes a point of departure for the audience's activities of recognition, remembering, and comparison, as well as for conditioning. The film's several well-known pieces of music stand in stark contrast to the less familiar ones and to the otherwise alienating world the characters inhabit. As such, the familiar music grabs the audience's attention, all the better to serve as the site for transformation. Alex's familiarity with Beethoven would ultimately effect a new response as a result of conditioning, just as Kubrick sets up music as a site for the audience's own responses and transformations. I take up this and other sites of experience Alex and the audience share in chapter 7.

Music participates in a variety of unstable dialectical pairs over the course of the film. The connotations of and responses to musical works—both for characters and the audience—seem in constant flux. The disposition of music in *A Clockwork Orange* constantly asks the audience to hear each iteration of a musical work in comparison to its other versions and in comparison to other music across the film. The musical works in the film assume a great deal of dynamism and even a sense of agency by their refusal to stay put, in terms of their sonic qualities, their connotations, or the way in which characters respond to them. As dramatic as these transformations may be, Kubrick is more interested in the audience member's awareness of change in her own perception. A listener's vulnerability to change searingly informs Kubrick's cautionary tale about the ills of a government that would control the minds of its people.

The habitual crossing of traditional sonic boundaries in *A Clockwork Orange* involves more than switching between diegetic and nondiegetic registers; that some of the music comes from the real, familiar world opens up the realm of the audience's subjective memories, associations, and opinions to bear on what the works mean in each instance, and how they effect emotional responses. Real-world music plays out in the film in unexpected appearances—first for the audience, then for Alex and the audience—both diegetically and nondiegetically. Beethoven's music is always diegetic in the film, suggesting that even though Alex can play it on his stereo, or applaud a spontaneous performance at the milk bar, he cannot ultimately control it any more than those in the audience can from their seats in the theater, or in so many other unbidden encounters.

Alex's Connection to the Audience through Sound and Image

Unlike *Lolita*, whose opening credits have recognizably tonal, orchestral music, *A Clockwork Orange* establishes no such stability. The most recognizable tonal quality of the first gently percussive, electronic, and dissonant sound is that it contains a tritone—a destabilizing force in Western tonal music. The screen remains red while the sound, heard three times like a tolling bell, slowly transforms by means of crescendo and glissando of various pitches, to converge on a C major chord. This unsettling music is Wendy Carlos's title music for the film, a synthesized arrangement of

FIGURE 2.3 Alex appears to fix the audience in his gaze, one of the many mechanisms in *A Clockwork Orange* that builds a sense of conspiracy between him and the audience. Warner Bros. Pictures, 1971.

the march from Henry Purcell's *Music for the Funeral of Queen Mary*. In addition to Carlos's original introduction, her arrangement also incorporates dissonant and rhythmically unpredictable electronic sounds, and a hint of the chant melody, *Dies irae*, upon which she based her main title for *The Shining*.

The fanfare elements impart the feeling that a show, albeit a grim one, is beginning. The basis in Purcell also nods to the film's setting in England, itself an object of the story's critique. A close-up of Alex appears, the whites of his eyes visible under his irises, and he appears to gaze, menacingly, straight at the viewer (see Figure 2.3). The "eye contact" Alex makes with the viewer is an invasion of the viewer's customary personal space that onscreen characters typically cannot invade. As the camera tracks out, Alex remains at the visual center of the mise en scène and of our attention, though his friends and the décor of the milk bar gradually come into view.

Nicole Rafter describes how "eye contact" builds complicity between the viewer and protagonist in the example of Hitchcock's *Psycho*: "The haunting terror of *Psycho*, and a factor that lifts it far above other psychological thrillers, lies in the way it implicates viewers in Norman's beastly acts. Through the very act of watching the film, we emulate Norman's creepy voyeurism, a parallel he forces us to acknowledge in his closing scene as he (and his mother), smiling complicitly, return our gaze."[5]

As the title music continues, we hear Alex's voice. In speaking to the audience as a narrator, though he remains motionless on the screen, he becomes an acousmêtre, like Davey and Humbert before him. But Alex is not like Davey or Humbert, who have immediate and clear agendas and who are in the midst of story events when they first speak in voice-over. As with Davey and Humbert, we see the body that produces the voice, though what we see represents a narrative past that Alex retells, and what we hear is the narrative present: Alex recounts his story. In this way, his presence seems double, and doubly eerie, in a way that it would not if he were actually speaking from his position onscreen. Alex's power and ubiquity are further amplified by this spatio-temporal ambiguity. Alex's physical stillness, in addition to the "eye contact" also makes it seem as though he is willing his voice-over narration to us like a telepath. Aside from this complex contact with the audience, the continuation of the title music, though slightly faded down in volume so that his narration can be clearly heard, further encourages the audience to attend to Alex's narration with unbroken attention.

Alex's copious narration, particularly in the first third of the film, establishes the importance of the soundtrack and Alex's freedom to use it. Alex's voice-overs have a poetic lilt, owing largely to Anthony Burgess's fanciful original dialect, and a host of unfamiliar words in *A Clockwork Orange*'s dystopia. Before each episode in the opening night's adventures, Alex shares his opinions and describes the events themselves—the encounters with the drunken tramp and Billyboy's gang, and playing "hogs of the road"—through his voice-over narration. In the last of these, he addresses the audience conspiratorially as "my brothers." Twice in his voice-over upon the gang's return to the milk bar, he speaks these words again, strengthening the semblance of a bond. The words pepper many of his remaining voice-overs, which, like Humbert's in *Lolita*, generate a sense of familiarity and camaraderie.

Kubrick designs all of the scenes in the opening sequence of *A Clockwork Orange* to solidify Alex's central position and agency in the story and establish a certain "proximity" and access to the audience via the soundtrack, following from Alex's initial gaze. At the same time, the opening scenes disturb the boundaries between nondiegetic and diegetic sound. As Alex walks home at the end of the night, he whistles along to Wendy Carlos's variation on her opening music. The synthesized background music and Alex's melodic whistling would seem nondiegetic and diegetic respectively (Alex is visibly whistling), but what does this combination of diegetic and nondiegetic sounds mean? Has his whistling spontaneously engendered the nondiegetic accompaniment? Or does Alex have the special power to hear nondiegetic music, even though it is not motivated by any source on the screen? In either case, this unusual sound disposition endows Alex with a power to come into close proximity to the world of the audience. Alex's supernatural power to cross into nondiegetic areas privileges him and intensifies the audience's response to him because of the tension it creates—a tension exacerbated by the audience's inability to reliably distinguish between "here" and "there." Furthermore, that Carlos's music appears as a variant of the opening music signals change as an operating principle for the soundtrack and for listening subjects both within the film and outside it.

Eyes Wide Shut: Sad, Rigid, and Ceremonial

The ambiguity of source music and underscore stands out once again in *Eyes Wide Shut*, showing the freshness and longevity of this approach at what would be the final stage of the director's career. The disposition of Ligeti's *Musica ricercata* in the film bears a remarkable resemblance to that of "Lolita Ya Ya" in *Lolita* in that it occupies one half of the film (in this case, the second) and recurs in a particular way with regard to the drama (see chapter 5). Kubrick's approach to the diegetic-nondiegetic line is simplified here by the omission of voice-over narration, which helps preserve the film's preoccupation with experiences (and limitations) of realization; the characters grapple to understand each other, and one of the film's objectives seems to be the cinematic realization of this aspect of human communication, particularly the emptiness of Bill and Alice's marriage.

The film's uncanny pattern of sonic interruption and inhibition keeps the drama in motion, as do the simple rhythms of daily life. After Bill presumably has told Alice about what he has seen and done, the couple realizes that their daughter will wake soon and they will not be able to talk freely. The daughter's presence also precludes conversation during the shopping trip later that day. If the sonic dynamics of *Eyes Wide Shut* seem subtle in contrast to *A Clockwork Orange*, and with an air of secrecy more urgent than in *Lolita*, Arthur Schnitzler's preoccupations with the repressive frustrations of life in the age of the nuclear family play out in appropriately restrained tones.[6]

Eyes Wide Shut, the most musically eclectic of Kubrick's films, opens with the second waltz from Shostakovich's *Suite for Variety Stage Orchestra*. By the time Bill turns off the stereo (see Figure 2.4), there has been a long enough overlap between the credits and the first scene in which the couple prepares to go out for the audience to be settled into a particular perceptive state. The music allows this transition, as in many opening title sequences, but when Bill turns the music off, this unremarkable act yields the curious revelation that the music was diegetic all along. The discovery itself disrupts the audience's complacency, and making sense of this is complicated by the need to attend to action, dialogue, and quick changes of mise en scène. When Bill turns off the music, it is as though he were severing the audience's connection to the "outside" or nondiegetic world (in other words, the audience's world), sealing the audience into a space much closer to the drama. Being privy to the world of the characters seems, in this way, to cost the audience the privilege of nondiegetic

FIGURE 2.4 Bill turns off the stereo, revealing the surprise that the
music had been diegetic. *Eyes Wide Shut*, Warner Bros. Pictures, 1999.

knowledge, such as that provided by a nondiegetic music track, by voice-over, or by
an omniscient camera; the film announces its request to the audience to see and hear
the world only as Bill does.

When Bill turns off the stereo, the music is not only revealed as diegetic but is
also imbued with an experiential slipperiness akin to the music of a clock radio slipping through the veil of sleep. The dreamlike ambiguities arising from Bill's limited
knowledge of his situations are an essential feature of the film and tie into the central
themes of fantasy, reality, and doubt. The "clock radio effect," however, works backward; we slip into a dreamlike world rather than wake from one. Dreams, wakeful-
ness, and consciousness are preoccupations of the film and inform its tone and style.
When Shostakovich's music appears several scenes later as nondiegetic music in the
scenes of Alice and Bill's daily routines, it gives us the sense that the characters have
been sleepwalking through their lives. After Alice's confession, Shostakovich's waltz
is not heard again until the ending credits, which leaves the audience wondering
how daily life will seem after the events of the film; indeed, the tunes and rhythms
of Shostakovich's waltz sound the same, yet they sound different after all that has
happened.

In addition to ambiguous moments regarding the diegetic-nondiegetic border
with music by Shostakovich and Ligeti, Chris Isaak's "Baby Did a Bad Bad Thing"
and the Oscar Peterson Trio's rendition of "I Got It Bad (and That Ain't Good)" also
are unclear. The first plays as Bill and Alice, home and undressed after Ziegler's party,
begin to make love in front of a mirror. The scene quickly fades, and though Alice
at first moves rhythmically, almost dancing as she removes her earrings, it remains
unclear whether or not the song comes from a space within the scene. The status

of "I Got It Bad (and That Ain't Good)" is also not initially clear; in close shot, Domino slowly moves toward Bill and kisses him as the jazz creates a dreamy atmosphere that the audience may not even think to question. Bill's phone rings, leading to the outing of the music as diegetic; he turns Dominic's stereo off, much as he did at the start of the film, though here for the purpose of concealing his location and activity.

In the same manner that the jazz creates, by virtue of its idiom and romantic context, a sensual atmosphere in line with cinematic convention, some of the music at the orgy behaves the same way. Though shots of Nick playing the keyboard establish diegetic status for the music of the first scene in the ritual, and guests later dance to "Strangers in the Night," the music by Jocelyn Pook, heard as Bill wanders through the mansion's rooms, is not provably diegetic until Bill's conversation with Mandy in the hallway, which establishes a sense of aural distance from the rooms where the music comes from (through relative volume and realistic reverberation).

Bill experiences several moments of recalling a woman's voice. In one scene, Bill looks across the kitchen at Alice, who is patiently helping Helena learn mathematics, and the audience hears her voice and words nondiegetically as she recounted her dream. Bill seems to be recalling her words in something like an internal voice-over, but one that entails another person's voice. This acousmatic echo, simultaneous with the body that produced the original words, seems to be less a trick of cinematic ambiguity than a device that replicates the common human experience of being haunted by another's words. Important here is Bill's futility in resolving the problems Alice's fantasies represent. It is as though the words must remain trapped in Bill's mind, since he cannot speak freely to Alice with Helena present. A similar trapped voice of the past arises in the morgue scene. Bill remembers the woman at the orgy saying that revealing her identity could cost her her life, and possibly his. Her death seals these words—further obscured by the muffling effect of the mask—to a fate of irresolution and mystery.

In the broader soundscape of *Eyes Wide Shut*, Ligeti's music becomes especially useful for gauging Bill's emotional state because his emotions are not expansively demonstrated. As with "Lolita Ya Ya," the import of the *Musica ricercata* movement is not immediately clear, but the audience is more likely to attend to it, because of its sheer volume, than to "Lolita Ya Ya" on its appearance (for details on how both pieces act in their respective films via a process of inscription, see chapter 5).

Musica ricercata debuts in the intense scene of Bill's interrogation and unmasking at the orgy, then appears four more times in the film. Though no musicians are visible in this scene, the music seems to carry diegetic gravity. There is an initial absence of other sound, and the crowd is motionless, as though listening. The master of ceremonies speaks only when the first phrase of the music ends, as though he had waited for—and therefore can hear—this musical silence. Likewise, when Mandy yells, "Stop!" the music ends midphrase, as though it has been part of the diegetic sound world all along. This interruption parallels the musical interruption that begins the drama, when Bill shuts off the Shostakovich and when he turns off Domino's stereo to take a call from Alice. Each break in the music of these moments invites the realization that music has been diegetic and necessitates a shift in perceptual frame on the part of the audience.

These perceptual shifts disrupt assumptions relating to the mode or guise of music as well as any connotations it may carry. They serve the idea of the uncanny, a great creative preoccupation of Schnitzler. Using the sonic register is a cleverly subtle way of fostering the audience's mistrust of "reality." Kubrick's play at the diegetic-nondiegetic boundary—a sort of laying bare of the device in aural form—creates an audience experience that parallels Bill's; he cannot rely on words (people lie to him and withhold information), and belated truths, like Alice's confession and moments in the last conversation with Ziegler, bring about troubling realizations.

Ligeti's music falls in line with a thematic-aesthetic pattern throughout the film that highlights its central questions about reality and perception. Michel Chion notices, for example, the replacement of one actress with another at Bill's side in a scene at the orgy and notes that because the audience does not dare to look closely, they miss the substitution completely.[7] I add that the audience's willingness to accept Kubrick's not-quite-right version of New York's village neighborhoods and the implication of diegetic music in the inquisition scene maintain this mode of reception for the film that pushes beyond—and is much more interesting than—run-of-the-mill cinematic suspension of disbelief. All of this fits well with the thematic concern with reality and perception thereof. Both for Kubrick's characters and his audience, reality is elusive and, in the end, somewhat beside the point.

Another unusual quality about the disposition of Ligeti's music is that its first appearance happens so far into the film that we are not likely to anticipate recurrence; films with recurring music tend to introduce it early. Finally, the piece's musical characteristics make for unlikely film music: its main subject doesn't have a tuneful melody one would go away whistling, its phrases are mechanical and halting, and no readily recognizable emotion emerges—save perhaps for the climactic buildups of the thick octaves, which create tension. The melody is simplistic and repetitive, yet sounds somewhat like a Medieval chant rendered on a piano. One could easily sing each of its phrases in one breath.

Ligeti's *Musica ricercata*, and in particular the movement featured in *Eyes Wide Shut*, stubbornly resists typical modes of musical description and classification. Though unfamiliar (as film music) in its sound, the work as a whole does have functional and historical associations to consider, such as those that figure into the analysis of the *Blue Danube* waltzes in *2001: A Space Odyssey*, taken up in chapter 6. "Ricercata" suggests that the music will resemble the Baroque ricercar in some way. John Caldwell notes, "The few modern composers who have used the term have generally implied by it a severe fugue with archaic mannerisms," and "severe" does seem apt to describe this movement, though fugue does not;[8] rather, the idea suits Ligeti's interest in limiting himself, as had the late Medieval and Renaissance composers he admired, to a small set of rules for composition.

Ligeti provides in the score few clues beyond the work's overall title, whose literal meaning implies searching. The marking of the second movement, used in the film, is *mesto, rigido e ceremoniale*: sad, rigid, and ceremonial. The material is extremely distilled and bare and as such, seems to be an anti-ricercar in comparison to the busily loquacious keyboard passagework of Baroque essays in this genre. On the other hand, the ricercar was employed in the seventeenth century as a replacement for the liturgical offertory—a function that readily resonates with the function and feeling of the second movement's debut scene in Kubrick's drama, at the circle ritual.

Musica ricercata does not sound like movie music, and its purpose, perhaps as a sonic epigram or symbol, is somewhat like a riddle. In form and function, Ligeti's music resembles the simplistic and wooden phrases of repeated dialogue in *Eyes Wide Shut* that yet fail to disclose meaning. Like the film's linguistic poverty, Ligeti employs an economy of means—several pitches, two main thematic areas. The listener puzzles out its meaning and purpose much the way the film is a meditation on the meaning and purpose of dreams and fantasies in human psychic life. Like dreams and fantasies, Ligeti's music appears unbidden and inscrutable. Only over the course of the film's second half does it attain meaning by establishing a pattern with relation to the drama (see chapter 5).

Ligeti's music attains meaning, as much music in film does, through context, and in comparison with other musical selections; this is especially true for *Musica ricercata* because of the difficulty of relating it to other music, or musical conventions that point to particular emotions or settings. Perhaps the most incisive instance of the *Musica ricercata* gaining focus through context and comparison occurs the fourth time it is heard, in the café Bill enters to elude the stalker.

It is worth pointing out here, however, that *Musica ricercata* is not such a fish out of water as it may seem. It is one of several musical selections in *Eyes Wide Shut* that prominently includes a stepwise melody. Jocelyn Pook's music for Bill's fantasy of Alice and the naval officer has a half step as its main melodic unit, like Ligeti's music does, and centers on the key of F, the starting note of Ligeti's piece.[9] The song "Strangers in the Night," the accompaniment for masked dancing at the orgy, also features the alternation between two notes, both a half step and whole step apart, throughout the verses of the song. These structural similarities tie the music—original and existing, diegetic and nondiegetic—into a larger structure that underlines the film's interest in recurrence and contrivance.

The "Rex tremendae" movement of Mozart's *Requiem* plays diegetically as Bill sits down and discovers the newspaper article about Mandy's drug overdose, which will result in her death; the sense of this coincidence is that the music "knows" just as the newspaper "knows" something more than its bold letters disclose. The choice of this particular requiem, as opposed to others in the Western repertoire, is poignant. The work is haunted by questions of authorship, stoked by the interests of composers tempted to take credit for parts of the work, and questions about how much of the work was completed at the time of Mozart's death.[10] The difficulty of determining the hand that wrote the music is a ready metaphor for the enigmatic relationships between the characters in the film and the absolute irretrievability of unseen events. For the Mozart *Requiem* as for the newspaper headline, origins cannot be surely located; they are as displaced and elusive as their surface gestures are bold, immediate, and moving, and they recall the film's masks that hide the faces that speak. The *Requiem* provides a clue that though the subject of the article is "lucky to be alive," she will not be for long. This somewhat dramatic yet plausible choice of café music also contributes to the impression that the film's drama is staged, which Ziegler later confirms.

A second important function of the *Requiem*, however, is to get pushed out of the way by Ligeti's music. As Bill focuses on the article, Mozart literally fades down and the insistent tones of Ligeti once again pierce the quiet. The musical shift in itself indicates a change of frame from diegetic reality to Bill's interior subjectivity. The fade-out of Mozart indicates not that the *Requiem* no longer plays in the café, but that Bill's attention to the article drowns it out. What's more, the appearance of Ligeti both conveys Bill's psychological state and, by association, connects Mandy to the stalker and to the orgy.

Each film—*Lolita*, *A Clockwork Orange*, and *Eyes Wide Shut*—offers an experience of music that appears to be nondiegetic and, for the audience, exclusive of the characters. The revelation of a diegetic source for the music effects the startling realization that characters and audience belong to the same sonic and emotional world. The realization in turn prompts a change of frame by which to understand the music—both with regard to the characters' world, and from the viewpoint of sound shared by characters and audience, which collapses the apparent distance between the characters and audience, as when one realizes that a pane of glass between two spaces is in fact missing. The ambiguity of diegetic and nondiegetic sound spaces leaves the audience particularly vulnerable to the affect of the drama. Music, and the entire narrative mode, cannot be trusted to maintain a steady guise; it becomes a rogue element that packs an emotional punch. For Kubrick, such uses of the soundtrack, and music in particular, were vehicles of impact and his way of toying with the "fourth wall."

Music-Cinematic Topics

3

MYSTERIOUS MUSIC WITH INVISIBLE EDGES AND THE

EMERGENCE OF MUSICAL FORM IN *THE SHINING*

MUSIC AND FILM depend on time and mark its passage. Time is the framework over which an ever-shifting relationship emerges between present, past, and future sounds. This essential feature of music works in a number of ways, even when only an excerpt is heard. Listeners frequently happen upon music in progress—for example, when switching to a radio station—and when they do, they know from experience and general familiarity that the music has been playing since before they tuned in and that what they hear represents part of a longer song or work. When a listener hears a song for the first time, she can probably deduce what the rest of the song sounds like based on her knowledge of similar songs and an understanding—even if intuitive—of common patterns like song forms and chord progressions.

Unlike a painting, which a viewer can take in as a whole or in parts in any order and at any pace, music and film meet the audience one moment to the next. The audience experiences both music and film—together or individually—as linear, pro-cessural media; images and sounds pass in and out of view and audibility.

While narrative is a clear and common organizer of film form, musical form comprises a procession of chunks (distinguished by melody, key, tempo, instru-mentation, and other elements), each of which can be understood by comparison with what precedes and follows it. Music theorist Heinrich Schenker identifies a distinguishing privilege of music, one that supports a linear, time-bound concept of musical form, when he says repetition is music's "most striking and distinctive characteristic."[1] Proving Schenker's claim is as easy as turning on the radio, and it will apply equally to Mozart and Motown. In Kubrick's oeuvre, the repetitive "I don't know but I've been told…" and other chants of the soldiers in training in *Full Metal*

Jacket readily illustrate the maxim that once music establishes a pattern, listeners expect it to continue. In this way, these perpetual chants handily convey the fatiguing, relentless, and mindless physical repetition of the training.

Even more basic than repetition is music's propulsion through time. Because we hear music in everyday life in a moment-by-moment way, music imports wholesale into film a real-world feeling of time passing that a series of filmed scenes and images might otherwise lack. The convention of montage, for example, depends greatly on this quality. Music's tendency to continue, simply put, contributes to the audience's identification with, and acceptance of, what they see onscreen. Continuation, a quality listeners intuitively know, is an important precondition of the more nuanced questions of form that have to do with the identification and order of discrete musical sections, such as those that animate Kubrick's work. Kubrick is well aware of listeners' tendency to anticipate, expect, and predict while they listen to music, and he relies on this habit to shape audience receptivity to, and interpretation of, his narratives.[2] Music's ability to hypothesize a past and future with relation to the filmic "now" is also crucial in spectator experience and plays important roles for Kubrick.

To help show that music has certain temporal privileges, it is worth pointing out that while image repetition is exceptional in narrative film, musical repetition, even note for note, is typical. Musical repetition across a film creates opportunities for the listener to recall the past, recognize its relationship to the present, and anticipate the future in a way that is unavailable or at least awkward by visual and verbal means.

Kubrick uses music in the cases discussed here to generate both an experience and a metaphor that can induce the audience to conceptualize and feel a scene in a particular way. In the examples in this chapter, music is cast as the invisible master of the filmic world. Aspects of musical form—the progress of pitches, rhythms and harmonies, contrasting sections, repeated passages that thus set up expectation, recognition, and a sense of logical, organized process—imbues film with abilities it otherwise would not have, for example to refer to other moments or elements within the narrative; to point beyond the narrative; to suggest a growing or waning force; to evoke the idea of memory or premonition; to convey a particular energy, tempo, or gravitas; to focus the audience's attention on a particular object or idea; and to excite physiological responses and emotions.

Music as Master of Time

Some directors have relied greatly on musical continuation and form in their work—notably Alfred Hitchcock in his own remake of *The Man Who Knew Too Much* (1956), where a musical score, and its execution in concert performance, provide the blueprint and cover-up for a would-be murder. Unlike other music-and-murder examples in Hitchcock, this one happens in real time—it is fully vectorized in the world of the film and in the time of the performance, and the deadly strike can only be sufficiently masked in one specific loud moment—a crash of the cymbals—in the piece.[3] The music's linear nature here serves to proscribe and guarantee the action, thus upping the physiological ante considerably; the effect is akin to being on a roller coaster, whose journey follows the absolute design of the tracks, and at specific, pre-determined speeds. Once you're strapped in and leave the station, you're on until the end of the line. The real-time countdowns of innumerable movie explosions also trade on this vectorization of time, and they often lead up to the moment of truth with intense volume, pitch, and texture in the sound and music tracks alike, but rarely do they employ the musical form of a piece of music wholesale.[4] The presumed degree of participation of musical form in *The Man Who Knew Too Much* is unusual. Practically, it is only the crash of the cymbals the audience need know about; the form itself assumes importance only as the path to the ineluctable moment of truth.

Along with an interest in musical repetition within works, Edward T. Cone has studied the experiential aspects of listening to a piece of music repeatedly. Regarding repetition within a work, Cone observes that the impact and effect of each statement of a repeating or recurring section depends on what has already been heard and what will be heard thereafter. Cone then notes that when the same piece of music is heard twice, the experience differs the second time around because the listener's knowledge and circumstances have changed.[5] While these notions about listening seem native to classical music, which presumes repeated listening and study, these conditions and changes in perception apply to film, and particularly to Kubrick's. Kubrick observed the affinity of good films and musical works in this way: "Don't you think it's true of all good films; you should be able to see them like you re-read a book or hear a piece of music. If a film has any substance."[6] That rewatching and relistening enact change can be illustrated if one considers a startling moment in a horror film; a member of the audience will respond a certain way to the film initially, and probably quite differently on returning to the theater a few days later, equipped with the knowledge of what will happen and when. An audience member's changing memories and expectations effectively make the film, and its music and other components, different every time.

Repetition even simply conceived takes various guises in film. Most common, the repetition of aspects of mise en scène, dialogue, or scenario might bring a story full circle or resolve it, for example in Kubrick's scenes of James Mason entering Quilty's mansion in the beginning and end of *Lolita*.[7] Another common use for such repetition is to measure changes in a story; in Hitchcock's *Spellbound*, there are two highly similar scenes in which Dr. Petersen (Ingrid Bergman) climbs the stairs to a closed door. In the first, she is delighted when she realizes "Dr. Edwardes" (Gregory Peck) is inside; in the second, she is full of trepidation for the same reason. On viewing the distinctive yet doubled scene the second time, the spectator has the opportunity to remember the first and to compare the two; this reference point helps measure the drastic change in the story's circumstances since Dr. Petersen first ascended the stairs. If a spectator attends to images and sounds, she can notice their repetition and remember what they meant before; the film affords a richer experience through these aspects.

Kubrick uses repetition in the strict symmetry of story events in the first and third sections of *A Clockwork Orange* so that there is an unlikely repetition of events (but with an inversion of victims' and attackers' roles). The repetition dashes any claims the film might have made to realism and displays Kubrick's love of form. His love of form also comes through in the clearly articulated musical tableaus of *2001: A Space Odyssey*.

But the literal repetition of a strip of celluloid usually suggests something abstract, bizarre, or unbelievable rather than narrative. The Wachowskis, for example, cleverly use a clip twice in succession to represent a glitch in the system of fabricated reality in *The Matrix* (1999). And Kubrick literally repeats moving and still images in Alex's bedroom fantasy in *A Clockwork Orange* and in the confused calamity of Jack's encounter with the lady in the bathtub in *The Shining*.[8] These two moments, both of which could be considered montages and therefore entail music, relinquish normal time in favor of a fantastic mode that suits the liminal states and situations of their respective characters.

In Kubrick's wordless scenes especially, musical form often comes to the forefront as a gauge of narrative logic and, of course, mood. The courtship scene in *Barry Lyndon*, taken up in the following chapter, and the spaceship waltz in *2001*, are two prominent examples; they rely in particular on conventions of dance and the attentive listening that accompanied the emergence of stylized music. Kubrick's deployment of *Also sprach Zarathustra*, particularly at the beginning of *2001: A Space Odyssey*, succinctly displays the director's reliance on music (see chapter 5). And for *The Shining*, the main subject of the present chapter, musical formal characteristics supply much more than structure; they are nothing less than the keys to the story's major themes and ideas, and their visceral manifestations.

Where Sound Meets Music

Talking about form (the sequential and synoptic relationships of musical events) is all well and good, but it assumes the music is recognized as such. Across Kubrick, however, are several striking moments of sonic ambiguity—instances in which sounds do not immediately sort into "sound" or "music"—and which generate some slippage or disorientation.

Kubrick plunges into a world of unusual sounds for the beginning of *2001: A Space Odyssey*. György Ligeti's *Atmosphères*, the first sound the spectator hears, begins with a mass of sound—not a beginning that announces itself as such, nor as something immediately obvious as "music." Ligeti's luminous synthesis of orchestral timbres foils attempts to identify the conventional instruments participating. This inscrutability and the lack of a conventional melody and metric rhythm leave the spectator, who has only a black screen to contemplate, in a position of relative disorientation.

After Ligeti's music, the MGM logo appears, accompanied by a new, rumbling sound. An organ, a contrabassoon, double basses, and a bass drum, all on Cs in the depths of the orchestral register, create this rumble, though again the instruments are difficult for even musically trained listeners to discern. Though the sound belongs to the opening fanfare of Richard Strauss's *Also sprach Zarathustra*, the listener might not label the sound "music." Many things could generate a low rumble (machines and engines come to mind), and other markers of music like harmony, melody, and rhythm are absent. Both Ligeti's and Strauss's works in the opening moments of *2001* are apt to inspire the spectator to wonder, "What *is* that?"

A Clockwork Orange benefited greatly from Wendy Carlos's disorienting synthesized sounds, particularly in the opening sliding dissonance that resolves into Carlos's version of Henry Purcell's *Music for the Funeral of Queen Mary*. Carlos keeps the listener unsettled by peppering Purcell's music with unpredictable, off-key stingers.

Like the bare sound of Strauss's low C in *Also sprach Zarathustra*, the unfamiliar, bare sound of drums, divorced from other musical elements, causes some momentary disorientation for the listener in *Barry Lyndon* when Captain Feeny robs the title character. The handheld camerawork in the scene and the vulnerability of the hero work together with the raw pattering of the drums to keep the spectator on edge.

The audience's first likely reaction to the existing pieces by Béla Bartók, György Ligeti, and Krzysztof Penderecki in *The Shining* is to recognize it as typical horror movie music, and this is perfectly correct.[9] The sounds that comprise the music by these composers, and by Wendy Carlos for the film, are those associated in cinema with horror and the supernatural, and the music of horror films probably employs what we might term "sound effects" more freely and frequently than any other genre. Sound editor Gordon Stainforth makes apparent efforts to hide the musical nature of music in some cases: while Dick drives a Sno-Cat up to the overlook, the status of what we hear is ambiguous; it is not clearly noise or music, especially as Ligeti's *De Natura Sonoris No. 2* mingles with what is ostensibly the noises of the Sno-Cat and the wind.

But the danger of equating the film's music with "horror" is that we may miss other ways in which the music is working. Recent scholarship on *The Shining* entails a host of varied creative approaches to interpretation, approaches that break well beyond stylistic generalities. In an example of such an approach, David Code observes that the procession of modernist composers' work in the film, and its ultimate replacement by mass-produced popular song, is not simply a timeline but the articulation of one of the film's central anxieties. Code's use of musical notation in his discussion—particularly its graphic and irrational alternatives in the decades following World War II—shows well how the theme of literacy is embattled in *The Shining*. In Code's analysis, the popular songs, finally, mark the dissolution of cross-generational understanding (especially relevant to Jack and Danny's relationship) in a postliterate world. In the present argument, the theme of remembering is of greatest importance, and placing this theme at the center of a discussion of musical form frames Kubrick's film as more faithful to King's novel than is usually perceived.

Making an Entrance

In making sense of musical form—say, for the purpose of singing along—a listener orients himself in a song on the radio according to the point at which he tuned in; he will quickly figure out whether a verse or chorus is under way, and might even know *which* verse or chorus it is, according to clues in the lyrics or instrumentation. The initial moment of orientation is crucial for the listener's navigation. A spectator of *The Shining*, however, is unlike the radio listener. She does not control or even know when music will begin. Potential moments of listener orientation stray further out of reach because of music's tendency to fade in. As the volume grows, the listener may eventually become aware of music's presence. It can be a disquieting surprise, somewhat like realizing someone is standing next to you though you cannot recall his approach. The listener will scramble to recall the beginning of the music and try to make sense of it, but Kubrick and Stainforth make these tasks particularly difficult. Because the music habitually fades in, the spectator realizes only retrospectively that it has begun; she will not know the precise moment it started, much less be able to use it as a point for aural orientation. Such a realization creates feelings of uncertainty, disorientation, and vulnerability with respect to the film. The unfamiliarity of much of the music further alienates the listener and denies her points of orientation in melody, harmony, and even meter, much less any more complex aspects of form.

Musical continuation exerts a strong force in *The Shining*, both within and outside moments in which the music is heard, and so many of the musical excerpts begin and end in a gradual manner that this sound shape constitutes its own form in the sound world of the film. The surreptitious appearance of music—especially in the opening half of the film—heightens the listener's awareness, much as a snippet of conversation might; one strains to hear the whole thought, or what might be said next. At the same time, the fact of fading in begs questions about where the music is coming from, when it began, and why we are not privy to these origins.

Kubrick also had used the technique of fading in for the second scene in *2001: A Space Odyssey* that features the *Blue Danube* waltzes. This is notable for two reasons: first, it implies that the spectator is catching up in medias res, thus creating the peculiar feeling that the music has been playing continuously and unheard. Adding to the impression that this music could in fact be some kind of space Muzak is that the music has backtracked to an earlier spot in the waltzes compared to where they had left off in their last appearance. Are we to think that it is playing on an endless loop?

In *The Shining,* the fading in and out of music—not unlike a fading in and out of visibility, or consciousness, or other experiences with "soft edges"—suits the theme of temporal confusion and animates the central character's ambiguous relationship with time. The music's "subject" in most cases is not carefully specified in the diegesis, as in cases of inscription (the subject of chapter 5), nor does it rigorously accompany a character or other discrete aspect of the narrative. Structural and sonic features of the music in *The Shining* represent creative solutions to the problem of conveying ideas that are difficult to visually depict, and for that reason they deserve special attention.

Depicting consciousness, a central interest in *The Shining*, has occupied several directors in recent film. Christopher Nolan has inventively portrayed and inspired in his audience the experience of becoming conscious of something. *Inception* (2010) plays with beginnings, endings, and consciousness, for example in the scene where Ariadne (Ellen Paige) fully realizes she is dreaming—and the audience too realizes it and reclassifies the scene as such. She is convinced she is dreaming because she is unable to recall how she arrived at the sidewalk café where she sits; the audience is likewise unable to trace the scene's origins. In *Memento* (2000), Leonard (Guy Pearce) lacks short-term memory and periodically struggles to orient himself in his surroundings. As in *Inception*, Leonard cannot remember how he got where he is, though the audience can piece it together.

The phenomenon of music, especially when it appears in medias res, serves as a metaphor for the supernatural or another reality; it is a manifestation of the film's supposition of a realm that is present—we need only "tune in" to it. The strains of Edith Piaf's rendition of "Non, je ne regrette rien" in Nolan's *Inception* creep mysteriously into the characters' dream worlds to prompt them to wake up. In the context of the dreams, the song seems otherworldly and curiously reverberant, as though echoing in from an adjacent room. Even in everyday life, a song's sudden appearance on the radio can evoke in the listener memories of another place and time (another world) quite powerfully, at the expense of his attention to his present surroundings.

In *The Shining*, the music that fades or creeps in—including Ligeti's *Lontano*, Bartók's *Music for Strings, Percussion and Celesta*, and the dance hall music first heard from a distance by Jack—suggests the "other world" from which it comes. Likewise, the forms of this music extend across the film—even when the music is not audible—like a skeleton underlying and animating the film's central ideas. When music is inaudible—especially when it fades out or stops before it seems finished—its presence lingers because of music's essential temporality and because of the film's thoroughgoing emphasis, for example in the acting, on the quality of hesitation.

The use of several popular music recordings from the 1930s and '40s for scenes in the ballroom help pinpoint the provenance of former caretaker Delbert Grady (Philip Stone). This music, particularly "Midnight, the Stars, and You," refers to that time period but also to the fact that the Overlook Hotel is uniquely bound to it. The film's parting photograph shows festivities in the ballroom in 1922, with Jack among the revelers, with a reprise of this song. The canned quality of the recording of the song, and the unseen, unexplained sounds of applause and chatting heard after the song, while the credits roll, are intriguing indicators as to the importance of sound and music in Kubrick's cinematic conception of *The Shining*. Unlike other music in the soundtrack, for reasons of context, style, or both, it is a song the audience is likely to remember and take home with them.

Continuous Musical Form, Fragmented Film

In his widely inclusive approach to film sound, Rick Altman argues that sound must be considered well beyond cinematic exhibition, and furthermore considered well beyond what seem to be its origins.[10] K. J. Donnelly's sensitive and richly imagined work on *The Shining* answers to Altman's call to expand inquiry and at the same time illuminates the potential for diverse and inventive interpretations on the part of active listeners as they both anticipate and recall the music in and beyond the film. Donnelly takes up questions of portions of music that hang over the edges of the frame, unheard, and he notes that when only part of an existing work is used—for example, one movement of Bartók's *Music for Strings, Percussion and Celesta*—the parts that are *not* in the film are also implicated in it and affected by it.[11] Yet because the unused movements have no clear relationship to the film, they provide an especially rich site of film-related imaginative activity. These kinds of creative listener activities haunt *The Shining* with particular persistence, and Kubrick seems to want them to.

Donnelly's position specifies the view, most thoroughly explored by Edward Cone, that the perception of musical form and repetition is contextual and subjective. Cone illustrates his theory with musical works that contain passages that recur or repeat, but his observation handily applies to any number of sounds or other experiences that could come before or after our hearing a piece of music, such as a movement, in its entirety, or to the very common occurrence of hearing a work on one day and hearing it again on another, any number of days later. Donnelly identifies a special potency in the movements of the Bartók that are not in the film—the two movements before the movement in the film, and the one after it:

> When I listen to the piece, I think of the film. Moreover, when I listen to the sections of the piece that are not in the film, I still associate them with the film. I imagine them as parts of the film that I have not seen…so perhaps there are further missing or incomplete versions in the mind or in the ether. I envisage whole episodes that do not exist, or imagine the music providing the character for the entire film, to the extent that it becomes the unheard soundtrack for the film, the two conjoining somewhere in my mind rather than on a piece of celluloid or videotape.[12]

Donnelly's description of an imagined world connected to the film via other pieces of music suggests a whole extra dimension available to the attentive spectator. Donnelly's description resonates with Wendy Carlos's own statement on the new release in 2005 of some her unused tracks from *The Shining*: "Some of the music will be familiar to those who know the film, and some will not…Other tracks hint at a lost world of possibilities for the film left unexplored on its release."[13] Carlos's statement underscores music's generative capacity in Kubrick and in film overall and hints that such lost worlds lie waiting for the listener to discover, with the help of the music, in the cinema of imagination.

"Much Is Going Unsaid"

Though *The Shining* offers up what might be manifestations of the supernatural in visual terms, and more so as the film progresses, from the beginning Kubrick had to solve a fundamental problem: how to portray the supernatural and unseen forces in the story. Music was on his mind in the earliest stages of the process—or at least by the time he reached page 373, as evidenced in the notes he made in the margins of the novel, which I will examine below. The solutions to cinematically conveying some of the invisible and elusive aspects of the story are answered by musical form, particularly in the hands of the sound editor, Gordon Stainforth. The spectator's susceptibility to form in *The Shining* is enhanced because of two tendencies: the small amount of dialogue, and narrative fragmentation. As a result, musical form—primarily the fade-in and fade-out, and secondarily the forms within and surrounding the second movement of Bartók's *Music for Strings, Percussion and Celesta*—comes to the fore like a perceptual life raft.

In the course of his work on issues of adaptation in Kubrick, Greg Jenkins observes that "the minimalist give-and-take of the film...comes to nurture a terrible apprehension that much is going unsaid; the want of words speaks as loudly as the words themselves, and creates suspense."[14] To be sure, the paucity of dialogue in the film prompts the spectator to hear differently and perhaps to work harder to find meaning in sound and music. It also leaves the spectator waiting for—and perhaps steeling himself against—the next sound. Jenkins's description of a coyote heard in an early scene as "a grim aubade" suggests an active and imaginative mode of listening.[15]

The Zoom-Out Effect

Stainforth helped Kubrick choose music for the film, then took great pains to place it in the film, as has been well documented by Leonard Lionnet, Jeremy Barham, and Julia Heimerdinger.[16] As remarkable as the chosen works are—by Bartók, Ligeti, and Penderecki—the manner in which Stainforth excerpts them is crucial. In addition to maintaining soft edges around musical entrances, Stainforth's sensitivity to musical architecture and sound quality is evident in his careful coordination of music to picture so that climactic moments in music have a sense of dramatic justification or narrative alignment. Lionnet's dissertation details these moments and their service to visceral effect. It is in these "hits"—moment of synchronization of sound and image—that Stainforth's hand is most discernable.

But there is another aspect of Stainforth's approach to excerpting that serves the film's deeper thematic substrates: each of the existing works recurs and, upon recurring, plays for a longer time. The works seem to reconstitute before our very ears as the film unspools. The partial presentation and progressive lengthening of excerpts, and the precipitous disappearance of space between them, sounds out the themes of realization (or awakening), consciousness, and remembering. That Stainforth starts somewhere in the middle of the works the first time and backtracks to earlier spots to start from in subsequent hearings—an unusual film-music tactic—intensifies these effects. It is as though the film were piecing together a memory out of scraps.

"Awakening" is even part of the title of one work, Penderecki's *The Awakening of Jacob*, though it is sometimes translated as *The Dream of Jacob*; in either case, the title names states of consciousness that are experienced ambiguously. The gradually forming musical works aurally realize the gradual awakening of the ghosts in the hotel, Jack's growing cognizance of his violent tasks, and Wendy and Danny's growing realization and fear of the dangers they face.

Stainforth's method practically amounts to a "zooming out" effect on each musical work. This scheme repeatedly provides the spectator with scraps of the music that share passages, yet a conventional point of orientation (such as a clear beginning) is categorically denied; the listener is aware it is out of range—somewhere in the past. It also enacts the progressive nature of remembering, realizing, or taking form, and it rhymes with Kubrick's famous tracking shots. The zoom-out effect is clearest in the third movement of Bartók's *Music for Strings, Percussion and Celesta*. One important aspect is its own symmetrical formal structure, and another is its inclusion of the first movement's fugue theme. The symmetrical formal structure falls into an ABCBA configuration—a real palindrome. As such, it is balanced, but on the other hand, it is closed, and destined in its second half to regress, which profoundly affects an interpretation of the narrative. Stainforth keeps the excerpt relegated to the relatively quiet first hour of the film. The middle section of the movement, C, is never heard in the film, probably because of its overall loudness and distinctive, firmly stated motifs, which would work against the film's initial commitment to quietness and hesitation.

Bartók's debut in *The Shining*, when Danny and Wendy are running toward the maze on a sunny day and Jack seems to see them in the model maze, begins with the blurry, atmospheric start of the first B section (the movement having an overall form of ABCBA). The string trills might give a sense of something gathering and create suspense (see Figure 3.1). The wispy timbres of the glissandos—which lead nowhere in particular but seem to vanish in thin air—have a disembodied quality; they could practically illustrate in a cartoonish way the spirits slipping by unseen in the Overlook's corridors. Bartók adds a melody in violins that has a wandering, floating gait, suitable accompaniment to Danny and Wendy's turning and doubling back in the maze (see Figure 3.2). Bartók's wonderful string trills, which enter one after the other, convey a sense of gathering and of suspense. There is a cut back to Jack, inside; the xylophone and timpani here, instruments that are identified most strongly with the A section of the work, signal a memory or a sense of suddenly recalling the past for those familiar with the movement—in this moment, the melody ceases its meandering. It is a moment that recalls focus and imparts awareness, as though one has just been daydreaming, but because the audience has not heard the A section of the work by this time in the film, the aural "reminder" renders a sense of amnesia.

FIGURE 3.1 An extraordinary passage from Béla Bartók's *Music for Strings, Percussion and Celesta* animates, first, a sense of gathering force, and second, in the maze scene, a sense of wandering.

As Jack looks at the maze, a fragment of a slow melody in the strings emerges; it is part of the fugue theme from the first movement of the work, a movement not featured, per se, in *The Shining* (see Figure 3.3). Bartók places the "out-of-body" fragments, already remarkable for their anachronism within the context of the present movement, as frames around the wispy violin music, above, and the thrilling celesta figures. The recollections of the fugue in this way become apt signals of the supernatural and seem to cast the spell that conjures simultaneous realities.

Jack looks at the maze and seems to see Wendy and Danny there. The music itself contains the sound of the unhinged (the celesta) and the uncanny (a melody

FIGURE 3.2 Wendy and Danny wander in the maze, unaware of the coming danger signaled by Bartók's wispy music. *The Shining*, Warner Bros. Pictures, 1980.

from another place). The celesta figures spiral out of the control of any discernible meter—music's typical temporal guarantee gone haywire—and end with an ominous crash and cut to "TUESDAY" (see Figure 3.4).

The second appearance of Bartók accompanies Danny's attempt to open the door to room 237. The movement begins just a bit earlier than in the maze scene so that it includes the first five-note phrase of the fugue theme from movement 1. As in other scenes with the Bartók, Stainforth has clearly taken pains to coordinate action and sound; in this case, Danny discovers that the door is locked just as the wandering melody reaches its highest point. There is a brief image of the twins, but they do not appear in the same place in the hotel that Danny is, and Danny does not see them; instead, he continues to back away from the locked door, and rides away on his Big Wheel with haste. The camera glides toward Jack at his typewriter; typing sounds tap to the accompaniment of Bartók's fanciful, swirling celesta figures and glissandos in harp and piano. The flurry of activity in the music reaches its height when Jack

FIGURE 3.3 The emergence of the fugue theme from the first movement of Bartók's suite in the middle of the third—literally music from another time and place—gives musical substance to the ideas of temporal disruption and multiple realities.

FIGURE 3.4 The celesta figures in Bartók's music unhinge Jack from his normal orientation in time and place.

pulls a sheet from the machine, seemingly bringing the music to a sudden, crashing end (see Figure 3.5). This time the Bartók plays for two and a half minutes, about fifteen seconds more than in the first scene.

The last appearance of the Bartók—one Kubrick did not initially want—is the longest, at four minutes, thirteen seconds. It starts from the beginning of the third movement and plays through the first A and B sections of the work, minus a few bars at the end that Stainforth cut to bring music and scene to a synchronized end. Danny tiptoes into the family quarters to get a toy and discovers Jack sitting on the bed, awake. Jack calls Danny to him and holds him on his lap. Bartók's music

FIGURE 3.5 Gordon Stainforth carefully coordinates image and music in many scenes, for example aligning a climactic hit in Bartók's music with Jack pulling a sheet of paper from his typewriter. *The Shining*, Warner Bros. Pictures, 1980.

renders an emotional strain hidden by the banalities of their conversation. Kubrick had told Stainforth that the scene could not have music, but Stainforth's use of the Bartók persuaded Kubrick.[17] Stainforth's and Kubrick's collaboration on this scene reprises a similar one twenty years earlier when Bernard Herrmann wrote music for a shower murder where Hitchcock insisted he did not want any. Hitchcock decided to include it at the last minute, and Herrmann's shrieking string music in *Psycho* contributes greatly to its place among the most celebrated moments in all of cinema.

Danny first inquires, "Dad?" and an upward glissando breaks the pattern in the strings and upsets the atmosphere. When Jack says he feels a little bit tired, his aspect changes, a small smile forms on his face, and he gazes off camera in a new direction (see Figure 3.6). The fugue theme from the first movement suggests an uncanny source for Jack's malaise, just as it had for his strange power to see Wendy and Danny in the maze.

A gradual change, one that depends on the music, comes over the scene. Elizabeth Mullen describes it aptly: "Were it not for the eerie music, what follows would seem tender at first… Imperceptibly the dialogue… becomes more strained, each phrase becoming more charged with menace as Jack's expression becomes more and more calculating and his tone more alarming." Mullen hears the tinkling sound of the celesta here as a link to the maze from the music's previous appearance and as fore-shadowing the final chase in the maze that would prove false Jack's fatherly assurance that he would never do anything to hurt Danny or Wendy.[18] Jack's startled response at Danny's question renders quizzical the tritones in the piano. Of all the intervals in Western music, the tritone is the most harmonically unstable, a quality that earned

FIGURE 3.6 Bartók's music marks the dips and swirls of Jack's state of mind in the bedroom conversation with Danny. *The Shining*, Warner Bros. Pictures, 1980.

it a reputation as the *diabolus in musica* in the Renaissance and that has appealed to composers of many eras for its signature pungency. In the nineteenth century, the tritone became portentous and symbolic. In Bartók's movement, the tritone is more mysterious and inquisitive than menacing, largely because of the music's overall languid pace and smooth surface. The sudden piano interjections, however, create a dangerous feeling of suspense in the context of the scene—one that makes the spectator wonder if Jack's growing rage will burst out at any moment.

The recollection of the fugue theme throughout the third movement is literally a memory—and a recurring one—in terms of the work, but Bartók exaggerates its remembered and past status by letting it float along, tenuous and somewhat distant, free of any strong metric pulse. Even as an absolute work, there is something ephemeral and disembodied about this version of the melody; it has no clear connection to the "present tense" of the third movement. It simply materializes in what seems an almost absent-minded, spooky manner (see Figure 3.4).[19] The tune sounds as though it were trying to remember itself, perhaps under hypnosis; Bartók uses slower rhythms in this instance compared to its incarnations in the first movement so the pitches become drawn out, as if to imitate an effort to recall. The music itself is about memory in this moment; the attentive listener knows she is in the third movement, for example, but hears and remembers the first at the same time. As Stainforth frames it in *The Shining*, it is a harbinger of Jack's rehabilitation to his former violent and alcoholic ways.

The zoom-out effect is a thoroughgoing principle in the first portion of *The Shining*, one that creates an impression that the Overlook is increasingly occupied by ghosts and that a dangerous force is taking form. An excerpt of Ligeti's *Lontano* and the beginning of Penderecki's *Awakening of Jacob* are deployed in similar ways to Bartók's movement, and notably, all three works disappear after the first hour and fifteen minutes of the film.

Sonic Continuum, Psychic Continuum

Stainforth's notable treatment in the film's first half of gradually fading in excerpts rhymes with other sonic features in the film and with several of its central themes. Sonic continuum describes the pitch material in many of the works used: Bartók's breathtaking glissandos in timpani and strings; the many throbbing, melting brass tones and sliding strings in Penderecki; and the way Wendy Carlos's stunning cue "Rocky Mountains" grinds down as it fades away. Penderecki's richly inventive use of instruments evokes many stylized vocal qualities—sounds that all have some glissando in them—like sudden shrieks, slow screams, or growls.

Continuous sound qualities in *The Shining* provide aesthetic continuity and evoke ideas of the organic, living, and conscious, perhaps because continuous sliding pitches are more idiomatic of vocal music, and of course speech, while most Western instrumental music is more pitch-discrete. Vocal sounds point back to the beings that make them—Jack himself makes a "wooooo" sound when he tells Wendy he felt like he'd been at the Overlook before. The theremin's habitual cinematic accompaniment of all manner of mysterious to threatening unfamiliar forces illustrates and reinforces the connection between continuous sound and the spooky and alien.

In *The Shining*, continuous sound is a useful metaphor for telepathy, and connected with the idea of an invisible frequency that some can tune in to. Soft-edged sound shapes contribute to an overall theme of dynamic continuum, as though the audible sound arises from a sleepy, ancient depth, crosses into our threshold of hearing, and then out again to return to its distant origin. As the film goes on, this shape gives way to sudden, jolting sounds that jump out of silence.

Continuous sound also points to the humanly inaudible reaches and liminal edges of sound where the spectator can just begin to perceive it. The appearance of Ligeti's *Lontano* in the pantry scene is a wonderful case of sounds overlapping and pointing to broader continuums. The sound is initially ambiguous—the spectator might think a fluorescent light or something electric is making the high-pitched whistle. When Dick sends a thought telepathically to Danny, the volume of his speaking to Wendy at the same time fades down, all the better to hear his telepathic vocal close-up. The message to Danny seems to be pushed along a wave represented by the simultaneous crescendo in *Lontano*. Danny's moment of "shining" creeps up on him without his bidding or apparently his full consciousness (see Figure 3.7), just as the sound in the first half of the film surreptitiously comes and goes. Sound is the best bridge *The Shining* provides into the experiences of the characters. For this

FIGURE 3.7 Thoughts seem to be transmitted along the waves and swells of György Ligeti's *Lontano*, as in the pantry scene when Dick sends Danny a question. *The Shining*, Warner Bros. Pictures, 1980.

moment, and the earlier appearance of *Lontano* when Danny sees the twins in the games room, Stainforth has plucked an exquisite passage from the work and pressed it into the service of central but elusive qualities of the story.

The Bartók is the first music in the film to disturb the smooth edges of dynamic continuum—by coming to a crashing cadence as Jack pulls paper from the typewriter, at which point there is a cut to "WEDNESDAY," and at the end of his unsettling bedroom conversation with Danny. Our act of reading is made violent by the accompaniment and again emphasizes the potential violence represented by the written word (see chapter 1).

Just as Bartók's form makes a symmetrical ABCBA shape, and therefore features continuum in its large scale and local structures, it has qualities of palimpsest as well. *Music for Strings, Percussion and Celesta* is thus able to play pointedly with "memory" and the superimposition of multiple musical realities.

Palimpsest

In the early stages of developing *The Shining* for the screen, Kubrick was concerned with how to convey "the simultaneity of a hotel plus time layered on itself."[20] He apparently compared the advantages of different modes—visual, verbal, sonic, and musical—as evidenced in the marginalia, clearly in Kubrick's hand, in his copy of Stephen King's novel. Kubrick gave particular thought to passages in King that describe realities of decades past occurring all at once. Kubrick's lucid brainstorming nearly fills all the empty spaces around several such passages, while many of the novel's pages go by without comment.

Regarding bringing multiple realities to life, he writes, "This is an imaginative concept. Can it spark off visuals." And at the top of the same, much-annotated page, "Surrealism? Escher? Can this be expressed." Kubrick's idea of using visual superimposition, mentioned in the margins, did not end up in the cataclysmic final scenes but seems to manifest itself in the lingering, sleepy visual dissolves during the family's initial tour around the hotel. The fuzzy edges of these images provide a ready rhyme to the prevalent sonic and musical continuums and play into the idea of awakening consciousness.

In the middle of the page where Kubrick writes in the right margin, "The simultaneity of a hotel plus time layered on itself," he also asks a question and admires King's writing in the left margin: "ARE THE ACTUAL *'WORDS'* FOR THIS PAGE THE BEST WAY TO DO IT? IT IS QUITE WELL WRITTEN." In the right margin, he speculates, "THIS COULD BE LIKE THE TRIP SEQUENCE IN 2001" (see Figure 3.8).[21] The meaning of this comment is not clear in terms of

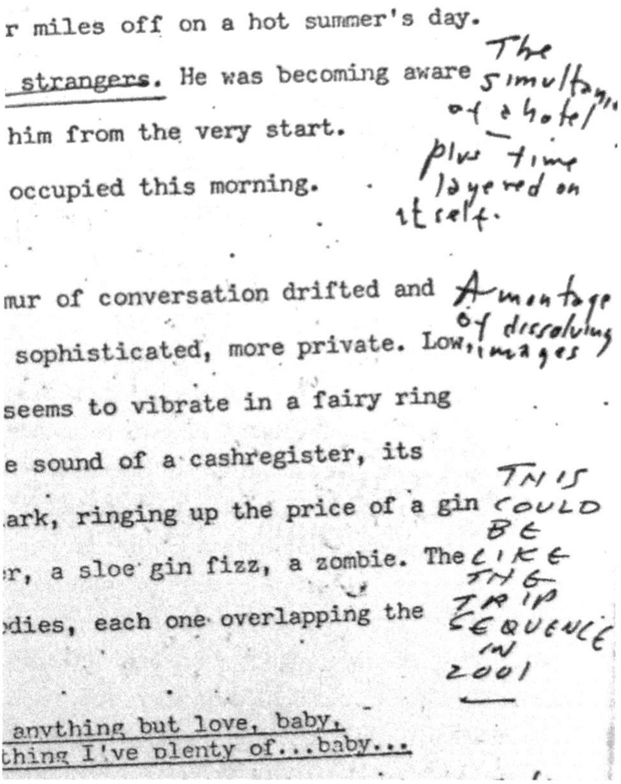
r miles off on a hot summer's day.

strangers. He was becoming aware

him from the very start.

occupied this morning.

mur of conversation drifted and

sophisticated, more private. Low,

seems to vibrate in a fairy ring

e sound of a cashregister, its

ark, ringing up the price of a gin

r, a sloe gin fizz, a zombie. The

dies, each one overlapping the

anything but love, baby.
thing I've plenty of...baby...

The simultaneity of a hotel plus time layered on itself.

A montage of dissolving images

THIS COULD BE LIKE THE TRIP SEQUENCE IN 2001

FIGURE 3.8 Kubrick nearly fills the margins of this page of King's novel with ideas about music and about how to convey some of King's creative ideas. Stanley Kubrick Archive, used with permission.

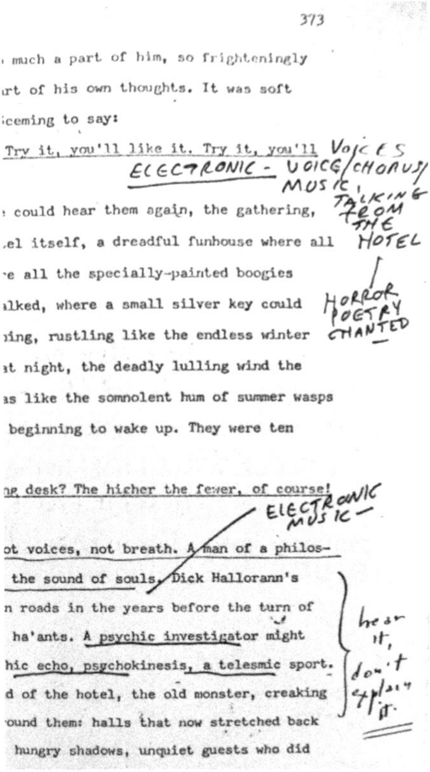

373

, much a part of him, so frighteningly
rt of his own thoughts. It was soft
:ceming to say:

Try it, you'll like it. Try it, you'll *Voices*
ELECTRONIC - *VOICE/CHORUS*
MUSIC,
: could hear them again, the gathering, *TALKING*
FROM
.el itself, a dreadful funhouse where all *THE HOTEL*
·e all the specially-painted boogies
ilked, where a small silver key could *HORROR POETRY*
ling, rustling like the endless winter *CHANTED*
it night, the deadly lulling wind the
is like the somnolent hum of summer wasps
beginning to wake up. They were ten

ng desk? The higher the fever, of course! *ELECTRONIC MUSIC -*

ot voices, not breath. A man of a philos—
the sound of souls. Dick Hallorann's
n roads in the years before the turn of
ha'ants. A psychic investigator might *hear it,*
hic echo, psychokinesis, a telesmic sport. *don't*
d of the hotel, the old monster, creaking *explain*
·ound them: halls that now stretched back *it.*
hungry shadows, unquiet guests who did

FIGURE 3.9 Kubrick's reliance on music for the concept of multiple realities in *The Shining* is pointedly acknowledged in the imperative he appears to have written to himself in the margin of the novel: "Hear it, don't explain it." Stanley Kubrick Archive, used with permission.

cinematic realization but might suggest a large-scale, fully absorbing audiovisual set piece; indeed, rather than following a clear timeline or forming causal relationships, the final calamities in the film seem more like fragments in a tableau. Music provides the evidence of unification.

In notes next to King's prose explaining what shining is, Kubrick explicitly rejects the verbal; he writes "ELECTRONIC MUSIC" and "hear it, don't explain it" (see Figure 3.9).[22] True to form, Kubrick seems to have wanted to foster nonverbal experience and allow his audience to experience something out of the ordinary, free of the "strait-jacket" of words.[23] In his efforts to put these ideas in our heads, he relies largely on overlaying sound and music.

The concept of palimpsest well describes the technique of sonic overlay in *The Shining*. This most obviously includes Stainforth's virtuosic and minutely designed overlays of multiple tracks at the film's end. But it extends as well to Wendy Carlos's opening *Dies irae*, a layered work based on Hector Berlioz's already-layered rendition of the chant in his *Symphonie fantastique*, plus Rachel Elkind's vocal line. Palimpsest—whether a feature of an existing work or created from multiple tracks— seems very much in the spirit of Kubrick's goal to convey simultaneous realities.

If the gradual sound—or continuum—indicates something is coming, palimpsest indicates something is *here*. With the exception of Carlos's opening *Dies irae*, palimpsest very gradually takes over as the evil forces gain ground, and even corporeality. Continuum is first destroyed when sounds enter and exit suddenly, calling our attention to the threat of a change, and it is further destroyed as it is drowned out by Stainforth's ever noisier palimpsests, which themselves benefit from Penderecki's thick and sometimes chaotic textures. Stainforth reaches a virtuosic climax when he mixes as many as four works at once for the film's last scenes.

The full reanimation of the hotel ghosts and Jack's murderous rage culminate with the increased occurrence of sudden, loud entrances—the stuff of horror movie startle, with increased extended techniques in the music and with increasingly layered sound and music. The recurring opening phrase from Penderecki's *Ewangelia* explodes with awesome and terrifying percussion sounds, exploited to full effect for the horrific revelations and acts that puncture the final scenes inside the hotel. Penderecki's sounds play well with important elements in *The Shining*, such as the evocation of ancient and unusual-sounding church music and the use of whispering voices.[24] In the context of *The Shining*, the work's original sense of religious ecstasy is disguised as the supernatural and horrific and is dramatically upstaged by the sheer sonic impact of the percussion passage that shatters the film's quiet.

Tracing the formal and sonic shapes in *The Shining* clarifies and makes visceral the increasing presence of the ghosts and Jack's violence. This analysis also illuminates a reading of the story that seems truer to King's novel than some commentators hold. An often-made observation is that Kubrick locates the evil in the hotel, while for King, Jack's own demons figure more heavily into the bloody equation. But Jack's first signs of transformation happen in the musical company of Bartók—music that is destined to regress and that recalls former habits, indicating that Kubrick too locates a major source of the evil in Jack himself. The overall musical design of the film generates a precipitous drive that may be tied to the image of the wound-up grandfather clock from King's novel. King's clock, which would be wound up and then run its course, is a handy analogy for the way music at times measures, and at times pushes, the drama.

Kubrick employs broad two-part structures elsewhere, with great impact. This would be an especially important distinction in *Lolita* as the absence of Nelson Riddle's tune, "Lolita Ya Ya" marks the characters' loss of innocence in the consummation of their relationship—something that could not be said or shown in the film. The switch in *The Shining* from extensive music to formally dissolute music is no less shocking than the procession of his two-part approach to the narrative of *Full Metal Jacket*; in *The Shining*, however, the shift happens in the register of music. The film's story and soundtrack rides an irreversible wave until the action has concluded. It is only in the epilogue that tonal 1930s dance music fades in for one last reprise.

Of Kubrick's films, *The Shining* is among those most daringly reliant on its music. The music is integrated in unique and sophisticated ways to *dynamize* the film's unseen forces—whether lurking in the hotel, floating in the air, or brewing within Jack himself—and to substitute for what cannot be seen. *The Shining* relies on the forms, in terms of the large scale as well as isolated moments, to point beyond the frame and stir a sense of memory by cleverly backtracking to successively earlier points in the music; this temporal intrepidity rubs off on the spectator's experience as a whole and ensures that it will linger in the mind. It is a statement about the attendant anxieties and horrific aspects of realizing and remembering. The existing concert music in *The Shining* also gradually yields its continuous mode of entrance and exit—its soft, surreptitious edges—to suddenness and superimposition. These are the musical techniques most responsible for our investment in, and our understanding and experience of, *The Shining*.

4

REIMAGINING MUSIC IN *BARRY LYNDON*

KUBRICK'S FILMS DISPLAY many ways in which music can be altered from its most familiar form. *Dr. Strangelove* includes instrumental versions of "Try a Little Tenderness" and a recurring and varied rendition of "When Johnny Comes Marching Home Again." For *A Clockwork Orange*, the notes and harmonies, rhythms, and tempos of Beethoven's Ninth Symphony are intact, but the work's instrumentation and timbres are altered. In *The Shining,* passages again appear by and large in original form, however, end with tiny modifications, or mingle with other works simultaneously.

In their respective scenes, the *Blue Danube* in *2001*, the Ninth Symphony in *A Clockwork Orange*, and the musical works in *The Shining* reproduce what one sees in published scores and hears in recordings of the works because these are, in fact, the sources on which they are based, or from which they were derived, and the structural integrity of the excerpts remains intact. The treatment of selected musical works in *Barry Lyndon* strays considerably further away from the letter—and in some cases the spirit—of their sources.

The substance of Handel's Sarabande from Keyboard Suite No. 4 in D minor, HWV 437, arranged by Leonard Rosenman (and its instrumentation and timbre) and Schubert's Piano Trio in E-flat, op. 100, revised by Jan Harlan, appear uniquely changed—down to the level of the notes and lengths of phrases. These two pieces were newly recorded during production.[1] In this way, the musical activities of Kubrick and his team go beyond selection and excerption and into the realm of composition and recording. One could argue that this film's use of music represents just another kind of music editing, but in no case up to this point had musical material been so substantially changed for Kubrick's work; the treatment of Handel entails a difference of degree as the work's structural components are repeated well beyond the length of Handel's original composition. The wearing effect of this repetition constitutes

87

a distortion of the original in which a sense of musical time is traded for a sense of endlessness. The treatment of the slow movement from Schubert's piano trio in *Barry Lyndon*, however, marks a difference in kind. That Kubrick and his team went to such lengths to rework the music attests to its particular importance for the film.

Adaptation and Artistic License

William Makepeace Thackeray's *The Luck of Barry Lyndon*, written in 1844 and set in the later decades of the eighteenth century, is a work of historical fiction with an unreliable narrator-protagonist. Thackeray's episodic structure follows the Irish title character's adventures on his quest for peerage in England, something he hopes his marriage to Lady Lyndon will secure. Kubrick's adherence to accurate detail in some cases, and inventive disobedience in others—in regard to both history and Thackeray's novel—make for imaginative retelling, and Thackeray's unreliable narrator-protagonist seems to give Kubrick the license.

Kubrick's version preserves selected episodes from the novel, though Redmond's marriage to Lady Lyndon and relationships with his stepson, Lord Bullingdon, and with his son, Bryan, supply more cohesive trajectories in the film's second half. After marriage, Redmond is unfaithful to Lady Lyndon, who spends much of the film in resigned solitude, or with her sons. Redmond clashes with Bullingdon, who in turn clashes with his young half-brother, Bryan, which ultimately leads to the climactic yet drawn-out duel between Bullingdon and Redmond. The concentration on these relationships has the effect of slowing down the overall pace of the story. The replacement of Redmond's boasting voice in the novel with the film's omniscient and apparently honest narrator is one of several choices that signals a change of mode, and the reliance on music is another.

In seeming accord with the stately pace and downcast mood of Kubrick's take on Thackeray's story, the general musical tempo across the film lists toward the slow end of the metronome, save for a few moments, like the dancing in Redmond's home village, the military marches, and music during scenes of Bryan's birthday party. The preference in the film's second half in particular for music with long, lyrical melodies, string textures, and smooth articulation encapsulates the drama in its subdued tone and leaves little hope that the characters might rise above their circumstances or resolve their conflicts. Schubert's late works—the slow movement from the E-flat trio, op. 100, and the opening measures of his Impromptu No. 1 in C minor—contribute substantially to this effect, with the help of the more melancholy variations on Handel's Sarabande. Schubert and Handel occupy the portion of the soundtrack populated by Baroque and Classical composers, alongside Vivaldi, Bach, Paisiello, and Mozart. These art-music works are counterbalanced against folk music and functional music, such as for dancing and military marching, yet it is the art music that seems to have won the lion's share of attention in the working process. The following sections examine the processes of selecting works and adapting them for the film, and evidence of Kubrick's efforts to shape the audience's experience—both in highlighting music within the film, and beyond, in the movie theater.

Music for *Barry Lyndon* and the Evidence of Process

Kubrick chose pieces and particular recordings that he loved to use throughout the films he made, and he tackled musical matters with gusto. Evidence of the care taken over the music for *Barry Lyndon* comes in a large, dedicated three-ring notebook full of correspondence, typed notes describing each of the film's cues by reel number and sequence (some of which differed from the finished film), and other notes relating to musical matters, such as the engagement of musicians to record works anew. A piece of graph paper is taped onto the very first page that lists, almost entirely in Kubrick's hand, music under consideration (see Figures 4.1 and 4.2).[2]

Kubrick made special lists of Baroque and Classical era works to consider for the film, a task to which he devoted much care, while there is relatively little evidence of process regarding the other music, let alone a process of narrowing down. This suggests the relative importance of classical works in particular, here and elsewhere in Kubrick's oeuvre.

Though Kubrick ultimately used music that existed before or up to the time frame of the drama (with the notable exception of Schubert), early considerations include twentieth-century film composers, including Nino Rota, Ennio Morricone, and André Previn.[3] There is also a lone reference to The Chieftains, whose performances of Irish music are heard in the film. Kubrick considered Donizetti's *Don Pasquale* and Verdi's *Atilla*, though these were not selected, perhaps because they were written too late. He annotates some items on the list with comments about tempo or melody, but it is not clear whether he had a priori criteria in mind. The different colors of ink for various entries or groups of entries in the list suggest that the list came together not all at once but over time.

In order to search as widely and hear as much music as possible, Jan Harlan wrote to Deutsche Grammophon in August 1973:

> We will need a large amount of all types of 18th century and 17th century music—dances, folk songs, minuets, gavottes, etc. I think it would be a marvellous [*sic*] idea if Deutsche Grammophon could provide us with a large choice of what is available along these lines, including all the big master works for orchestra and chamber music of this extremely rich period.[4]

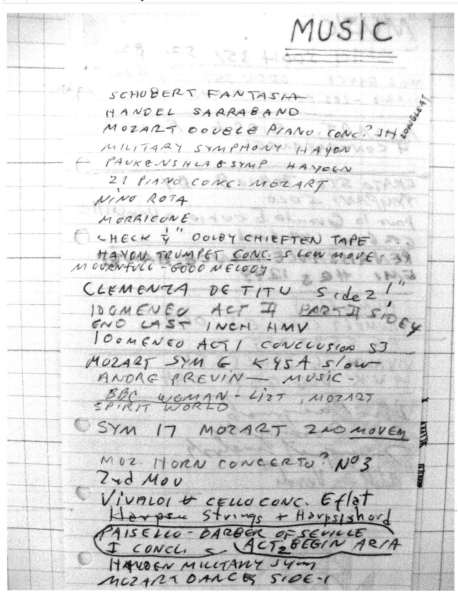

FIGURE 4.1 Kubrick's list of music under consideration for *Barry Lyndon* appears at the front of a large binder of notes and documents pertaining to music, attesting to the importance Kubrick accorded the task. Stanley Kubrick Archive, used with permission.

In addition to this omnivorous search came the question of which recorded version of a work to use, or whether a new recording should be made. The National Philharmonic Orchestra recorded Leonard Rosenman's creative variations on the Sarabande for the film, and there are notes relating to nearly all the newly recorded

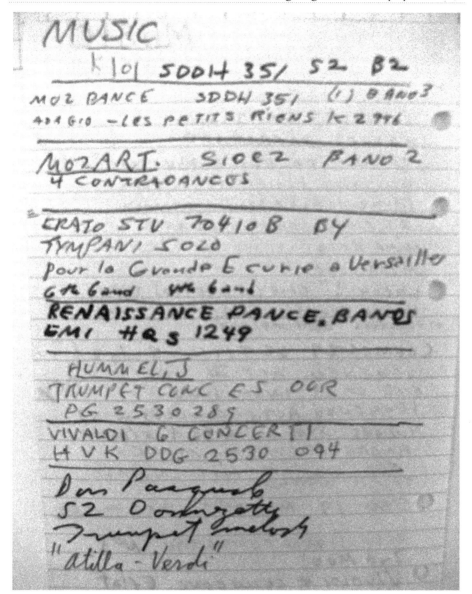

FIGURE 4.2 Kubrick's list, back. Stanley Kubrick Archive, used with permission.

tracks in the film, and even to music that was recorded but not used. The notes
weigh the merits (appropriateness of length, performance qualities, background
noise quality) of different recordings.

Though it is not clear who authored the notes, Kubrick attended all recording
and transfer sessions. Notes from recording sessions in October 1975 include details
about balance, buzz sound, mistakes, sloppiness, false starts, and length. Notes in

connection with the recording of the aria by Paisiello are typical in their attention to detail. Comments include "must be in excess of 4 minutes" and "Clar too
loud = pizz lost with orchestra," indicating that clarinet was initially chosen as the
melody instrument. Once viola was chosen instead, such comments appear as "viola
phrasing like a singer," "viola played too modestly," "2 x wrong notes on mandolin,"
and "mandolin trill at end of phrase better." The aria, which went through thirty-one
takes, is one of several tracks Kubrick had recorded rather than borrow from an
existing recording.[5]

   In the interest of music coming across in the context of the action, his actors at
least mime playing instruments convincingly. For Marisa Berenson, who plays Lady
Lyndon, Kubrick went a step further by scheduling harpsichord lessons for her during production.

   Kubrick apparently went beyond the efforts of most directors to ensure a particular experience for his audience by writing a letter to the projectionist (see chapter 1).
The letter suggests that each copy of the film went out to a theater accompanied by
the letter and a record of music related to the film. The letter instructs the projectionist on technical parameters of exhibition such as the strength of the projector lamp
and aspect ratio, but also advises the projectionist to play the enclosed record before
the start of the film, during the intermission, and afterward. The Kubrick Archive
contains a thick folder full of copies of this letter, translated into many languages.
But Kubrick's involvement and oversight did not end here; he sent men, like spies,
to theaters all over the United States and Europe to check that these conditions were
met. Several documents in the Kubrick Archive report on these conditions.

Barry Lyndon's Musical Landscape

Traces of Kubrick's hand emerge in yet other ways regarding music and its importance in *Barry Lyndon*. Clues manifest in several prominent sync points (most notably, the two kisses Redmond and Lady Lyndon share), and in protracted dramatic
moments that minimize other audible elements in favor of music. The music also
falls into a two-tiered class system that divides the stylized works of the aristocracy
from the functional, bodily music of the lower classes.

   The music, overall, helps define and juxtapose characters and tells a deeper story of
what is gained and lost as Redmond Barry makes his progress, a story that speaks to
Kubrick's perennial concern with class divisions and the question of a man's ability
to improve his circumstances. The Baroque and Classical era works, military music,
and Celtic folk music round out the soundtrack and sort clearly into two types: the
functional, physically active, and joyful music of the lower classes, on one hand, and

the stylized, still, restrained music of the aristocracy, on the other. In the early scenes of *Barry Lyndon*, the music Captain Quin and Nora Brady dance to is an artifact of daily life, much like the military music that accompanies Redmond's activities in the army. Accordingly, Kubrick's camera privileges physical activity—marching, fighting, dancing. Schubert's German Dance No. 1 (1813), one of many such works meant for private social enjoyment, underscores the magician's act and the miniature carriage ride at Bryan's birthday party.

Musically, Redmond seems at a disadvantage; there is no evidence that he even notices music when it plays, though he is presumably listening during the concert at Castle Hackton, and he adheres to the rhythm of the drums when marching in the military scenes. In the case of the dance music, Redmond is a jealous, sullen observer of Quin and Nora, and he never dances in the film.

Kubrick's film saliently dramatizes the eighteenth-century rise of stylized music; the Irish folk music of modest means and carefree dancing in scenes of Barry's youth give way to the still orchestras and audiences in the music rooms of high society. Redmond moves in environments of functional music in the film's first half. In his quest for peerage, he marries the Countess of Lyndon and enters a terminal atmosphere of stylized music—chamber music, to be attended to with care and silent admiration.

Musical activity in aristocratic life furnishes a major arena for power dynamics; the scene in the castle's music room seals Redmond's ruin. Lady Lyndon, Lord Bullingdon, and Reverend Runt seem perfectly at home playing chamber music, sometimes for an attentive audience. In this particular scene, Lady Lyndon and Reverend Runt play an adaptation of the second movement, Adagio ovvero largo, from Bach's Concerto for Two Harpsichords in C minor (BWV 1060); here, the solo parts are adapted for harpsichord and flute. Such substitution of one instrument for another was common in Baroque music and continued in domestic music making thereafter.

Lord Bullingdon, fed up with his stepfather's treatment of his mother, protests during the concert by bringing in Bryan, who stumbles along in Bullingdon's too-large shoes, making loud, clunking noises against the orderly, measured peace of the music (see Figure 4.3). Redmond sits in the audience, trying his best to impress his company. The music trails off, dissolving into silence as Bullingdon and Bryan enter. Bullingdon speaks out against his stepfather, Redmond explodes in a rage at his stepson's insults, then handheld camera captures the dissolution of order as father and stepson fight, and the room's calm yields to shrieks, gasps, and shouts. The sonic disposition—and interruption—of the scene bears similarities with the turf war played out in music, sound, and words between mother and daughter in *Lolita* (see chapter 2); music and sound often gauge power in Kubrick's work.

FIGURE 4.3 The disruption of Bach's music with clunking sounds articulates the shifts in power among the family members in *Barry Lyndon*. Warner Bros. Pictures, 1975.

Musical Sync Points and Transformation

Barry Lyndon displays the impulse to transform musical works through new arrangements and interpretations, and through revisions, such as in the curious case of Schubert, the anachronism. As in other films by Kubrick, music calls attention to itself in moments of synchronization with images. In *Barry Lyndon*, the synchronization is focused in a pair of scenes that feature the kisses the title character shares with Lady Lyndon, and harmonies that stand out in the context of their respective works. The lengthy scene that provides the double introduction of Schubert's trio movement and of Lady Lyndon follows her through the gardens with her then-husband, Charles, her young son, Bullingdon, and Reverend Runt. The scene continues to the card table, where she sits across from Barry, who gazes unabashedly at her. In a rare solitary action, she excuses herself from the table and walks outside into the moonlit evening. Without a word, Barry follows her and approaches her where she stands; she turns, and the two kiss just as Schubert's music arrives in the sunny sounding key of E-flat major. The alternating melodies in the cello and violin lines provide a tempting sense of a lovers' duet, while the triplet arpeggios in the piano part expand the movement's range into new expressive territory. In comparison with the opening theme of the trio movement, this major-key music sounds free, radiant, and delighted.

The couple's wedding is soon followed by a carriage ride in which the Lady's request to Redmond to stop his pipe smoking for a while is answered by his blowing smoke in her face, and a small kiss. Vivaldi's reorchestrated cello sonata casts a gloomy emotional atmosphere in the carriage scene and several others that follow, confirming the narrator's prediction that Lady Lyndon would become a background fixture in Redmond's life. Redmond neglects his wife in favor of philandering with her servants, though he apologizes in the scene that brings about the couple's second musically synchronized kiss. As in the couple's first kiss, Redmond approaches her, this time in her morning bath. As they kiss, the music's most dissonant, bittersweet chord sounds, like sympathetic commentary on Lady Lyndon's misplaced love and trust.

Throughout *Barry Lyndon* are subtly transformed versions of classical works. The effect is a bit like seeing a familiar person in a dream, then realizing he is not whom one had thought. The small changes make it seem as though very good replicas are standing in for the real thing, creating an unsettling sense that handily conveys doubt as to whether Redmond will ever attain peerage. The choice of a piece by Vivaldi is not in itself remarkable, but in the guise of Paul Bazelaire's (1886–1958) lush, romantic arrangement of his modest sonata movement, and the expressive rendition of the solo part by Pierre Fournier (1906–86), "the aristocrat of cellists," it is quite transformed. This little-known work of Vivaldi comes from a set of six sonatas, RV 40 (see Figure 4.4). Fournier, admired for his interpretation of Bach's cello suites, infuses Vivaldi with pathos and dignity.

In this rendition, the music takes on an aching yet restrained beauty that seems an apt fit for Lady Lyndon. It could almost be Brahms. We have not heard Vivaldi like this before; its style and expression make it new and intimate, and surprisingly accessible to contemporary audiences for its affinities with more familiar styles of film music. It is crucial in making Bullingdon and Lady Lyndon sympathetic. Kubrick places this Romantic Vivaldi in scenes of Lord Bullingdon's anguished tolerance of Redmond, who has intruded into his and his mother's lives, and of Lady Lyndon's lonely idleness.

While alterations of music for scene length, and sync points between drama and musical events are trademarks of Kubrick's oeuvre, here alterations are more

FIGURE 4.4 Vivaldi's music carries the pain and pathos of Lady Lyndon and her son, Lord Bullingdon, both of whom suffer when Redmond appears in their lives.

drastic. Handel's music is subject to broad repetition and variation beyond its modest, original form, and Schubert's music is distorted along the lines of repetition in some passages, while other passages have been excised. Elongation in both cases is not a mere matter of making the music fit the length of a scene; it substantively changes the affect. Likewise, musical omissions have profound consequences for Schubert's music and its appearance in the film. Such effects stand out all the more against the drama's remote temporal setting, trim dialogue, and lingering pace. These recurring works animate through their real and reimagined musical structures the cyclic and cumulative events of Redmond's life, such as the painstakingly slow and stubbornly recurring duels and the effects of his relationship with Lady Lyndon.

Kubrick's tack is neoclassicist; just as Igor Stravinsky wrote directly on eighteenth-century scores to create his *Pulcinella* ballet, Kubrick's films have a way of rewriting and repurposing music. In *Barry Lyndon,* this occurs on the level of the notes, the instruments, the phrases, and other material facts of the works in play.

The Sarabande

Film composer Leonard Rosenman subjected the sarabande to numerous variations according to scene length but, following the dictates of drama and tone, also according to mood, and intensity (see Figure 4.5). His variations play with deep timbres and short, percussive articulation and rhythmic variety—the creative proving grounds of the twentieth century. His use of timpani as a melody instrument places his variations firmly in the twentieth century, and well out of Handel's time, but deeper timbres such as these and the low strings Rosenman favors in many instances also root the variations in twentieth-century film music. The choice of any work built on a clear repeating pattern exacts a fateful, forward-driving sound and a sense of destiny, because once the audience hears the first sixteen bars, they know that whenever the music recurs, it will follow this pattern. In this way, the sarabande in

FIGURE 4.5 Despite Leonard Rosenman's inventive variations, Handel's Sarabande circumscribes the characters and their fates in *Barry Lyndon*; it attends scenes of death, grief, and loss from the very beginning.

Barry Lyndon has much in common with Kubrick's proscriptive waltz in *Paths of Glory* and falls in line with the tradition of Ophüls's use of the waltz (see chapter 8).

The sarabande took on a variety of forms and moods since its emergence in the sixteenth century and was one of the most expressive movement types that a composer might include in the suite, an important keyboard genre of the High Baroque. The Handel sarabande featured in *Barry Lyndon* embraces the slow, serious English style, the typical, two-bar ostinato rhythm, and a concluding pattern with hemiola that brings about a feeling of grand finality. The Handel sarabande chosen for *Barry Lyndon* bears a harmonic progression and key (D minor) very similar to a famous related type of music called the folia. The folia is a persistent form traceable to the early seventeenth century that bears a stately triple meter and an emphasized second beat, like Handel's Sarabande. "Folia," meaning madness or folly, may also bring meaning to *Barry Lyndon* as a comment on the futility of the characters' lives, or the folly of man in his material pursuits, a message made explicit in the final title card.

Handel's Sarabande frames the film in the main title and end credits and appears in several pivotal scenes that involve death or the threat of death—for example, during Redmond's duel with Captain Quin. It is always nondiegetic and has the power to transcend local moods in the film, for example, casting an ominous cloud over the scene of Bryan and Redmond happily parrying with swords, and the scene in which Bryan innocently asks for a horse for his birthday. The sarabande seems to finally fully arrive when Redmond retells Bryan the story of sneaking up on the French fort, and—in full volume—during Bryan's funeral procession.

Redmond's retelling of the story of the attack on the French fort is especially striking here in contrast to the first time he tells it, to the accompaniment of Schubert's jolly German Dance no. 1, which rendered it an exciting tale of adventure. In the retelling, Barry struggles to keep his tears at bay, his voice breaks, and the music stands at a distance from the story and its teller to give the scene its pathos. This twice-told story with different music recalls the twice-shown opening of *Lolita*, both of which show Kubrick's awareness of the power of music to recast drama.

The sarabande's ultimate equation of ambition with death manifests itself most obviously in the death of Bryan, which the film via the sarabande frames as a result of Redmond's materialism and ambitions for peerage. A remarkable version of the sarabande plays after the funeral scene, reduced in volume and energy, the melody now sounding like a worn-down song of grief; Rosenman depends on sustained harmonies in low strings to achieve this effect. One feels at the end of the scene not that the music is over, but that the music has simply stopped playing—an important difference in a film centrally interested in portraying characters' power, or lack thereof. Even after Redmond ceases to care about peerage, or anything else, the forces he set in motion (by disgracing the Lyndon name, mistreating Bullingdon) must play out to their conclusions; the unrelenting repetitions of the sarabande in several too-long scenes helps make this clear. For example, the slow passing of time, matched with the cruelly measured and seemingly endless iterations of the sarabande, conveys the suspense and suffering of both Redmond and Bullingdon in their final duel.

Copious notes from the recording sessions show that the sarabande was carefully planned to fit the length of each of its scenes so that in each case, the music would stop at the end of the musical phrase.[6] This logic preserves the sense that the music represents both the endless, nonnegotiable flow of time, and the numbered days of the characters, somewhat in the manner of a clock.

Choosing and Changing Franz Schubert (1797–1828)

Among the works selected for the film, Schubert's require special attention, first because he is uniquely anachronistic among the composers of art music, being the only one who lived and composed after the time frame of the drama. Why did Kubrick allow this in a compilation that otherwise conforms to the dramatic time, and in which other details pertaining to the late eighteenth century—clothing, daily routines, societal mores—are so carefully re-created? Schubert's music may have appealed to Kubrick too much to leave out, but there are yet other reasons Kubrick made an exception for this composer's music—particularly works from Schubert's distinctive late style, which includes those written between the onset of syphilis in April 1823 and his death in 1828.

The second movement of Schubert's trio, op. 100, D. 929, and the few notes of the Impromptu No. 1 in C minor, op. 90, D. 899, are the most emotionally expressive music of the film, in terms of genre and content.[7] True chamber music, especially in the vaunted string quartet and piano ensemble genres (piano trio, quartet, quintet), was meant for private enjoyment and study in the early nineteenth century. Schubert's music furthermore bridges into the era of subjective individual expression in music, the Romantic era—the kind of expression Kubrick smuggles into the film via Bazelaire's Vivaldi. Yet little of Schubert's music is allowed to play as it was written; for the film, it has been carefully limited—and, in the case of the trio, made over.

The bare opening bars of Schubert's impromptu signal intermission in *Barry Lyndon*. The music plays just through the monophonic antecedent phrase, ending on the note D, which both here and in the context of Schubert's work, hangs in the air like the word before a comma; Schubert's consequent phrase, however, which would bring both harmony and a clear cadence in C minor, is omitted. This simple truncation renders the phrase a compelling fragment, well suited to creating a melancholy, lonely suspense for the second half of the film.

Producer Jan Harlan oversaw the more drastic alteration of Schubert's trio and made changes that would sacrifice a central principle of the movement for the sake of the dramatic needs of the film. His solution for the trio movement would transpire unnoticed by anyone unfamiliar with this work—or even by those somewhat familiar with the work but absorbed in the story or the beauty of the images. If the changes are subtle, the meanings of these changes are even more nuanced with respect to moviegoers who are unfamiliar with the history of musical styles. The remainder of this chapter offers a discussion of the contexts and facets of Schubert's late music, which supports a particular interpretation of the musical alterations for the film and their role in shaping the story.

Form and Flexibility in Early Nineteenth-Century Music

Formal expectations began to give way to a focus on musical content as music's classical period drew to an end; subjectivity and individual, emotional expression through melody would become central tenets of the Romantic era. Another condition in the rise of concert music based on dance forms (in other words, stylized music) was that because there were no dancers to consider, composers changed established forms. It was the substance of these changes—and even violations of the rules—that distinguished a composer's style and creativity.

Thomas Allen Nelson's observations of the broad changes in literature in Thackeray's time also help explain why Schubert could have been a particularly attractive choice:

> Thackeray toyed with fictive forms and point of view in an age no longer impressed with an 18th century addiction to decorum in language and behavior; the language of good sense was being replaced by a fascination with the various forms and dynamics of language and thought as a means for exploring complex modes of perception.[8]

Nelson's "addiction to decorum" is a handy parallel for what nineteenth-century composers may have thought about the classical preoccupation with musical form and syntax, and "complex modes of perception" would well describe a strong trend in the discourse on Schubert's late works. In the context of Schubert's late style, any deviation from formal norms becomes the stuff of analytic import, a "way in" to the work. In other words, *how* the rules are broken becomes part of how we understand composers of this time period.

For his slow movement in the trio, op. 100, Schubert used sonata form, a form that routinely gets more scholarly attention than other movement types and is often considered a prime site of the composer's best ideas and abilities. Questions about meaning, drama, and emotional expression proliferate in analytical discussions of sonata form, a fact that only brightens the spotlight on questions of the potential narrative meaning of this music for *Barry Lyndon*.

Though composers could bend form for the sake of expression, the role of the performer often became more strictly proscribed and subjugated to the singular authority of the composer, but performing works from Schubert's time—or any time, for that matter—is more than a simple matter of following the score as though it were a script. Performances lie somewhere in between the law and letter of the composer's score and performance practice, a collection of decisions made and passed on by musicians. The long tradition of omitting a repeat of a section, either for the sake of time or to move the "story" forward, for example, conflicts with the call to follow the score to the letter. In a case that hinges on this very problem, vigorous disagreement surrounds the ending measures of the first repeat in the first movement of Schubert's B-flat major sonata, D. 960, another of the composer's late works. Pianist Alfred Brendel, who omits the first repeat, stands at one end of the debate, holding that this unique material is too different from the rest of the work, and thus disruptive to its overall coherence. András Schiff, on the other hand, protests that omitting the first repeat and its provocative ending measures constitutes a transgression equivalent to "the amputation of a limb."[9] The tenor and terms of this debate mark the tension between viewpoints that differ over how to account for all the aspects of Schubert's music: essentially, an argument between disruption and cohesion. These issues apply as well to Schubert's other late works, especially if they are altered, as in the case of the trio movement in *Barry Lyndon*.

Schubert's trio movement is in sonata form, though Schubert did not give it a true development section; still, he supplied stormy, vigorous passages that serve this function. For its appearance in *Barry Lyndon*, these stormy passages are precisely those which have been omitted. In light of the radical effects of the omission of just a few measures of a Schubert sonata, as in Schiff's view, the question of the much more drastic surgery on Schubert's trio movement for *Barry Lyndon* must be explored.

Schubert's Late Style and Why It Matters

Formal experiments were common in music in Schubert's time, but Schubert's remain some of the most difficult to describe; as Walter Frisch puts it, "Their 'concrete values' are not easily elucidated by the methods developed for other composers."[10] For Schubert's late style (1823–28), things get even more complicated. There has been a greater urge in Schubert studies than in those of most other composers to locate evidence of the man in his late music; the language in such studies ventures into the psychoanalytical and describes the music in terms of states of consciousness, memory, and other feelings that evoke the passing of time, a sense of bittersweetness, distance, and ambivalence—all of which Kubrick treats in *Barry Lyndon*.

In the commentary on Schubert's late works, certain trends emerge, such as great length and amplified proportions. Charles Rosen remarks with undisguised weariness, "The accusations of excessive length continue to surface, and will not go away."[11] Schubert's late style refuses to drive forward through its sections and keys like music by his contemporaries, particularly Beethoven. Rosen implies that those who deride Schubert for this trait have missed the point: "This destruction of large-scale direction, however, can be the occasion for some of Schubert's greatest inspirations."[12]

Schubert's late style in particular discloses a host of experiments with form and tonality that push the edges of recognizable formal shapes and proportions and undermine a normal sense of scale and orientation. In this way, it flirts with metaphysical questions of form and its relationship to meaning and experience. On the particular quality and dynamic of Schubert's music that again recall the notion of landscape, Theodor Adorno offers a paradox: "The language of this Schubert is in dialect, but it is a dialect from nowhere. It has the flavor of the native, yet there is no such place, only a memory. He is never further away from that place than when he cites it."[13]

Though Adorno was writing about Schubert in the 1920s, his work finds resonance in the emergence of late style as a broad subject of study in recent years. Edward Said's work *On Late Style: Music and Literature against the Grain* seeks to characterize the special quality and mode of works by artists who are cognizant of their approaching death.[14] The recognition of such a mode aids an understanding of how Schubert's music participates in *Barry Lyndon* as well. Schubert began composing his trio in 1827, when he was aware of his approaching death from syphilis, and it was published in 1828, the year of his death.

Words often used in connection with late style include "serenity," "nostalgia," "economy," "abstract," "severe," "translucent," "exile," "austerity," "anachronism," "immobilized," and "unresolved," among others.[15] In short, late style is essential, but also aberrant. Joseph N. Straus's formulations about late-style music in terms of physical and mental deterioration, including that which results from age, are particularly relevant and illuminating for Lady Lyndon, Redmond, and Bryan in *Barry Lyndon*:

Late-style music is understood as having certain distinctive attributes, often including bodily features (fractured, fissured, compact, or immobilized) and certain mental or emotional states (introverted, detached, serene, or irascible).

It may be that in writing music describable in such terms, composers are inscribing their shared experience of disability, of bodies and minds that are not functioning in the normal way.[16]

Physically, Lady Lyndon moves little. She sits or reclines in many scenes. When she does move, she walks slowly, delayed by a child, an old man in a wheelchair, and burdened by her elaborate and heavy clothing. The scent of death follows her from her first appearance with her aging, ailing husband. Emotionally, she deteriorates through the drama, her state gauged roughly by her outward appearance, the narrator's descriptions, and music. Redmond likewise resigns himself to limited mobility following his final duel with Bullingdon, and experiences social immobility in his failure to gain a title.

Bryan's vignette within the story is couched in the exuberant strains of Schubert's youthful, human, earthly German Dance, which accompanies the birthday, and then Handel's Sarabande rudely intrudes and escorts him to death—but not before he lies, immobilized and without physical sensation, on his deathbed.

Schubert's Trio in *Barry Lyndon*

Though the slow movement from the trio appears midway through the film—one of Kubrick's musical trademarks—it is, unsurprisingly, at the film's troubled emotional center. It balances against the churning mechanisms of peerage and upward ambition represented in the sarabande—a piece that threatens to crush or obscure the more delicate, breathable trio. The trio, whose major section brings some of the only contented music in the film's second half, seems to remind the audience of the first scenes of Lady Lyndon's appearance in Redmond's life and of the happiness for which she had hoped (see Figure 4.6).

The trio most closely accompanies intimate interactions in the lives of the main characters and seems to track emotional trajectories, their few moments of warmth, and subsequent loss, disillusionment, regret, and nostalgia. The insistent rhythm of the trio—a light shadow of the repeating rhythms of the sarabande—press ahead through the scene at the card table in which Redmond cheats Lady Lyndon out of some money, and gazes at her. She becomes aware of his look and returns it, then he follows her outside. Their kiss coincides with a move from the sorrowful, pensive-sounding C minor to a splendid E-flat major in which the piano arpeggios bring a feeling of abundance and happiness, and the violin and cello carry on their dialogue (see Figure 4.7). This counterpoint sounds carefree and content in its moment; there is no problem to solve, and no hurry to move ahead. This untroubled

FIGURE 4.6 Franz Schubert's Piano Trio in E-flat, op. 100, second movement; this work was subjected to considerable alteration to fit the needs of the film, including scene length and subtle nuances of tone and meaning.

feeling, however, is illusory and fleeting. The music represents an impossible ideal, as unlikely as a kiss that coincides with a shift from minor to major.

To sustain the initial pensive mood for the length of the opening of the scene, then coordinate the kiss with the change in key, adjustments were made. The first alteration, in film order, comes in the repetition, made possible with the addition of a few new transitional notes, of the first twenty measures of the piece, which include the cello's rendition of the main melody. Like Brendel, who appeals to cohesiveness as his authority, Harlan wanted the work to sound relatively consistent in tone across the film, a time-honored aesthetic in film music to which the other preexisting works in *Barry Lyndon* already conform. Harlan worked out a solution for the Schubert, first with an audiotape, then with Schubert's score, and even composed a handful of new transitional notes. In a letter to Ralph Holmes, one of Britain's premiere violinists and a player on the recording, Harlan explains his changes:

> I made a provisional cutting of the tape again, for the end of the Adagio, going roughly from Bar 83–103, then 129–153, and then 187 to the end, as we discussed on the telephone.

FIGURE 4.7 Redmond Barry kisses Lady Lyndon as Schubert's music lands on a sunny, major chord. *Barry Lyndon*, Warner Bros. Pictures, 1975.

The problem is that the less sombre variations of the theme are not quite suitable for the very quiet scene on the screen, and it would be much better to have the main theme repeated first, and to continue from Bar 187 to the end.

I made another cut starting from Bar 1–40, going directly from Bar 40 into 187, which then would have to be played very quietly and in the same mood as the previous part: if this can be done, it would be much better and would indeed work extremely well.[17]

Harlan's description of "not quite right for the quiet scene" seems an understatement in light of the wildly dynamic, stormy developmental material he omits. The development even takes on a heroic character prescient of Brahms, with triplets playing against duple eighth notes in contrary motion. Likewise, the intense piano tremolos would exceed not only this scene, but the emotional tone of the entire film. Also in this omitted passage are repeated dissonances that locate the work squarely in a nineteenth-century idiom and leave the eighteenth century behind. As music for this film, Harlan knew that it could not work as Schubert wrote it.

Schubert's main theme and minor mode reappear in a variant by Harlan that sustains a half cadence—for a suspended feeling—to introduce the conversation of Redmond and Charles Lyndon. Where Schubert's original quirks and ambiguities prevail to great effect and without alteration is in the last scene in the drama, where Lady Lyndon signs a note for Redmond's annuity; here the trio's slow movement plays out to the end of its natural life. The plodding nature of the accompanying

instruments mirrors the endless procession of bills and locates the cause of her financial and emotional ruin in her relationship with Redmond. Lady Lyndon's enfeebled
state and painful memories, suggested visually only by her weathered appearance,
blank stare, and hesitation, sound through the idiosyncrasies and delays in Schubert's
music. Twice Schubert sidelines the progress of the now-familiar melody with a low
cello trill, an element that introduces doubt and disruption at a late stage in the
movement when it ought to be wrapping up and resolving. There is also a fleeting
major version of the trio's main melody that, strangely enough, does not sound like
a happy resolution at all, but "wrong" and uncomfortable, like bending a limb in the
wrong direction. This passage, complete with its ingenious quirks, fits what we may
guess to be Lady Lyndon's ambiguous memories.

Schubert's late style seems fitting for the dissolutions and estrangements of the
film's end: for the distress of Lady Lyndon, the amputation of Barry's leg, and the
uncertain end to his story, short of the equality the characters achieve in death,
announced in the final title card and sealed away with Handel's Sarabande. But the
expressiveness of Schubert's music—particularly in its incomplete arrangement—
speaks to the film's preoccupation with absence and disconnection. The courtship
scene lacks dialogue, after all, then communication fails in the carriage (to the
accompaniment of the much more melancholy-sounding Vivaldi) when Barry,
upon the lady's gentle protest to his smoking, blows smoke in her face. The absence
of development effects a perpetual stalemate between the two characters, despite the
scenes of early courtship; without developmental material, there can be no negotiation and thus no growth or new understanding.

The rhetorical failures and impoverishments of the characters' lives benefit from
similar qualities in Schubert's music as edited for the film. While Schubert's developmental material at least goes through the motions of dramatic build-up, suspense,
climax, and progress of some kind, Harlan's cuts keep it out of the film, rendering
this version of Schubert even more truncated, dismembered, and disabled. The cuts
affect Lady Lyndon the most; the promise of change represented by Redmond's
appearance in her life remains unfulfilled.

Coda: Sounding the Changes

With the shift from the body to the mind and the accordant shift from dancing
to listening in art music, new conventions of meaning arose in connection to the
unfolding of musical form. Kubrick's films would follow musical form closely, but
not always with respect to original function (where an original function other than
listening exists)—indeed, much of Kubrick's borrowed music turns out to be both

symbolic and functional, like Richard Strauss's *Also sprach Zarathustra* in *2001*, Beethoven's Ninth Symphony in *A Clockwork Orange*, and Schubert's late works in *Barry Lyndon*.

Jan Harlan's alterations for the dramatic and practical needs of *Barry Lyndon*, though they may seem tantamount to erasing part of one's memory or—as some might have it—removing a limb, intensifies the pain of Lady Lyndon's unfulfillment. Schubert's main theme becomes all the more ghostly and inscrutable for appearing without the context of the rest of the movement by which the listener can make full sense of it, but this works to the film's advantage; the partial presentation a work that "isn't all there" in the first place is even more attenuated and distilled. Schubert has been out-Schuberted.

Schubert's departures from developmental expectation in favor of juxtaposition and repetition, emphasized in Harlan's arrangement, resonate with Kubrick's experiments with symbols, sounds, dialogue, and music in *The Shining* and *Eyes Wide Shut*. In *The Shining*, more and more of the music is revealed to sustain a physiological response and stand for a central theme, but only nominally to elucidate meaning. The events of *Eyes Wide Shut* inherit some fundamental problems of communication from *Barry Lyndon*, as well as its lack of connection between the characters.

Finally, the altered nature of Schubert's and Handel's music renders the events of the drama somewhat unverifiable by making references to the real world that are, after all, inaccurate. These are the kinds of changes that should prompt the attentive spectator to wonder about Kubrick's goals in adopting strategies of distance. These have elsewhere signaled a particular narrative mode; Wendy Carlos's flagrant, synthetic transformations of Beethoven underline the inversion of power between Alex and the world around him to mark the shift from antagonist to victim and, for the audience, attend new and unexpected responses relating to Alex's changing circumstances.

It is ultimately the implication of futility and worthlessness of the final title card that sends the strongest message about sacrifices the characters have made at the expense of an economic system that both serves and enslaves them. Schubert's music—and its loudly missing parts—has quietly aided in stripping the characters of their occupations, fortunes, family members, minds, and limbs. Kubrick's verdict on the rules of society as *Barry Lyndon* depicts them hinges on the film's successful portrait of irretrievable loss and isolation; Schubert's problems—both inherent and enhanced—show them to be a valueless and costly invention.

We've Met Before: Familiar Pieces and
Their Histories

5

THE MUTUAL INSCRIPTION OF MUSIC AND DRAMA

IN THE PREVIOUS chapter, music was an important source of orientation and structure and a means for understanding characters and themes in *Barry Lyndon*. The present chapter concerns Kubrick's technique of mutual inscription, a design of recurring music that entails extraordinary coordination of drama, narrative, and images with musical events. The music in these cases recurs and forms a clear and sustained moment-to-moment correspondence with unique dramatic elements. In inscription, each instance of Kubrick's dramatically cohesive music brings additional images, drama, and ideas, with attendant meanings that prompt the spectator to redefine the meaning of the narrative and the significance of the music. The audience must actively seek and "read" for meaning—it is not neatly quantifiable and, though occasionally allied with words, is not easy to verbalize. This kind of interpretation is essential to the high level of engagement Kubrick expects of his audience, and it helps account for the enduring richness and acclaim of his films. The mechanisms of inscription—both Kubrick's strategic deployment and the audience's inference—display and achieve perfectly Kubrick's goal that the audience determine the meanings of the films for themselves. Furthermore, Kubrick's marriages of music and image discussed here take on such salinity that the meanings of the musical passages, vis-à-vis Kubrick's dramas, strike the listener as native; it is as though a secret dramatic import were there in the music all along, awaiting verification and discovery in cinematic form. Musical-dramatic pairings that display mutual inscription are indispensable in the following two cases: *Lolita*, in which content was limited by the censors, and in *Eyes Wide Shut*, in which it could not easily take verbal or visual form.

Inscription and Its Impact

The impact of inscription lies not only in its provocation to recall previous contexts and emotions, but also in its ability to embellish, develop, and *more deeply impress* these. The process of embedding meaning in the music through careful synchronization and recurrence takes on a nearly palpable quality, especially for the demands it makes on the audience; an acute listener will recognize the music, recall its previous context, compare the current scene with the previous one, and process these responses in a way that is both linear and discrete and, on the other hand, synoptic and organic. In other words, the listener understands how the parts interrelate and contribute to a whole.

In limited respects, inscription is similar to the leitmotivic score. But while leitmotifs may accompany the appearance of a character or object, their melodies and rhythms tend not to be tailored to every movement or spoken word. Furthermore, inscription is something Kubrick employs for subjects that cannot be quickly and easily summarized or verbalized: *Also sprach Zarathustra* does not simply signify celestial alignment; rather, it implies a constellation of interrelated ideas having to do with evolution, intelligent extraterrestrial life, and other things implied but not shown, or even showable in any recognizable way. Even though the audience sees the apeman use the bone as a tool, they must still infer that he has made a leap in intelligence.

Kubrick did not believe that things handed to the audience would be at all effective. Inscription becomes effective when we struggle to "read" it. That Kubrick never defines the content of his recurring music cues the spectator to continue reflecting on meaning—the films compel ongoing engagement. As Kubrick's narrative aesthetic relies so often on endings without definitive answers, or answers to larger problems (war, for example), musical form and particularly inscription become all the more important as loci of not only coherence through semblance or repetition, but the film's logic center and emotional core.

Musical and contextual features collaborate and guide the audience's perception and interpretation. The audience's gradual awareness of the technique of recurring music with complex or invisible meaning further lends to the music's increasing gravity across an experience of each film that uses it and to subsequent viewings of each film. But Kubrick does not always mark the puzzle pieces obviously. Like other Kubrick devices, such as the ambiguous introduction of diegetic music (see chapter 2), the most developed and extended examples of inscription, in *Lolita* and *Eyes Wide Shut*, present surreptitiously.

The first moment one can realize that the music is recurring, of course, is on its *second* instance. The second instance is therefore the one that confirms the presence of a pattern and does so by virtue of engaging recognition, prompting the spectator to recall the music's earlier context and meanings, and simultaneously make sense of new contexts and meanings. Discovering the potency of recurring music in Kubrick is akin to realizing that a magic trick has occurred for which one was unprepared, and the impact is astonishing.

The Announcement of Conspiracy: Music in Main Titles

Moment-to-moment music and image relationships often occur in Kubrick's opening credits sequences when words, images, and music are synchronized in formal patterns. The opening of *2001: A Space Odyssey*, featuring Richard Strauss's *Also sprach Zarathustra*, furnishes a case in point. The moment-to-moment relationship between *Zarathustra* and the initial images is marked by the synchronized appearances of text or objects and obvious musical events, like sforzandi, cymbal crashes, and chord changes. Without any dialogue or story to follow yet, the audience is undistracted from the copresentation of music and image. In the opening of *2001: A Space Odyssey*, the combination of Strauss's music with the images seems irrefutable. The music boasts the hallmarks of majesty, grandeur, and triumph— rendered all the more awesome at high volume—but the audience cannot yet understand these qualities in relationship to the images or to the film overall; the music and the images, on a very basic level, inscribe each other with their respective qualities.

Strauss's music furthermore enacts inscription by virtue of its accruing contexts over the course of the film and the new meanings each instance of the music brings. Each time the music returns, the audience gains more insight into the significance of both the music and the images. The contexts share symbols—objects in alignment, the monolith—and other symbols remain local—the apeman's bone tool, and the star child floating in space; it is the aggregate that suggests what the music means. In all three instances of *Also sprach Zarathustra*, but most obviously in the opening credits, there are moments of synchronization or near-synchronization of images with musical events. This fusing draws attention to the surface level of the film's narrative, in this case, the appearance and relative movement of objects, while the recurrence of the music invites the spectator to connect images across the film. Thus, inscription entails both a technique of filmmaking and the spectator's detection and understanding of it.

While the image-rich main titles of *2001* furnish one example of careful coordination between the appearances of written text with musical events, the openings of several of Kubrick's films present readily evident patterns with a similar logic. There is nothing to distract the spectator from the white-text title cards that announce *Barry Lyndon*, or the white, all-capital lettering on bright colors in *A Clockwork Orange*. In both cases, the music is made to seem as though it were propelling the obedient appearance of the title cards, as these appear with strong downbeats. In *Full Metal Jacket*, each of the two first title cards and all of the shots of recruits getting their heads shaved are treated to equal time, dictated by the four-square rhythm of Tom Hall's "Hello Vietnam" as sung by Johnny Wright. Music, specifically the troops' chanting, likewise serves to organize the young men in groups in later scenes. The main titles are thus used to signal the importance of the music as a force in the drama to come.

The opening credits of *Eyes Wide Shut* offer an illuminating exception to the patterns in *A Clockwork Orange* and *Barry Lyndon*, and even though they would seem to have the most in common with *Full Metal Jacket* in presenting both title cards *and* images cut to musical rhythm, they forge a new path. The opening title cards each occupy the screen for the same amount of time, measured to the music so that each appears in conjunction with a strong downbeat. The card reading "a film by Stanley Kubrick" is in turn replaced by a shot of Alice undressing. The mere interruption of the white credits on a black screen with a color-rich image makes for an unexpected, jarring shift. Alice is shown for a longer time than any of the title cards, followed by a cut to black screen. This cut to black seems to come early—happening a full bar *before* the strong downbeat that would follow the initial pattern. It is not the appearance of the image of Alice undressing but its *disappearance* that is most remarkable in this case. The effect, akin to a reflexive looking away, comes from both the music, and from the camera. This introduces the sense of an independent watcher, and at the same time makes the spectator aware of her own condition as a watcher. The screen remains black for one measure of music before "EYES WIDE SHUT" appears on the screen. No cut after this point respects the rhythm of Shostakovich's music, contributing to a sense of spontaneity and instability, even as the film presents a conventional enough establishing shot of a New York City street.

Hand-held camerawork in the first scene, in Bill and Alice's bedroom and bathroom, and their hasty preparation for the party, unravels any stability pretended by the initially music-bound credits. Music participates in this dissolution when Bill turns off his stereo. In this simple, swift act, he at once ends the music *and* reveals it as source music—a status not likely to have been consciously suspected by the audience (see chapter 2).

Order is thus briefly established in the opening credits through the coordination and therefore the cohesion of image and music, only to be precipitously unraveled by the subsequent decoupling of music and image that begins with the shot of

Alice—the shock of the sudden sight of a beautiful naked woman and its disruption of the visual rhythm are an apt symbol of the film's theme of unbidden desire and its effects. Order is further confused when the appearance of the stereo divides the spectator's attention between contemplating the discovery of the music's source within the story and trying to keep up with the characters, who have abandoned the bedroom and are rushing to leave the apartment. While music is proposed as a governing, stabilizing force in the opening of *A Clockwork Orange* and *Barry Lyndon*, Kubrick proposes, then undermines, the same convention of stability afforded by moment-to-moment music and image in the opening of *Eyes Wide Shut*. The result is that the spectator is left in an uncomfortable position from which she can well empathize with the destabilizing forces of jealousy and other uncertainties that will threaten Bill and Alice's marriage. It is the moment-to-moment coordination, then dissolution, that sets the thematic stage.

Hidden in Plain Sight: Inscription in *Lolita*

In *Lolita*, music takes on a great deal of the connotative tasks of the film, because censors objected to what they saw as its most controversial scenes and topics before its release. While the provocative nature of the subject matter hindered production, it also generated excitement. The film's tagline, visible on one poster design and spoken in the trailer, play up the sensationalism: "How did they ever make a movie of *Lolita*?" Nelson Riddle's music takes on a critical role in conveying ideas that the censors deemed unshowable and unspeakable, and it answers to a large extent just how *Lolita* could be made. The heavy reliance on music, born of necessity in this case, would in turn become a staple of Kubrick's style. Riddle supplied original music, as well as orchestrations and instrumental versions of several songs: Bob Harris's title tune, the "Love theme from *Lolita*," Hal Hopper and Tom Adair's "There's No You," Paul Mann, Stephan Weiss, and Ruth Lowe's "Put Your Dreams Away," and Dolores Vicki Silvers's "Learnin' the Blues." The character Quilty (Peter Sellers) also plays the opening of Chopin's Polonaise in A, op. 40, no. 1, to which he spontaneously adds lyrics.

Kubrick introduces many cues in *Lolita* as source music, including the ubiquitous "Lolita Ya Ya," written by Riddle. The score builds meaning through repetition and association, an often-used film-music practice codified in Max Steiner's leitmotif scores in the 1930s. Riddle's score, like other leitmotif scores, hinges on the spectator's growing familiarity with the music, a technique that could become more subjectively potent with the potentially familiar classical music of his later films. It is in *Lolita* that music and drama first cohere in Kubrick's work on a recurring *and* moment-to-moment basis.

To make music follow action on a moment-to-moment basis was also a feature of Max Steiner's early sound era scores, and the most extreme and literal examples were called Mickey Mousing, after the manner in which music in cartoons amplifies physical actions. Though it fell out of favor in the 1940s as a technique for dramatic film, it has continued in comedic and animated film. Kubrick's adoption of a moment-to-moment use of music with regard to *Lolita* helped him convey what would have been impossible on the screen, and awkward in language. Rather than evoking physicality, as in Mickey Mousing, Kubrick's use of recurring music in *Lolita* has the job of carrying psychological subtext.

Over the course of the film, a recurring moment-to-moment relationship between music and drama establishes and substantiates crucial ideas and pointed subtexts. The scenes with the recurring music—scattered across the film's first half—offer new dramatic situations for the audience to factor in to a conception of what the music means and how it functions. Taken together, these scenes contribute to a deepening emotional and thematic groove. This process of mutual inscription of music and drama (and, in turn, the collation and decryption by the audience that it implies) speaks to Kubrick's statement about the power of things one discovers for oneself.

Visual symbols and objects can be hidden in plain sight in film; a visual symbol may be displayed onscreen yet still unseen if, for example, it is shown among other objects that compete for attention. Still, one may re-view the scene and see how the important object had been hidden—either because of the mise en scène or because the spectator's knowledge of the story did not cause him to give the object any special notice. The thought of treating music with this kind of discretion may seem counterintuitive, yet Kubrick finds a way of hiding "Lolita Ya Ya"—a fluffy sounding piece of pop-style music that turns out to be very important to the spectator's understanding of the protagonist—in plain sight, as it were. Riddle's score hints as to what may be Kubrick's concern with the tone of this music and its unassuming first appearance; above the first measures of the drum part in the score appear the words "Ad lib. Rock and roll (cymbal, etc.—polite, not raucous)."[1]

"Lolita Ya Ya" is first heard when Charlotte shows Humbert around her house (see Figure 5.1). The music fades in under Charlotte's chatter, apparently as underscore, as she gives Humbert her phone number. Before he leaves, she insists he take a look at the garden. The music gets louder as they go outside, and Lolita is seen sunbathing with a radio by her side; in this way the audience learns the music is diegetic. In all subsequent scenes, however, this music is nondiegetic. Lolita, Humbert, Charlotte, and the film spectator all hear the music when Lolita first appears on camera. By virtue of this double presentation of her, physically, with the

FIGURE 5.1 Nelson Riddle's "Lolita Ya Ya" starts as the ephemeral stuff of Lolita's radio but takes on crucial connotative tasks—often to comic effect—in later scenes. The two different sections come to stand for Humbert's desire and strategizing throughout the scenes in which they appear.

only rendition of this music as source music, the music would seem to refer to her and to be, upon its reiterations, her leitmotif.

Since "Lolita Ya Ya" sneaks into the soundtrack, the spectator has no reason to suspect in the garden scene that the music will have any purpose beyond being the music coming out of Lolita's radio (it is incidental, right?). The musical style of "Lolita Ya Ya" also would seem to disallow its status as dramatically meaningful. There is no sign that this music is in any way special, so the spectator has no reason to seek or contemplate its potential meaning in relation to the drama. In this way the music—or, rather, its *importance*—is hiding in plain sight, waiting to be discovered as the film progresses.

Kubrick's approach makes a strong departure from that of many Hollywood directors and composers who would spotlight the status of important musical themes upon first playing. David Raksin's famous title theme for Otto Preminger's *Laura* (1944) plays in brazen, luxuriant reverie over the film's opening shot of Laura's portrait. The theme is subsequently worked into the rest of the film's music so that it becomes a ubiquitous presence and parallels the main character's magnetism and influence. Raksin's rhapsodic chord progressions, effusive melody, and lush orchestration set the tone for the film immediately and convey the notion of Laura as a woman who inspires desire. The sentiment and the importance of the music are immediately available. Preminger's and Raksin's straightforward choice regarding music is perfectly appropriate here; with a murder to solve and twists along the way, the audience has enough to keep it occupied.

"Lolita Ya Ya" is most effective because of inscription, particularly in the garden scene. Throughout Riddle's score, timings in seconds are noted consistently above bar lines in the cues of "Lolita Ya Ya" and in some of the other cues as well. These timings suggest that careful planning informed the relationship of the music with the drama. Some of the cues for "Lolita Ya Ya" include descriptions of action above the staves, such as in an instance of the version of the "Lolita Ya Ya" music titled "How Relaxed." Here, the words "Lolita appears" and "Humbert looks at her" are written over the fourth and eighth bars, respectively.[2]

The music is integrated into the film by repeated presentations of the theme's two sections with action and dialogue that signify two aspects of Humbert's experience. The A section, which features the eponymous nonsensical lyrics, stands for Humbert's desire. The character of this music had to symbolize both Lolita and Humbert's desire without being too prurient, in order to maintain a delicate balance in the audience of sympathy for and identification with Humbert, at one extreme, and moral objection and repulsion, at the other. The B section, by contrast, stands for Humbert's strategy and negotiation.

In the order the film presents it, the B section comes first. It plays in scenes in which one character persuades or outwits another in a matter of significance to the turn of events in the story, usually to Humbert's benefit. The phrases in the B section often line up extremely closely with lines of dialogue—so closely that they share a phrase-by-phrase correspondence. The first instance of the B section accompanies Charlotte persuading Humbert to rent the room in her house. In each phrase of the B section, the melody in the violins rises in register, creating a heightened sense of tension that ultimately resolves in a return to the A section, in a higher key to signify not just resolution, but Humbert's progress to a better set of circumstances. There is almost literal text setting in this scene insofar as the spoken phrases align with the music and inscribe it with clear meaning that will return (in the absence of other forms of explication) in later scenes. In setting the text to music almost in the way that words are set to music in opera, Kubrick goes far beyond typical practices of pairing music and cinematic drama.[3]

The pairing of musical and spoken phrases makes this the music of foregone conclusions in Humbert's favor. With the exception of the first line, which Humbert speaks, Charlotte speaks as each of the musical phrases begins. Of course, by this time, Humbert has seen Lolita sunbathing in the garden (see Figure 5.2) and decided he will take the room in their house, but he plays the part of a man considering his options, lest he arouse suspicions of his motivation (see Figure 5.3).

In subsequent scenes, the B section accompanies dialogue whose structure matches phrases in the music in a phrase-by-phrase fashion, though more loosely than in the garden scene. Examples occur when Humbert reassures Lolita that Charlotte is safe

FIGURE 5.2 Lolita sunbathes while listening to the radio. *Lolita,*
MGM, 1962.

when in fact Charlotte is dead, and when he negotiates with a hotel manager who
"convinces" him to take a room for himself and Lolita that has only one bed.

"Lolita Ya Ya," with both its A and B sections, underscores scenes of Humbert's
life with Lolita and her mother, in which his fascination with Lolita and distaste
for Charlotte become evident. The A section of the theme is heard even in Lolita's
absence, strengthening its role of signifying Humbert's preoccupation with her. The

FIGURE 5.3 Humbert plays the part of a man negotiating a fair rent when in fact he has already
decided to stay at the Hazes' house because of Lolita. The music, invisible but ever present, sounds
his distraction. *Lolita,* MGM, 1962.

process of inscription relies on the listener's recognizing the music and recalling the previous words, interactions, and contexts that came with it; these meanings gradually inscribe the music over the course of the film. The tune is heard while Humbert and Charlotte play chess and Lolita comes into the room. The convergence of the dialogue, action, and music, concerning the capture of Charlotte's queen—one of countless double meanings in the film—supersaturates this moment: there can be no mistaking that the music stands for Humbert's hopes of capturing Lolita.

Humbert marries Charlotte, and Charlotte is soon hit by a car and killed. The news of her death, however, seems only to lead Humbert to think of Lolita. The B section—the music of strategy—makes only one brief appearance in this scene, toward the beginning, signaling that Humbert has one final bit of acting to do: playing the role of the devastated widower, while friends Jean and John (Diana Decker and Jerry Stovin) and the driver of the car file in one after the other to console him as he soaks in the bathtub (see Figure 5.4). Meanwhile, the learned meaning of the A section and its light sound face off against the serious mood of Humbert's visitors in one of the film's most ironic moments.

Riddle initiates the music for the bathtub scene with a darkly comic twist of musical ingenuity. A stinger chord that follows the news of Charlotte's death functions as the preparatory chord for "Lolita Ya Ya." After a man on the street says to Humbert, "Are you the lady's husband?...I'm afraid she's dead," the stinger and then "Lolita Ya Ya" are heard. This shocking elision drives home Humbert's use of Charlotte to get to Lolita, to the extent that Charlotte's death itself, musically captured in one chord, is incidental. Kubrick's editing and Riddle's accompanying juxtaposition of the stinger chord and another rendition of "Lolita Ya Ya" cruelly cut Charlotte—literally and musically—right out of the picture. As Humbert drives

FIGURE 5.4 John offers sympathy to Humbert, who, the music indicates, is thinking not about Charlotte's death but about Lolita. *Lolita*, MGM, 1962.

to Lolita's summer camp, the A section of the theme modulates ever upward and undergoes transformation: boisterous trombones and saxophones join in, flutes play fevered-sounding trills, the rhythm becomes more active overall, and it gets louder. Here Riddle sends the music into overdrive; it seems barely able to contain Humbert's invisible glee and excitement at the prospect of unobstructed access to Lolita.

Once the ingratiating "Lolita Ya Ya" has appeared a handful of times, its absence—after Humbert and Lolita have spent the night together at the hotel—is striking. This effects a retrospective realization that the theme has really stood for Humbert's *desire* for Lolita, rather than attainment of her. Desire, however, will soon yield to Humbert's paranoia and jealousy. For the audience, the comfort of the theme's familiarity is also gone, and in the many scenes that have no music following the couple's first night together, the audience is left to grapple unassisted with Humbert and his actions and to consider him—in the company of the more melodramatic and suspenseful cues—more sympathetically.

"Lolita Ya Ya" is a two-part leitmotif that wears more hats and carries more weight than its teenybopper style and the seeming happenstance of its first appearance on Lolita's radio would intimate. In fact, its seeming to signify precisely nothing on its first appearance is what gives the song the ironic wind-up to its punch. The adhesive and cumulative mutual inscription of "Lolita Ya Ya" and its scenes in *Lolita* exhibits an interdependence evident in many of Kubrick's later moments, for example the alignment of space travel in *2001* with the strains of the *Blue Danube* (see chapter 6).

Necessity may have been the mother of invention when Kubrick devised the roles music plays in *Lolita*. After all, in the novel it plays only a very small role. Kubrick relied on music to convey *Lolita*'s unshowable and unspeakable aspects and, in so doing, invented what would become some of his signature soundtrack techniques—the mutual inscription of the drama and music from one moment to the next, and music of ambiguous diegetic or nondiegetic status (see chapter 2). More than tools in Kubrick's musical arsenal, these techniques and their consequences for Kubrick's later work constitute a distinctive musical ethos.

Ligeti's Psychological Map in *Eyes Wide Shut*

In *Eyes Wide Shut*, the two parts of the second movement of György Ligeti's *Musica ricercata* (1951–53) not only line up with, but recur with, two distinct emotional states of the protagonist throughout the film. Ligeti's *Musica ricercata*, like the other pieces in the film, are not likely to be familiar to the audience. It is furthermore difficult to place *Musica ricercata* in a familiar style or guess, based on its sound, when

FIGURE 5.5 The second movement of Ligeti's *Musica ricercata* constitutes, in combination with fragments of dialogue and images, a psychological thread of meaning throughout the second half of *Eyes Wide Shut*.

it might have been written. Its technical features disclose little by way of connotations or function; it is a perfect stranger, one that strikes listeners—in moments—as alarming or menacing, yet its unfamiliarity leaves it empty of associations through which the audience might understand the drama and images.

The second movement of *Musica ricercata* comprises simple sections that highlight contrasts in the ranges of the piano (see Figure 5.5).[4] The music consistently accompanies specific psychological qualities and events involving Bill so as to generate meaning, in much the same way that originally written leitmotifs attain their connotations through repeated appearances with particular characters, emotions, and so on.[5] But, again, this is a case of inscription by virtue of the repetition, the tight cohesion of music to drama from one moment to the next, and the extended scenes the music occupies; as such, it also implies a piecemeal process of forming an interpretation.

The pairs of tones in the melody and their inversions supply a ready analogy for the mirror images of the bright party at Ziegler's and the dark orgy at the mansion, as well as other, less visible opposites, such as Alice's lived fidelity and her imagined indiscretion, and the notion of reality versus fantasy at large. The two pitches seem at the same time to be in a relationship of opposition and symbiosis, both of which are apt analogies for the parallel fantasy and reality worlds inhabited by the characters.

The extremely deliberate and steady rhythms of the piece lend themselves to the scene, "First Warning," in which Bill's interrogation and the mysterious woman's intervention have the pacing and gravity of scripted rites.[6] The other important component of the piece is the sudden appearance and then repetition of the note G^2 in *fortissimo* (see Figure 5.6). In each case, the first of these notes—a real sonic surprise—signals the transition in the film from a general sense of foreboding to a

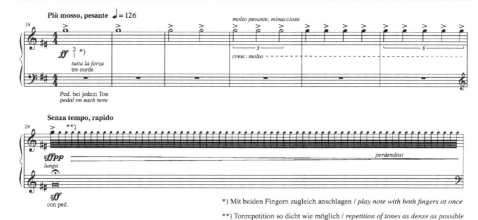

FIGURE 5.6 The high Gs that stick out of the texture sound alarm, often synchronized with the appearance of an image in *Eyes Wide Shut*.

pointed sense of panic and crisis. The moments of greatest tension in each scene coincide with the high Gs so that the relationship cannot be missed.

Ligeti's marking "ceremoniale" clearly resonates with the music's first appearance, the music's only appearance that could possibly be interpreted as diegetic, when

FIGURE 5.7 The man in red (seated) orders Bill to remove his mask. *Eyes Wide Shut*, Warner Bros. Pictures, 1999.

Bill is questioned by the man in red and made to remove his mask (see Figure 5.7). That the audience has seen Nick playing the keyboard to accompany the rites in this room in an earlier scene primes them to hear the first appearance of Ligeti's music as diegetic. The diegetic impression is reinforced when the woman's shout brings it to an end. The man in red begins to question Bill in theatrical, declamatory tones while a gallery of masked, robed figures silently looks on.

After this first appearance, surprisingly well into the film (1:24:19), it is heard as underscore in four subsequent scenes. Though the music is underscore in most of its appearances, little else is concurrently audible in its company, and the music plays at high volume.[7] This thrusts the music to the forefront of the audience's attention and allows for a sonic, musical experience of Bill's emotional reactions from one moment to the next. A close look at the interplay between the few distinct components of the piece's spare second movement with respect to the drama and images reveals surprisingly rich and consistent connections (see Table 5.1).

TABLE 5.1

György Ligeti's *Musica ricercata: Mesto, rigido e ceremoniale* in *Eyes Wide Shut*. Scene names and timings are given as they appear on the DVD.

1. "First Warning"	
Start time	1:24:19
Measures in the score	1–middle of 32, then 31–34
Description of scene	Bill is led back into the atrium, where a crowd is assembled around the man in red, who is sitting expectantly on a throne. He asks Bill for a second password, which he does not know. He must remove his mask. Before he is made to remove his clothes, a masked woman intervenes and offers to redeem him. The man in red threatens dire consequences for Bill and his family if he tells anyone about the events of the night.
Role of alternating semitone figure	The first four completely monophonic bars (not doubled) reflect Bill's isolation in the crowd. As the last note articulated in m. 4 decays, the man in red says, "Please, come forward," as if prompted by the pause in the music. There is the feeling of ceremony here, though Bill does not know his part. The addition of the other octaves (beginning m. 5) creates a sinister feeling.

(Continued)

(Continued)

Role of g^2	When Bill claims to have forgotten the password for the house, a gasp in the crowd fills the grand pause of m. 17, followed by the first of the alarming, lone high Gs. These notes are played forte, and in ever quickening succession, reflecting Bill's alarmed state as he removes his mask.
Role of semitones and high G^2s together	As the man in red orders Bill to take off his clothes, the two main elements of the music seem to gang up on him. The G^2s continue in what has now become a trill with sforzandi, and the semitones, in octaves, are menacing in their fortissimo. The tension builds, until a masked woman yells, "Stop!" at which point the music ceases for dialogue between her and the man in red.
Role of mm. 31–34	Bill is literally rescued from persecution by the woman, who is led away.

2. "Second Warning"

Start time	1:49:00
Measures in the score	1–30
Description of scene	Bill returns to the mansion for clues to the mysteries of the previous night. He is met at the mansion gates by a man who hands him an envelope. The threatening message orders him to give up his inquiries.
Role of alternating semitone figure	Already, these tones are like a leitmotif for the impenetrable mysteries and threatening powers behind the inquisition, and Bill's helplessness to understand them.
Role of G^2	The first G^2 punctuates the man handing Bill the envelope. The subsequent G^2s fill in a feeling of panic as we and Bill realize the letter was there, waiting for him, and the reiteration of a threat to him and his family.
Role of semitones and high G^2s together	Mounting panic, a threat.
Role of mm. 31–34	Bill reflects on the letter, puzzled, but not in immediate danger.

3. "The Stalker"

Start time	2:01:23
Measures in the score	1–32

(Continued)

Description of scene	Bill is followed by a man in a trenchcoat.
Role of alternating semitone figure	We only see Bill during the first four measures. When the octave doublings begin, we see Bill "doubled" by his silent pursuer, on the opposite side of the street, but clearly following him. When the octaves drop out, Bill has rounded a corner, out of the man's sight. The stalker reappears when the octave-displaced F-sharps begin in m. 10. The semitones act as a kind of walking music throughout the scene, and carry their leitmotivic associations with the mansion.
Role of G^2	After Bill steps out of the stalker's view a second time, the stalker's reappearance in the frame from around the corner of a building is especially shocking, as it coincides precisely with the first of the high Gs, m. 18. Here, the music conveys the alarm of confrontation between the man at the corner and Bill, standing at a newsstand in the middle of the block. They stare at each other. The man crosses to Bill's side of the street and pauses, but walks away. The Gs voice Bill's internal panic.
Role of semitones and high G^2s together	Mounting panic, a specific threat.
Role of mm. 31–34	This music is heard after the stalker goes away. Danger abates.

4. "Looking for Mandy"

Start time	2:05:43
Measures in the score	1–8
Description of scene	The "Rex tremendae" from Mozart's *Requiem* plays in the café but gives way to Ligeti as Bill becomes absorbed in what he is reading. He makes the connection between the woman who saved him and the woman in the news who died of a drug overdose. He goes to the hospital to find her.
Role of alternating semitone figure	Leitmotivic.

5. "I'll Tell You Everything"

Start time	2:40:05
Measures in the score	1–34

(Continued)

Description of scene	Bill wearily returns to his apartment. He walks slowly; his guard is down. He comes to his bedroom where he sees Alice, apparently asleep, and on the pillow beside her, the mask he wore to the mansion. Bill breaks down in tears and, when Alice wakes, says that he will tell her everything.
Role of alternating semitone figure	As Bill is slowly walking around in his apartment, and not seeming panicked for the first time in the presence of this music, it is the audience who panics. The music may mean one of his pursuers is lurking in his home.
Role of G^2	The first G^2 precisely accompanies Bill seeing the mask on the pillow. Though he is frozen to the spot, the whip pan from him to the mask conveys his shock.
Role of semitones and high G^2s together	The emotional denouement, before the resolution not of unsolved mysteries in the plot, but of Bill's solitariness in his bizarre adventures. His vow to tell Alice everything provides the solution to the mounting tension and threats.
Role of mm. 31–34	Alice wakes. She is safe. Bill cries.

The meanings of the alternating semitone motive include foreboding, gathering threat, and even mild forms of persecution, as when Bill is followed. The high Gs, which even sound like some kind of alarm, signal panic. Their ever quickening succession reflects the danger of a crisis and Bill's fear. Afterward the music calms down, and it always bring a release of tension as crisis is averted. In "I'll Tell You Everything," the music does not refer to anything we can see, though it will find its correlate in the mask on the pillow. In light of the threats made to Bill, which are drawing ever closer to him and his home, the music carries the sense that someone may be lurking in Bill's apartment. More important, it tells us Bill is completely in the grip of the mysteries he has seen and is struggling with his own actions and feelings. The crisis point of this scene, as compared with the other four, takes place on the most purely psychological level. There is little action and no dialogue before the G sounds, thus the meaning of the scene relies on the music and then the visual clue of the mask on the pillow. The whip pan, the cinematic equivalent of a gasp, from Bill to the mask comes with the first G (see Figure 5.8). Has someone killed Alice and left the mask on the pillow as a calling card? Did she find the mask in the apartment, put it on the empty pillow next to her, and fall asleep? The return of the semitone music fulfills its

FIGURE 5.8 Ligeti's notes pierce the air as a whip pan reveals the mask Bill sees on the pillow next to Alice. *Eyes Wide Shut*, Warner Bros. Pictures, 1999.

role of releasing tension, and Alice wakes up. Bill realizes with horror and regret that he put his marriage and family at risk. The film's greatest resolution comes with Bill's decision to keep no secrets from Alice, and the couple's resolution, the next day, to preserve their marriage in light of the belief that the reality of one night is never the whole truth and that "no dream is ever just a dream."

As with "Lolita Ya Ya," Kubrick exploits events in the music in *Eyes Wide Shut* to underline more subtle psychological occurrences in the dialogue and drama. Both "Lolita Ya Ya," in *Lolita*, and *Musica ricercata*, in *Eyes Wide Shut*, supply an indispensable layer of meaning. In each case, the piece is diegetic at first, and nondiegetic thereafter. However, despite the music's status as nondiegetic, its quality retains the memory of its initial appearance as diegetic music, conferring to the recurrences an uncanny quality—like a bug in the system, or an afterimage. This excessive repetition, which reads as persistence, helps inscription work. The nature of the music as a key to the drama, in both cases, is there to be discovered and explored. In *Eyes Wide Shut*, the content or meaning of Ligeti's music is much harder to quantify than that of "Lolita Ya Ya"; it reflects Bill's own limited understanding of the characters and places he encounters. His responses come across in degrees of intensity, vis-à-vis Ligeti, but exactly what he feels or thinks is never clear; it is impossible to know the substance of his experience, just as one can never truly know the experience of another. Considering how "sticky" music is in its ability to accrue meaning, it is remarkable that the recurring music keeps the finest details of emotional content just out of reach, a state that reflects Bill's and Alice's own emotional blind spots and limitations.

Beyond using music to organize and express that which would not have passed the censors and that which eludes easy visual and verbal means, the music in both cases here exemplifies Kubrick's perennial interest in the musical-thematic double frame. In *Lolita* and *Eyes Wide Shut*, the recurring works signal and substantiate the darker worlds that shadow the real ones, each in its own way. A sense of discrete territories in these scores would give way in the tumultuously changing dialectical relationships in *A Clockwork Orange*, the subject of chapter 7; such instability helped Kubrick undermine the tropes of Western ideology the story evokes. Kubrick's habit of creating a musical double frame was nevertheless done differently every time; additional patterns and nuances of organization—constructed by means of its deployment in the film, by its native structures, or by a combination of the two—motivate the music for the most remote and invisible regions. Meaning also arrives by way of history; the previous appearances of a famous work color new ones and carry the potential for strong emotional responses for listeners, depending on their respective memories and feelings relating to the music.

Taking *Lolita* as a lesson in Kubrick's musical methods, we know to suspect Ligeti's *Musica ricercata*, once it becomes nondiegetic, to portend Bill's downward spiral and the humiliating limits of his power in society in *Eyes Wide Shut*, and so it does. While "Lolita Ya Ya" provides a running commentary about the inappropriateness of Humbert's desire for Lolita in 1960s American society, *Musica ricercata* represents the working out of a more elusive central idea. The first appearance of Ligeti's music is more like an enigmatic prophecy than a clear commentary on the mode of the drama. In "Lolita Ya Ya," we have the music of a man in control who loses that control (and this music appropriately vanishes with it). But in *Eyes Wide Shut*, Ligeti's music appears when Bill is most lost; subsequently (and in the company of this music), he regains his way and his control. The final outcome of Bill's adventures, unlike most of Kubrick's endings, is resignation to an ugly status quo (see chapter 8). While music drives decisive moments that lead to Humbert's undoing in *Lolita*, it effects a clear-eyed view of the economics of Bill and Alice's marriage and the larger societal forces—such as the wealth and power of men of Ziegler's class—that they cannot overcome.

6

STRAINS OF TRANSCENDENCE IN *2001: A SPACE ODYSSEY*

IN 1968, *2001: A Space Odyssey* met with the early critical division that so frequently followed Kubrick's work. It gradually gained overwhelming critical and popular success. For some, the film meant nothing less than a new mode of engagement with cinema.[1] Others could not forgive Kubrick for what they felt was an alienating, boring, or self-indulgent film. On a longer timeline, *2001* has continued to gain acclaim, appearing sixth in the 2012 critics' top-ten poll by *Sight and Sound*, and second place in the journal's poll of directors.[2]

2001 earned praise for its technical achievements—particularly the meticulously designed and crafted visual elements and the pairing of impressive effects with philosophical themes. Several aspects of this science fiction epic, however, noticeably pulled away from generic expectations. The dialogue is slim and often mundane. The plot, whose trajectory extends across millennia, develops in rare, broad strokes. The soundtrack consists in music from the concert hall, an old approach to film music that stands out against the experimental and popular alternatives emerging in soundtracks of the late 1960s. Kubrick's choices of tonal, classical music were especially unfamiliar in the genre of science fiction.

The relative absence of dialogue and action opens the film widely to interpretation, in keeping with Kubrick's stated vision of the film as a nonverbal experience and his validation of the audience's subjectivity:

> I tried to create a *visual* experience, one that bypasses verbalized pigeonholing and directly penetrates the subconscious... I intended the film to be an intensely subjective experience that reaches the viewer at an inner level of consciousness, just as music does; to "explain" a Beethoven symphony would be to emasculate it by erecting an artificial barrier between conception and

appreciation. You're free to speculate as you wish about the philosophical and allegorical meaning of the film—and such speculation is one indication that it has succeeded in gripping the audience at a deep level—but I don't want to spell out a verbal road map for *2001* that every viewer will feel obligated to pursue or else fear he's missed the point. I think that if *2001* succeeds at all, it is in reaching a wide spectrum of people who would not often give a thought to man's destiny, his role in the cosmos and his relationship to higher forms of life. But even in the case of someone who is highly intelligent, certain ideas found in *2001* would, if presented as abstractions, fall rather lifelessly and be automatically assigned to pat intellectual categories; experienced in a moving visual and emotional context, however, they can resonate within the deepest fibers of one's being.[3]

Though Kubrick emphasizes the visual nature of *2001*, the plot's empty enormity and the paucity of spoken words force a perspective in which music comes to the fore as an important element in the audience's experience. Roger Ebert observes, "The genius is not in how much Stanley Kubrick does in *2001: A Space Odyssey*, but in how little," which seems an apt assessment of the film's bare salinity and its adoption of a mode more symbolic and suggestive than expository.[4] At the same time, the film is lavish in images and music, and it has generated a great amount of critical response.

Beyond simply suppressing other elements to make music stand out, Kubrick's engineering of this film via its music relied on a number of careful choices and coordinated efforts that help organize the film and, in turn, bring out structural, functional, and historical aspects of the music. Concerning what and how music means, interpretive methods and conclusions have ranged greatly; aesthetics, numerology, and pitch class indicate just some of the strategies applied. This chapter examines music's immediate and more abstracted relationships with images and meaning in *2001*; just as the film's visual elements have invited interpretive strategies that reach beyond the screen and into various areas of knowledge of art and design, a similarly focused attention on music is in order. Connotations of musical genre and style and the histories and characteristics of specific pieces play essential roles in forming an understanding of the whole. Kubrick's hope for the audience to see his films again and again justifies the close, multivalent attention this chapter pays to musical detail. The film's salinity, on the other hand, practically forces the engaged and curious audience beyond the immediate sights and sounds of the film; this chapter shows how historical and contextual aspects of musical works shape an understanding of the film.

When the music plays at length in *2001*, the effect is much greater than if the audience were simply attending to the music in the absence of dialogue and other sound; the music becomes the primary site of audience engagement by casting the film's structural integrity and shaping audience experience along the lines of connotative content and formal aspects. On the whole, music's role is generative—in other words, it controls, designs, and organizes what the audience sees and shapes the ways viewers make sense of the images. Kubrick adopts a similarly restrained approach to words in *The Shining*, *Barry Lyndon*, and parts of *Eyes Wide Shut*, likewise allowing music to assume the perceptual foreground in distinct ways.

The scenes featuring the classical works, particularly *Also sprach Zarathustra* and the *Blue Danube*, offer dazzlingly entwined relationships with their attendant images. Moments of coordination fuse the music and images together, much like in the opening credits, where musical and visual events are in sync. There is something virtuosic about the results of Kubrick's choices that eludes full explanation—like some aspects of the plot—but this seems to have only fostered discussion of the film, speculation about its meaning, and the sense of lasting impression.

In addition to the incorporation of classical music, *2001* marked the codification of an important technique that Kubrick would employ through the end of his career—the editing of the film both before putting in music and again afterward, to unite music and image in the most convincing and compelling ways. Music announces its authority and logic in its synchronization with images in the opening credits, as I have shown in chapter 5, and it aligns with visual events throughout the film. Coordinating the efforts of music and image may have allowed the audience to accept these largely atypical choices for the genre—Johann Strauss Jr.'s *Blue Danube* waltz (1866); György Ligeti's *Atmosphères* (1961), *Requiem* (1965), *Aventures* (1966), and *Lux aeterna* (1966); Richard Strauss's *Also sprach Zarathustra* (1896); and an adagio from Aram Khachaturian's ballet *Gayane* (composed in 1942, last revised in 1957).

Eclecticism across Millennia

Musical works in *2001* refuse to cohere in one group in terms of musical style and mood, though they all create local continuities. This mosaiclike design, which matches the discontinuity of the narrative sections, defuses any sense of musical centerpiece or climax. Indeed, it would be difficult to say whether the *Blue Danube* or *Also sprach Zarathustra* has left the greater impression, a matter only complicated by the endurance and reappearance of these pieces (often evoking Kubrick's film) in popular culture. Such an arrangement helps Kubrick reject a conventional narrative arc in favor of an accelerating line.

In addition to the tendency of some of the music to adhere to specific portions of the film, such as the *Blue Danube*'s accompaniment of spacecraft between earth and the moon, and Khachaturian's appearance in scenes of life aboard the *Discovery*, some of the works recur and transcend the divisions of the story; Ligeti's *Requiem* and Strauss's *Also sprach Zarathustra* share this privilege. While Ligeti's works as a group seem to signal the new and unknown, a closer look at the compositions helps explain why they might lend themselves to this interpretation.

Most important for the present discussion, the styles of the musical works enact a procession across the film of prominent ideas in aesthetic and philosophical history. In this film that throws a dwarfing perspective on themes of human existence, consciousness, and postindustrial society, the Romantic-style *Also sprach Zarathustra*, the *Blue Danube*, and *Gayane* come from a bygone earth-bound age preoccupied with individual emotional expression and the emergence of nationalism in the Western world. These works serve as persistent reminders of the enduring human, on whom the story is centered, and hint at a central anxiety of the film: how will humans measure up when encountering another form of intelligence? The Romantic music frames the human as slow and antiquated, traits that could work against humankind's own impulses toward progress. But Kubrick's musical choices do not denounce cultural achievement, old or new; rather, they celebrate it while dramatizing questions about the human in terrestrial and post-terrestrial life. They are works Kubrick might recommend to bring to a truly universal exposition. In *2001*, this earthly music helps qualify the difference, and perhaps measure the distance, between human intelligence and that of the monolith and HAL, both of which the human will confront.

Putting the Soundtrack Together: The Temp Track That Wasn't

Many ideas about music for the film came and went, and Kubrick benefited from the input of numerous people who worked on the film, as well as composers who ultimately did not.[5] It is difficult to say precisely when the process of selecting the music began, as evidence in the Kubrick Archive suggests ongoing searches for music suitable for a variety of projects; the main activities included determining best-selling recordings of various eras and genres, listening to music, and securing permissions. These activities continued with respect to *2001* until mere days before the premiere for the press on April 2, 1968. By November 1966, Kubrick had assembled a sizable collection of records to evaluate and had definite ideas about what he was looking for, as Jeremy Bernstein relates:

There was a phonograph and an enormous collection of records, practically all of them contemporary music. Kubrick told me that he thought he had listened to almost every modern composition available on records in an effort to decide what style of music would fit the film. Here, again, the problem was to find something that sounded unusual and distinctive but not so unusual as to be distracting. In the office collection were records by the practitioners of *musique concrète* and electronic music in general, and records of works by the contemporary German composer Carl Orff. In most cases, Kubrick said, film music tends to lack originality and a film about the future might be the ideal place for a really striking score by a major composer.[6]

It was Kubrick's wife Christiane's chance hearing of Ligeti's *Requiem* on a BBC radio broadcast on August 18, 1967 that set Kubrick on the hunt for a recording of this, then of other works by the composer.[7] Paul Merkley has established through his assiduous evaluation of archival evidence and firsthand accounts that Kubrick had decided he would use the *Blue Danube* by November 1967 (though not clearly attached to any particular scene) and *Also sprach Zarathustra* by December 1967. Jan Harlan, who helped Kubrick with music for this and subsequent films, brought the beginning of Strauss's piece to Kubrick's attention because it answered his search for a piece that would come to an end quickly.[8] From the notes in the score, Kubrick later learned of its program, which tied into some of the film's central questions about human achievement.

Also in December 1967, Kubrick engaged Alex North, composer of original music for *Spartacus*, to write an original score for *2001*.[9] Kubrick used none of North's music; instead he used concert hall works throughout. North recalls the situation in an interview in 1970:

> He was honest with me from the beginning. He made it clear that he had been listening to Ligeti (which was used for the "light show" at the end) and that he was very impressed with it. I also knew how set he was on the "Zarathustra"...After I had finished the first half of the film, he said that he was going to use sound effects, mostly the sound of breathing, for the rest of the picture, and so I was through and I returned to New York. At the premiere, I discovered that not one note of what I had written had been used...I regret what happened, of course; but I bear him no ill will. He just did in good conscience what he thought was the right move artistically.[10]

Henry Brant, who served as one of North's orchestrators on the project, further recalls Kubrick telling North that if he had been able to get permission early in the process to use the temp tracks, "the score would have been a *fait accompli*."[11] Nevertheless, any composer in North's position would have hoped against Kubrick succeeding in that regard, and hoped to sway the filmmaker with irresistible new music.

There are yet other ways the soundtrack could have gone, one intriguing possibility being the inclusion of a popular song. Roger Caras, first unit publicist on the film through April 1967, pushed for a hit song in a letter brimming with enthusiasm and evidence:

> I know that we have discussed this before but I am afraid I am going to be a pest about this and you are never going to get me to stop talking about it:
>
> Please note the attached top LP list from the current Billboard. The second most popular LP album in America is the sound track from Dr. Zhivago. They have sold over a million copies—it has been on the charts for twenty-six (26) weeks and just moved up from third to second position. Do you realize what this means in royalties? Do you realize what this means in free promotion for the film?
>
> Stanley, the Mitch Miller recording of the marching song from the Bridge on the River Kwai was a major weapon in the fight to put that film into the forty-million dollar category (I think it must be close to that by now). The Childrens Marching song from the Inn of the Sixth Happiness is another example.
>
> Do you want some more? The title song from the High and the Mighty. Do Not Forsake Me from High Noon—the list is long and impressive.[12]

Caras's letter, which continues for three more paragraphs, evidences the climate in the late 1960s for new alternatives to traditional soundtracks, and the new financial boon represented by a hit song in the uncertain and diverse film market of the later years of the decade.[13]

Kubrick succeeded in finding existing music he wanted and getting permissions in a process that took place over months. Though even Kubrick himself has referred to the music in the film as the "temp tracks" (for reasons discussed at the end of this chapter), the term is clearly inappropriate for a musical scheme he intended to use from the beginning. North's music was also not a temp track in the traditional sense of the word, though his music was temporary and was intended to be so. North's music was, in essence, backup in case Kubrick did not find or get the rights for the music he wanted.

Meaning at the Seams Where Music Meets Image, Familiar Meets Strange

Kubrick may have been a modernist on the whole, as James Naremore has elegantly displayed, but his approach to music in *2001* succeeds in a refreshing bid for populism and audience response long lost by classical music culture in 1968; the works are accessible and practically seem to invite interpretive and aesthetic responses. In Kubrick's efforts to create a different kind of cinema, I offer that rather than going back to a pre-sound-era style, as some commentators have argued, he attempts to forge new possibilities by making the most of the perception and memory of those in the audience; diverse and vivid responses to the film suggest that he succeeded in this regard. Responses to the music in the film, a thread in the criticism, constitute a tremendous range of approaches that clearly answer Kubrick's call for subjectivity.

The story follows two interrelated phenomena: discoveries of monoliths and progress of humans as an intelligent species. These two topics, in turn, illuminate the film's central question about human encounters with intelligent life beyond earth. As archival and anecdotal evidence shows, Kubrick's criteria and thinking regarding the music in *2001* is greatly varied and site-specific, yet all of the works serve the film's theme in some way.

Clues as to music's function, and evidence of the director's hand, lie in the sometimes-conspicuous editing of music and film alike. Examples include the stark severing of the "Kyrie" of Ligeti's *Requiem* to end the first scene of the monolith, and the gradual fading in of the *Blue Danube* in the middle of a waltz on this work's second appearance. The listener's familiarity with existing works allows him to recognize incompleteness, which has its counterpart in the narrative mode. The constant framing of the present as a slice of a larger totality that extends vastly beyond the perceptive frame may have helped justify both the selection and the excerption of stylistically and temporally diverse music.

Kubrick had to assume that some of his audience would not recognize the works in *2001*, much less specific connotations that might arise from them. *2001* affords a range of possible responses for each listener based on his or her familiarity and associations with the works. But choosing existing works over an original score also raised questions about Kubrick's film, which otherwise seemed "original." In defense of scores composed of existing works, Robynn Stilwell has pointed out: "There can be as much or more creativity in choosing the appropriate music as in composing a new piece. Of course, one runs the risk that the intertextual connections are not made by everyone in the audience, but that should not discourage one from making the attempt. There are levels of recognition."[14] Kubrick hopes not only for listeners' attention but also for their familiarity with at least some of the music.

For listeners familiar with the music, or those who will gain familiarity through recordings they purchase after seeing a film and through experiencing the film again, the music can take on layers of meaning that do not originate in the film, but may shape an interpretation of it. At the same time, familiarity can trigger strong emotional reactions; as Jonathan Romney and Adrian Wootton felicitously put it:

Selecting one forgotten number from among the B-sides of the unconscious instantly takes you back to the place and age you were when you first heard it…Moreover, every viewer comes to the cinema carrying his or her own juke-box ready loaded, waiting only for the film-maker to hit the right buttons.[15]

While Kubrick could not know what associations his audience might make, he knew that *something* would result from his button-pushing.

"A Place to Visit" and a Place to Dance

The *Blue Danube* of Johann Strauss Jr. provides a rare moment of contented play-fulness in Kubrick, one that admires human achievement at the level of both the spacecraft that so effortlessly transport humans in the solar system, and the dazzling display of the ships captured by moving cameras that seem to bask in the process. The act of animation is technically virtuosic yet still child's play, particularly in the hints of anthropomorphism in the spacecraft throughout. As an attendant of cel-ebrations and other rituals—notably courtship—the dancing evoked by the sound of the waltz provides a bodily counterbalance to the intellectual ideas connoted by *Also sprach Zarathustra*.

Kubrick's feat, for the sake of the present discussion, is restoring the waltz to its role as dance music. In a sense, it is Kubrick's obedience of the waltz that creates the greatest shock, borne out in commentary that continues to proliferate about this scene. Yet, as the commentary demonstrates, the essential identity of the work in this context is surrounded by doubt.

The great and lasting impact of the *Blue Danube* in *2001* owes foremost to the care-ful alignment of von Karajan's sumptuous recording of the waltzes with Kubrick's breathtaking images; the alignment turns out to be deeply faithful to form and func-tion—specifically, of waltz choreography. *2001* reaches new heights of cinematic ingenuity in the rendering of visual effects and inventing a striking yet familiar and plausible vision of the future.[16] Apart from furnishing an important visual motif, the circular designs of spacecraft in the second portion of the film confer an organic and even anthropomorphic quality that enhances their animation, at the very least, and paves the way for the film's major interest in artificial intelligence and questions about its claims to life. The waltz as a dance-music type is a particularly appropri-ate choice for this spectacular scene because of its distinction as the first dance that entailed a stimulating, unabashedly sensual—and multisensory—mode of specta-torship on the part of the (mostly male) crowd that watched the dancing couples (see chapter 8).[17]

Kubrick transposed the circular associations and physical proclivities of the waltz to superearthly dimensions with virtuosic effects in waltz scenes. The *Blue Danube* has been discussed in terms of irony, a view that supposes the waltz goes against the images. Irony may indeed lie in pairing the workings of a scientifically advanced world with the musical and choreographic discourse of an old, favorite tune, and perhaps partly in the very selection of a Viennese waltz for a scene in space—all ideas I will address in turn.[18] The present section establishes the ways in which the scene owes its organization and procession to the structure and conventions encoded in the waltzes. The music and images are carefully aligned so that they smooth over the experiential gaps between the audience and the unfolding visual events. Kubrick taps into the "music of the spheres" mythology, a long-running thread in Western intellectual history that connects—even equates—music with the workings of the universe.

For Kubrick, the waltz is a handy, ready-made framework and metaphor for many of the scene's movements and ideas (see chapter 8). But beyond its metaphorical qualities, the function of the music as music to *dance* to succinctly guides an interpretation of the images so that the audience gets distinct impressions and sensations of movement; these are helped along by some of the more obvious sync points of music and visual elements.

The *Blue Danube* sequence follows Dr. Floyd's two-part journey. The first part of the sequence takes Floyd to the space station for a brief layover, which has no music, and the second part joins Floyd in medias res on his way to the moon. The sequence begins with one of the most celebrated edits in all of cinema—a cut that replaces the bone thrown by the apeman with a similarly shaped spacecraft in orbit. Kubrick doubly shocks with this jarring cut and the drifting shot of the spacecraft, where one might expect a more static establishing shot; from the start, the celestial bodies—important as they are—are not stationary with regard to the frame. In fact, nothing in the frame seems fixed, which suggests that the real "stars" of this scene will be motion and gravity. The lack of a visually fixed point in this initial moving-camera shot evokes the rotation of celestial bodies on their axes and their rotation around the sun, the rotations of our solar system within the galaxy, and so on.

The first strains of the *Blue Danube*, its introduction in A major, come with the first shot of space. Though the choice of the piece of music gets much attention, also important is Kubrick's choice of this recording of the Vienna Philharmonic led by Herbert von Karajan.[19] Von Karajan's tempo leans toward the languid, effectively magnifying the music and giving certain passages a surreal, slow-motion feel. In this first part of the two-part sequence, von Karajan's recording plays continuously up to the cut to Floyd's layover; the work has played all the way through the second strain of waltz no. 4. When the music ends here, it does so on a strong F major cadence, which gives a semblance of closure, but indicates the music and the journey are not yet over; there has not been a cadence in the tonic, the D major of its most famous tune.

The second half of the *Blue Danube* sequence picks up von Karajan and his orchestra with waltz no. 2 and sees the piece through to the end.[20] Some of the same passages that played when Floyd traveled to the station are heard again, and the reason for this may be purely pragmatic; Kubrick needed music to fill each half of the sequence and aligned the first part from the beginning of the piece, and the second part so that the ending of the journey and the ending of the piece would coincide. But for spectators familiar with the *Blue Danube*, the effect of hearing some of the same passages again is somewhat disorienting and raises an issue: surely the music has not somehow gone backward in time (the images are new), but it is playing *again*. This detail evokes a canned music track, looping ad infinitum like Muzak out in space, something that would no doubt lend to the feeling Piers Bizony and others have had that "*2001* was…a *place to visit*."[21] This connotation even echoes through the end credits, giving a slight sense of exiting through the *2001* gift shop.

Kubrick posits the waltz as an experiential analogue for the audience since the audience (and Kubrick too, for that matter) does not know what it feels like to float in space. The sonic qualities of the waltzes—particularly the melodic contours, rhythmic profile, and transitional passages—make the space travel more convincing in alignment with the images.

Among the first clues as to the musico-visual alliance is the strong suggestion of ascent; the effortless, ascending arpeggios of the melody in the introduction each conclude with one note that remains afloat, almost always the highest pitch of each phrase. These high, held notes create an open feeling and keep the melody suspended with respect to its key (its "ground"). In these introductory measures, before the first waltz proper, the music likewise floats free of any marked rhythmic pattern. This passage may reflect the spectator's tentativeness and wonder upon making the leap from prehistoric man, seen seconds ago, to a future beyond his own (true both in 1968 and now).

A point of synchronization emerges when the highest pitch, an A (mm. 14–15) carried by cellos and horn, accompanies an image that guides the spectator's gaze upward from the lower portion of the frame, where the earth is visible, to the long spacecraft serenely gliding overhead (see Figures 6.1 and 6.2). The effect is all the more impressive on a large theater screen; the eyes catch sight of the image at the top of the screen, and the head tilts back to take it in. Kubrick is the puppeteer of the images and of his audience.

Collusion continues with a swell in the overall dynamic and a timpani roll, which seems to power the spacecraft and sound the roar of its engines. Following the brief

FIGURE 6.1 The long, high notes of Strauss's melody in the introduction of the *Blue Danube* help map out space and confer a sense of loft in the moving visual compositions in *2001: A Space Odyssey*.

FIGURE 6.2 The image of the gliding ship appears at the top of the screen, compelling the eyes and heads of the audience upward in a motion that parallels Strauss's melody. *2001: A Space Odyssey*. MGM, 1968.

timpani part, the range of the melody seems even higher, and, like the spacecraft, to be floating somewhat miraculously. As the tempo picks up, the camera slowly zooms in on the space station, as if introducing a young lady hoping to be asked to dance, which is exactly what would have happened during this passage in the music in its heyday as a dance tune in Strauss's time.[22] The music casts the spaceships as dancing partners and primes the audience for a sympathetic, anthropomorphic experience of the scene.

If the spacecraft can be said to be the dancers in this scene, it is the humans that seem, literally, out of step and behind. For the travelers in *2001*, the necessity of relinquishing familiar gravity entails slow, ungainly movements and clunky compensatory measures—for example, the movements of the flight attendant in Velcro shoes.[23] Her tentative steps in the long, narrow aisle of the space plane suggest the feat of a tightrope walker, which draws out the association of waltzes with circuses. The melody itself suits the idea of a back-and-forth between tottering forward (in the short, quick notes on chord tones) and regaining balance in place (longer, more precarious-sounding notes that careen a bit too high). Kubrick's scene felicitously exploits Strauss's inventive melody (see Figure 6.3).

The most dramatic sync point pairs the camera tracking out to reveal the majestic empty rectangle at the center of the space station with four measures of music that seem to make an announcement. These four measures, and others like them in the waltz repertoire, signal that a new waltz is about to begin; they are driving and homorhythmic and lack the waltz's characteristic oom-pah-pah accompaniment figure, though the overall rhythmic momentum continues (see Figure 6.4). In addition to the announcement of a new waltz, Sevin Yaraman explains another function of such passages: "In the context of the ballroom, these sections provided the dancing couples with an opportunity to catch their breath and to change partners."[24] Just as the individual dancers in the waltz align with new partners, so do the space travelers and their vehicles realign, and so does the spectator become uncoupled from one frame of reference and alerted to another—in this case, one in which people appear to stand upside-down on the ceiling. For the dancers of the waltz and the spectator of *2001*, the ground (musically and conceptually) seems to drop out dramatically from underneath during the transition. Strauss crafts a brief but gasping silence of two beats after the transition announcement, heightening the suspense.

Waltz no. 4, like waltz no. 1, and like the introduction, begins in a gentle, tentative way (notably, all of the waltzes that begin tentatively begin with ascending arpeggios); von Karajan luxuriates in these gestures by pulling the tempo back. Here is another moment where the waltz tempo seems to be making kind adjustments—waiting patiently and soothing the audience as it adjusts to seeing the inconceivable. On the repeat of waltz no. 4, which is even quieter than on the first time through, the space

Tempo di Valse

FIGURE 6.3 This passage, with its precariously leaning high notes and fluttering octave accompaniment, casts the flight attendant's careful walking in the cabin as a precarious yet entertaining undertaking.

plane aligns with the opening in the space station; the suave melody highlights the delicacy of the adjustments that make the maneuver possible and seems to say, "Easy does it." James Naremore detects Max Ophüls as the inspiration for the circular and turning images with this music: "The famous image of a shuttle docking in a revolving space station to the music of 'The Blue Danube' not only makes a sly Freudian joke

FIGURE 6.4 On the downbeat of the fourth measure in this transition Strauss engineers a surprising silence that would have delighted dancers with a sense of heightened suspense before the beginning of the next waltz.

but also evokes memories of Ophüls's *La Ronde* (1950) and *Lola Montès* (1955)."[25] Chapter 8 explores connections between Kubrick and Ophüls in detail.

Once the space station is aligned, the music snaps back into a regular, buoyant triple, lending both a sense of triumph to the accomplishment of the maneuvers and a sense that success is a foregone conclusion. The triumph is the audience's in catching up with future man and the spectacular beauty of the scenery he already seems to take for granted; for the pilots, it seems to be a routine flight. Dance music is not merely accompaniment; rather, it prescribes and causes steps and partner changes. There is a sense in which music is in charge, providing and manifesting the logic and structure in Kubrick's vision of space travel.

An even closer look at these two waltzes shows Strauss's mastery in this genre of clear codes and expectations, and how they create meaning in Kubrick's film. The first and fourth waltzes have an aspect of melodic rhythm in common. In waltz no. 1, the highest pitch in each of the ascending four-bar groups arrives on the third beat, then is rearticulated on the following downbeat and sustained. Likewise, the highest pitch of each eight-bar group in waltz no. 4 sounds on the third beat and is tied into a note held into the next bar. Waltz no. 4 seems to have evolved from its ancestor, waltz no. 1, in its greater length, in its greater variety in melodic direction, and in tying notes over the bar line into smooth arcs that hide the downbeat, evoking even more strongly something aloft. The coincidence of strongest (longest and highest) pitch with the weakest rhythmic position in the bar creates tension; the melody disobeys the metric gravity. This is an ingenious turn by Strauss, who unmoors the melody from the downbeats so it seems to roam and float on its own; it is a striking choice in a place where stability usually reigns. The similarities and the subtle differences between waltzes 1 and 4—especially the impression that Strauss is progressively shaping the angles of his melodies into curves—are significant for seemingly effecting the organic progression of the spacecraft from rectilinear and earthly to rounded and intrepid, regardless of gravity's pull. From the first image, of a long, rectangular craft to the more streamlined space plane, to the double-circle of the station, to the spherical craft that lands on the moon, the music has aided an impression of evolution in design and intelligence.[26] The likeness of the final craft's appearance to a round head with windows for eyes (see Figure 6.5) provides a basis for a stronger

FIGURE 6.5 The waltz seems to effect the ever-rounding shapes of the spacecraft, culminating in this sequence in the unmistakably anthropomorphic "face" of the spherical moon ship. *2001: A Space Odyssey*, MGM, 1968.

emotional reaction to the scene, supported by the waltz's ebullient closing, and thus prepares the audience for a more emotional response to HAL.

The spherical ship descends toward the moon to the strains of the coda—replete with cadential harmonic progressions and downward motion that answer to all of the ascents of the beginning. Even the reprised ascending melodies now have descending counterpoints, and the highest points of melodic arcs begin to sink. There is another striking silence in a grand pause precisely the moment one expects the final note of a phrase; the silence occurs just as the spherical ship touches down. This coordination viscerally confirms the end of the flight. That Strauss writes a grand pause rather than measured rests signals a true break in the dance rather than a transition. Strauss cleverly sets up the listener to be disappointed that the dancing is at an end by interrupting this music—heard several times before—in an abrupt way, and one note short.

The final bars crescendo and accelerate with a blooming percolation of eighth notes in the violins to not merely announce but celebrate the end of the sequence, and a task successfully accomplished. The *Blue Danube* sequence seems to be designed to dispel any fear or disquiet the audience may initially feel and replace it with the sense of the enjoyment and comfort of space travel. The waltzes ask to be heard, from moment to moment, as the manifestation of circular and spherical shapes and their gravities, and the images consistently reinforce the connection. But the waltz does not merely symbolize gravity (whether earth-centered or the "surrogate" gravity of the space station); it partners with Kubrick's fluid camera to induce sensations of gravitational ebb and flow. Though Kubrick revives the waltz faithfully in this instance as dance music, there are yet other associations that entail the visual designs and sensations of amusement park rides, the history of the waltzes, and anthropomorphization that compete for attention.

In its cosmic setting, the waltz is a vestige of life on earth and helps bridge the gap between our earthly present and an imagined future. The waltz focuses the listener's attention on gravity as she knows it, and it encourages her to re-cognize it in the new terms Kubrick sets forth. Though Kubrick strips away any human drama from the dance, he nevertheless renders dancing as such and shows his skills as an animator.

While the scene contains the most recognizably bodily music of the entire film, humans are marginalized and minimized by the ships that are slowly replacing them. There is a delightful and strange quality in the scene—and certainly some irony—a last moment of delight and familiarity before the dangers and mysteries that await humankind, portrayed in the character of HAL, and Dave's (Keir Dullea) journey through the Star Gate.

The diversity of the commentary on music in *2001*, especially concerning the *Blue Danube*, answers Kubrick's call for subjective response. David Patterson summarizes a trend in the opinions on the waltzes; they sort mainly along the lines of whether the waltz "imposes its meaning from its weight as a cultural artifact" or whether it "dispels the pre-existent cultural associations altogether."[27] While I agree that these are the two main forces magnetizing the scene, and they handily apply as a tool in deciphering existing music (classical, popular, or other) in films in general, *2001* drops the audience into a game of shifting and blending perspectives between old and new that speaks to Kubrick's idea of a nonverbal experience. This experience resembles the disorienting but not unpleasant mental acrobatics that occur, for example, when the eyes sort the images of a double exposure. The spate of associations the *Blue Danube* carries and the impressions Kubrick's visuals create with the music thus require a pluralistic approach.

A strong current in responses to the *Blue Danube* sequence evokes a sense of location, motion, and physical space. The most broadly available connotations of the waltz, and other triple-meter music, owe to associations in both stage works and film with circular objects and movement; the spindle music in Tchaikovsky's *Sleeping Beauty*, Schubert's song "Gretchen am Spinnrade" (Gretchen at the Spinning Wheel), Mendelssohn's "Spinning Song," and the second movement, "Fileuse" (Spinner), from Fauré's *Pelleas et Melisande* Suite all provided models for cinema, which included turning machinery of all sizes and kinds and a revitalization of the music of the spheres.[28]

The sense of place, beyond fairgrounds, in these comments is also overwhelmingly Viennese, locating Strauss in his home city where this music and the culture surrounding it thrived. Strauss was not merely considered a Viennese figure, however. In a time when the population saw rapid growth in size and ethnic diversity, Strauss's music played an intriguing double role; it was the face both of old Vienna and of cosmopolitanism—even beyond the Western world.[29] A poll taken in 1890 about the most popular figures in the opinion of the European public reflects Strauss's celebrity in his time: he earned a distinguished place in the top three, alongside Queen Victoria and Otto von Bismarck.[30]

2001 and its *Blue Danube* waltz scenes would appear to have particularly strong aesthetic and thematic connections to another "place to visit," Edmund Goulding's *Grand Hotel* (1932). Its cosmopolitan characters, interest in metaphors for a universal perspective that reduces human life to sameness, circular spaces and imagery, and the use of Strauss's music—the *Artist's Life* and *Blue Danube* waltzes—argue for its status as an antecedent. The *Blue Danube* plays over opening credits that show a rotating background of glowing spheres, stars, and beams of light. Spectacular bird's-eye shots of the hotel's concentric balconies and circular lobby establish the circle design that is in turn animated by its ever-revolving front door (see Figure 6.6).

FIGURE 6.6 The lobby in *Grand Hotel*, its concentric circles and waltzes symbols of life's repeating patterns. MGM, 1932.

The character Dr. Otternschlag, who appears mainly in the lobby, has distinctive dark and light sides of his face that echo the black-and-white checker pattern of the floor (see Figure 6.7); this striking visual scheme renders him a permanent fixture of the hotel (and a cinematic precursor, though benign, to *The Shining*'s Jack). Because he speaks as the omniscient mouthpiece of the hotel, his comment, spoken both at the beginning and the end, takes on an overarching perspective: "Grand Hotel. People come, people go. Nothing ever happens." His statement ironically reduces the emotional adventures of the other characters to blips on a universal canvas; personal stories have greatest significance for those who live them. *Grand Hotel* frames its events—births, deaths, affairs begun and ended—as universal archetypes through

FIGURE 6.7 Dr. Otternschlag, an omniscient, *jeu de meneur*-like figure and visible fixture in the hotel, comments on the sameness of life in his framing statement: "Grand Hotel. People come, people go. Nothing ever happens." *Grand Hotel*, MGM, 1932.

the suggestion that they recur. In a similar way, it is not Dave's transformation in *2001* that is ultimately important, but human breakthrough within and beyond the film that it represents.

Other character dialogue, too, highlights the themes of *Grand Hotel*; near the film's conclusion, Flaemschen (Joan Crawford) and Kringlein (Lionel Barrymore) plan to go to Paris. She asks, "How do you know there will be a Grand Hotel in Paris?" to which he replies, "There's a Grand Hotel everywhere." The weaving of Strauss's waltzes and the connotations of internationalism and repetition through the film codifies a sense of the universal, continuous, and repeating. The Viennese flavored internationalism that offers the characters a sense of comfort becomes, in *2001*, the extension of familiar brand names into space. It is difficult to qualify the sense of these brand names beyond a sense of believability in *2001*, though it is safe to say the profusion of franchises and brand names in Western culture reached a wearying excess that cinema reflected, perhaps by the time a Coca-Cola bottle played the role of an ambiguous catalyst in *The Gods Must Be Crazy* (1980), and undoubtedly by the critique of the proliferation of Starbucks shops in *Austin Powers: The Spy Who Shagged Me* (1999).

Piers Bizony's description of the *Blue Danube* sequence, particularly his aesthetic response to its realism and beauty, exemplifies the scene's power to convey an event and place:

> point. blue Danube makes audience feel the place visit. and it's exist!

> Vividly, I remember how Kubrick's giant space station seemed to tumble over my head. Its gentle rotation against a backdrop of stars was one of the most beautiful things I had ever seen, and I still get a lump in my throat when I see it today. I didn't know the name of the music it seemed to be dancing to—the *Blue Danube* waltz—but I thought it was much better than the usual electronic bleeps and wails you got in other space films. I thought the orbiting station and the other ships looked so real, I could never quite believe they didn't exist... *2001* was something different and important; not a "normal" film at all, but a kind of visual fairground ride; not a work of art just to go and look at, but a *place to visit*.[31]

Michel Chion echoes Bizony's tone of awe and recognition of fairgrounds in his response: "Who other than Kubrick has tried to make us feel what it is like to live in a world where there is no up or down? *2001* gives us time to shed our usual spatial and temporal orientations; to go round with the characters, not just watch them go round as gawkers at a country fair."[32] Michel Ciment also sees a Ferris wheel, and a specific one at that: "'The *Blue Danube*' not only evokes the music of the spheres with a deliciously buoyant humor but adds a dash of Kubrick's characteristic nostalgia for

FIGURE 6.8 The evocation of fairground rides in the image of the double-wheeled space station, affirmed by the presence of the waltz, renders *2001* "a place to visit." *2001: A Space Odyssey*, MGM, 1968.

a period when Johann Strauss's melody cradled revelers on board the Big Wheel in Vienna's Prater."[33] For Tanya Brown, the sounds recall rides: "The incomplete space station revolves to the strains of the waltz, evoking fairground rides with the faint echo of the oompah band in Strauss's glorious, predictable crescendo and rhythmic emphasis."[34] Claudia Gorbman hears not so much the fairgrounds as the ballet and considers the *Blue Danube* "both ironic and sincerely appropriate" in the film; the imagery "seems to invite the shimmering waltz to create an elegant ballet through the fusion of sound and image." (see Figure 6.8)[35]

Composer John Williams's reaction stands out for its description of the audience's reorientation from previously held associations to new ones:

It's largely cultural association. But what I think Kubrick has shown so wonderfully well is that the associations can be dispelled. Take a thing like the Strauss waltz in *2001*. The whole thing about a waltz is grace, and you can see that the orchestra can achieve this. Kubrick takes what is the essence of courtly grace, the waltz, and uses it to accompany these lumbering but weightless giants out in space during their kind of sexual coupling. And even though the Strauss waltz in my mind...it's the Danube, it's Viennese awful chocolate cakes and ghastly Viennese coffee...But Kubrick says to us, "Watch the film for more than five seconds and forget those association, and it will stop being nineteenth-century Vienna," and in the hands of Von Karajan the music becomes a work of art that says "look," that says "air," that says "float" in beautiful orchestra terms, and if you go with this film, the film helps dispel all of these associations.[36]

The space is less enchanting for Irwin Bazelon, who observes, "It functions as a kind of Muzak to get you up to the space station where Howard Johnson and Conrad Hilton have taken over."[37] My own observation, above, about the waltzes appearing for a second time, in progress, also points to the recognition of something like Muzak.

These responses convey a strong sense of the interdependence of the music and images. Questions of which came first are not consciously asked by many audience members; rather, connotations of works from their past contexts bounce around (sometimes unconsciously) and into new ones in a complex hall of mirrors. Rather than causing anxiety over the loss of the original, however, this aggregation of meanings, sounds, and images can weave together like a blanket; there is the constant comfort of at least partial familiarity, even when the piece is in a "new" context. At the same time, the deeper we inquire, the more we may discover.

Compromises and Mutual Transformations

The commentary on the *Blue Danube* seems to indicate that music renders the image somehow more accessible to comprehension and aesthetic response, and the specificity of the waltzes with respect to circles galvanizes this process, but Bizony's observations about "bleeps and wails" might prompt one to ask why soundtracks for "other space films" were often uncritically accepted. This point correlates to the relative lack of commentary on Kubrick's choice of Ligeti's music and why Kubrick's choice of Richard Strauss did not seem remarkable (because it seemed appropriate enough). Audience perception seems to skew along the lines of generic expectations and relativism; the audience notices what sticks out, such as an old waltz in outer space.

In addition to the recurring imagery in responses to music in *2001*, there is a clear sense of willingness to relinquish both disbelief and, more to the point, old associations in favor of Kubrick's new ones. Chion's remark about shedding our usual orientations is a case in point. The audience is asked in the scene to contemplate the process and watch it unfold. Roger Ebert describes how the scene works: "We know the music. It proceeds as it must. And so, through a peculiar logic, the space hardware moves slowly because it's keeping the tempo of the waltz. At the same time, there is an exaltation in the music that helps us feel the majesty of the process."[38] Ebert, content to attribute the success of the scene to the "peculiar logic" of the parts, adopts the attitude of abandonment seen in much of the commentary. Kubrick's scene requires an act of trust as spectators float adrift of what they know; for many, reward followed. Kubrick's recognizable musical choices likewise may give something up upon becoming part of *2001*.

The waltzes have long been known as purely instrumental music, but Strauss wrote the piece as a *Chorwaltz*. The waltzes assumed no less than three different poetic texts for choral settings over the years, but in Strauss's time, the popularity of the instrumental version, both at the Paris World's Fair and in performances in New York, eclipsed the choral versions; prominent music critic Eduard Hanslick, for one, was apparently unaware that the piece had ever had sung lyrics. His remarks about the piece are useful both for indicating how the work was understood in its time and for illustrating the very process of abandonment of meaning that Kubrick's later reappropriation would effect: "The *Blue Danube* not only enjoys unexampled popularity; it has also achieved a unique significance: that of a symbol for everything that is beautiful and pleasant and gay in Vienna. It is a kind of patriotic folk song without words." Clearly, the lack of sung words in the performances Hanslick heard did not prevent him from hearing meaning in the piece, and even a resemblance to texted music. He described its celebratory qualities as nationalistic in nature, calling the work "another national anthem, one which celebrates the country and its people."[39] The absence of words, and then Kubrick's transposition of the waltzes to space, dramatize the nature of survival (biological and aesthetic alike) that abandons what has fallen into disuse in favor of a replacement that suits immediate needs.

Aside from the reprise of the *Blue Danube* with the end credits, *2001* contains two other waltzes, and these imply that the technological advances and celebratory maneuvers buoyed by the *Blue Danube* have a dark side as well. David Patterson makes a compelling case for including in the overall conception of music in *2001* the rhythmic patterns of the pulsing alarms during the murder of the hibernating astronauts, which organize neatly into a mechanical waltz.[40] In this instance, HAL appropriates the waltz for his own purposes. Likewise, the deaths of the slumbering astronauts come, swift and invisible, from the very technology that humans built and that had sustained their lives in space up to this moment. This technological appropriation owes to a long tradition in cinema of relating the waltz to doom and death (see chapter 8).

HAL's own singing of Harry Dacre's "Daisy Bell (A Bicycle Built for Two)" presents as another death waltz, albeit rendered as a melody without characteristic waltz accompaniment. The gradual slowing of tempo and sinking pitches of HAL's performance convey a clear portrayal of the computer "winding down" toward death as Dave shuts down his systems. The song nostalgically recalls its late nineteenth-century origins and innocent words and pays homage to the IBM 7094's feat of singing the same song in 1961; but in the context of the *Blue Danube*, it becomes a sour commentary on the human price of technology and its great risks. These scenes afford a brief glimpse at the fraught ethics of artificial intelligence, including the mysterious and unsettling matter of its death.

Lonely Vignette: Khachaturian

The Adagio from Khachaturian's *Gayane* introduces the audience to the mission of the Discovery, heading toward Jupiter. The intertitle marks the time as eighteen months after the scenes on the moon; the music seems immediately magnetized by this human concept of marking time, and the relative brevity of human life. The glacial, gliding movement of the ship indicates that these months have passed very slowly.

Armenian composer Aram Khachaturian wrote music in the twentieth century, like Ligeti, but his style employed tonality and a self-described nationalistic quality. His style takes a traditional and lyrical approach to the orchestra, and a wide range of moods and energies and many ingratiating folklike melodies animate his works; he is best known for his popular "Sabre Dance," which also comes from *Gayane*. Khachaturian was an important Armenian cultural figure and the first Armenian composer to write music specifically for film, a career option for which he was well prepared by his experience writing ballet, opera, and other stage music. By the time of his 1957 revision of *Gayane*, he had written nearly a dozen original scores for Armenian films, an activity that he found particularly rewarding and that showcased his sensitivity to dramatic nuance.[41]

Compared to the other works in *2001*, the nondiegetic Adagio assumes the most traditional roles: establishing a mood that is melancholy and resigned, and imbuing this scene with pathos. The sound of this string-dominated music is tonal and lyrical. The Adagio's initial, bare cello melody lacks any accompaniment to ground it in a clear harmony or obvious meter. In time, violins join in with a separate melody, creating counterpoint and moments of dissonance that sound more strained and hopeless than aggressive. The musical style bears similarities with Dmitry Shostakovich's quieter moments and has a sensibility and timbre akin to Samuel Barber's Adagio for string quartet, which, in its full string arrangement, became one of the most popular works of the twentieth century. Barber's music was used at funerals of high-profile figures, to accompany solemn radio broadcasts, and in film, perhaps most famously in *Platoon* (1986).

Khachaturian's initial melody accompanies shots of the ship, then of Frank (Gary Lockwood) running in the centrifuge; the music may convey his unexpressed loneliness and despair and other feelings the audience may imagine the astronaut to have after so much time in space. More important, the music invites a sense of pathos about the state of Frank's life, devoted to the mission. His likeness to a hamster in a wheel is an incisive reminder of man's physical nature as an animal—one that must exercise to maintain itself to carry out its tasks and remain healthy. The effects of life in space on his emotional state—a topic hinted at in HAL's psychology report on the crew—remain unclear.

Frank's running and the music are out of sync, the music's pulse being more lan-guid, which makes the shots of Frank seem relatively dispassionate compared to those of the *Blue Danube* sequence. The opening minutes of the piece play again when Frank receives a video message from his parents, who chatter excitedly to him about mundane details of life on earth and wish him a happy birthday. The awk-ward fit of Khachaturian's music with the diegetic "Happy Birthday," which is not particularly in tune itself, again creates a sense of detachment. Frank's face registers no response as he listens to the message, a believable response of someone accus-tomed to this mode of communication, but one that hides the emotional world of the astronauts from the audience's view. Khachaturian's music points to this absence and laments it.

Khachaturian's music also contributes to the sense that humans are outmoded. Juxtapositions of HAL's superior intelligence and perpetual awareness with the humans, whose lives are measured in only so many birthdays, makes the humans' needs seem like embarrassingly short-sighted design flaws. Khachaturian's music helps render a sense of the human costs of scientific ambition, and the stubborn dis-tance that remains between these ambitious plans and the smallness of an individual human life, bound in a watery body that still needs to feed, rest, and breathe. This music focuses a sad attention on humans' most human qualities and questions their place in a future with intelligent computers and interplanetary exploration.

Though most of *2001*'s musical homages and parodies refer to or include *Also sprach Zarathustra* or the *Blue Danube*, this moment too has some notable prog-eny. James Horner reworks Khachaturian's music in several of his original scores, most notably *Aliens* (1986), and several scenes in *Mystery Science Theater 3000: The Movie* (1996) feature a compelling stylistic imitation of Khachaturian's Adagio by Billy Barber. In *Mystery Science Theater 3000*, Khachaturian-like music accompanies images of the bone-shaped ship (a clear *2001* nod) slowly drifting across the screen, left to right, and of Mike (Michael Nelson) running in a centrifuge and drinking from a giant pet water dispenser, at once explicating and spoofing the associations viewers might make with hamsters in this scene and its progenitor in *2001*.

Ligeti at the Limits

Of the music in *2001*, György Ligeti's seems to get the least attention. Its apparent fit for the science fiction genre has kept deeper inquiry at bay and kept its nuances hidden in plain sight. Ligeti's *Atmosphères*, *Requiem*, *Lux aeterna*, and *Aventures,* all written in the 1960s and likely unknown to all but the most enthusiastic followers of new music, would have practically seemed to the audience (with notable exceptions, including the composer himself)[42] to be original film music. It is for this reason, perhaps, that Ligeti's music in the context of the film has been the least investigated. In addition, the distinction of Ligeti's works as a group, as atonal and modern, compared to the tonal, traditional sound of the works by the other three composers, seems to have discouraged further scrutiny. In any context, however, Ligeti's music presents challenges, and even the savviest of listeners of 1968 would have found existing musical concepts and vocabulary insufficient for discussing the composer's sound world.

The formulation "Behind every man alive stand thirty ghosts, for that is the ratio by which the dead outnumber the living" became a prominent catchphrase in the press material for *2001* and represented a thematic concern for Kubrick. Questions about the mysterious and inexplicable aspects of the universe and human experience creep in at the edges of *2001* wherever Ligeti's music appears, and Kubrick's interest in the spiritual ramifications of the statement may have compelled him to keep an ear out for music that might suggest them. Ligeti's music may also have answered Kubrick's need for "unusual and distinctive" music and "a really striking score by a major composer," Ligeti having achieved international critical renown since the premiere of his experimental sonic drama *Apparitions* in Vienna in 1960.

Ligeti's music in *2001* comes from a period of intensive exploration and invention in the composer's eclectic career that bears coincidental interests with Kubrick's film. Inspired in large part by the experimental electronic music of Karlheinz Stockhausen and Herbert Eimert of the Darmstadt School, Ligeti was keenly interested in limits—the limits of listener perception, instruments, performers, and technology. Ligeti's music of the 1960s is further shaped by the composer's experimental energy and by techniques and concepts in the music of fifteenth-century composers. On first listen, the intriguing *Atmosphères*, an ambitious work for eighty-nine instruments, seems an unlikely choice for overture music, especially in comparison to the grandiose, tonal scores of contemporary film epics, of which Kubrick was well aware. *Atmosphères* is conventional, however, in providing a sample of music to come, and hinting, through its challenges to listener perception, at perception itself as a central interest of the film.

The slightly abbreviated version of *Atmosphères* at the very start of *2001*, with black screen, ushers in Ligeti's sonic world; the work is among Ligeti's first to use his technique of micropolyphony. In micropolyphony, Ligeti creates complex textures with dense clusters of sustained pitches and gradual additions and subtractions of layers to create a dynamic texture. The density of this music challenges the ear to discern where one pitch ends and another begins, or when one group of instruments disappears and another enters. The distinctions between pitches are often finer than the human ear can hear, and in terms of constituting an unconventional and distant relationship between individual parts and whole, they have something in common with impressionist painting, whose component parts cohere only when the viewer stands at some distance.

Ligeti seems more concerned with the aggregate effect of his many tiny component parts than with the details themselves. Jane Piper Clendinning explains how Ligeti's use of great speed effects an illusion at the limit between two perceptions: "The small units are repeated quickly enough that the pitches almost fuse into a chord, creating a compound melody, complete with voice leading within each melodic line connecting adjacent harmonies."[43]

As Ligeti pushes his approach to tonality toward complexity, his approach to rhythm and time is much more simple. Ligeti's de-emphasis of pulse and meter in the sound of his music may account for the serene quality commentators have noted. Though these techniques seem opposite, both work to disorient the listener with regard to "real time" and to the overall piece; it is not clear, in the midst of listening to a piece by Ligeti, how much time has elapsed since it began, how long it will continue, or where (in terms of range and intensity) it is heading. The various challenges Ligeti poses to his listeners in his micropolyphonic music amount to a kind of modern sublime. A full understanding of the style requires some detachment, and its effect is often overwhelming, though also beautiful.

Several scenes in *2001* benefit from the floating temporal quality and disorienting effects of Ligeti's music. It could be the temporal and harmonic aspects of Ligeti's music that make it suitable for suggesting a life form above and beyond our own and for casting a dizzying perspective on the human experience. In playing with limits of materials and perceptible qualities, Ligeti's modern sublime serves Kubrick's themes and modes well. It is worth noting that two of his works in the film, "Kyrie" from *Requiem* and *Lux aeterna*, are the only ones with voices in the score.

For *Lux aeterna*, Ligeti relied on the traditional technique of setting the voices in canon, but the canons—spread among the sixteen voices—are complexly interrelated, as their proportions eschew meter in favor of numerical ratios. The result is that this work, like *Atmosphères*, seems to float freely through time rather than musical measures or beats. It also creates the impression of a gradual accumulation of energy. *Atmosphères* plays as the apemen contemplate the appearance of the mysterious monolith, giving this encounter a sense of protracted time and intensification, while *Lux aeterna* contributes to the opposite effect when it accompanies shots of the moon bus that takes Dr. Floyd from the moon base to the monolith. The moon bus glides very quickly in the frame, and without a distinct meter, the music takes on the visual tempo of the image; suddenly, Ligeti's music is not slow, as it might sound without the accompanying image, but compressed, its distilled lines zooming past the ear as though at the speed of light. The combination relies on the audience's assimilation of qualities in both image and music to perceive qualities of atmosphere, time, and motion.

The composer's own dynamic description of his style in the 1960s reveals a rich imagination and sensitivity to qualities of sensory—and cross-sensory—experience:

> Sounds and musical contexts continually bring to my mind the feeling of colour, consistency, and visible or even tastable form. And on the other hand, colour, form, material quality and even abstract ideas involuntarily arouse in me musical conceptions. That explains the presence of so many "extra-musical" features in my compositions. Sounding planes and masses, which may succeed, penetrate or mingle with one another—floating networks that get torn up or entangled—wet, sticky, gelatinous, fibrous dry, brittle, granular and compact materials shreds, curlicues, splinters and traces of every sort—imaginary buildings, labyrinths, inscriptions, texts, dialogues, insects—states, events, processes, blendings, transformations, catastrophes, disintegrations, disappearances—all these are elements of this non-purist music.[44]

Ligeti's description conveys an intuitive, freely associative, and abstract approach that erases differences in the scale and nature of its topics. The description helps explain the music's availability to "extra-musical" aspects and its relevance for *2001*. Ligeti's words might also serve as a verbal approximation of the journey through the Star Gate, which evidently challenges and overloads Dave's fundamental abilities of perception. Kubrick's chaotic procession of images, colors, shapes, and a sense of endless motion combine with *Atmosphères* in his attempt to create a unified musico-visual sequence. The liminal and microcosmic aspects of Ligeti's music—both the "Kyrie" and *Atmosphères* after that—are indispensable in this final set piece.

The "Kyrie" from Ligeti's *Requiem* and his *Lux aeterna*, by virtue of their generic origins in the Requiem Mass, impart notions of their original functions and the divine. The "Kyrie" of the *Requiem* is heard with the monolith on earth, with the monolith on the moon, and finally with the monolith that floats near Jupiter, and the first images of the Star Gate beyond. The ideas relating to death and its attendant customs and mythology in Ligeti's vocal works resonate with Kubrick's interest in the residual souls, or ghosts, suggested by the "thirty ghosts" statement. The "Kyrie," *Lux aeterna* (a stand-alone work for sixteen voices), and *Aventures* are well disposed to evoke the human, and perhaps the superhuman, by virtue of the presence of voices and the way Ligeti writes for them. The micropolyphonic treatment of the voices stretches pitches to unusual proportions and great lengths, but also renders the sung words nearly unintelligible, save for the rare exposed consonant.

One may wonder at the purpose of sung words that are not set to be discernible, but Ligeti's approach owes a debt to traditions in Western music that, over time, had so fully absorbed liturgical texts that these became secondary to musical craft and aesthetics. The extraordinary length of the sung pitches in the twelfth-century works of Léonin and Pérotin, for example, hides the syllables and words they contain in a way that especially prefigures Ligeti's approach.

Ligeti wrote *Lux aeterna* (heard during the flight to the monolith on the moon) not as part of a larger mass but as a stand-alone work, yet its text preserves that of the portion of the mass devoted to Communion. This piece had an intensely personal resonance for the composer. Ligeti, who was slowly recovering from surgery for a perforated intestine, wrote the piece on commission for Clytus Gottwald, director of the Schola Cantorum Stuttgart. During this time, Ligeti was often sedated with morphine and may have felt he had come close to death.[45] It is difficult to imagine Ligeti's approach would not have been colored by his sense of mortality; one might consider *Lux aeterna* to have some of the qualities of a "late" work in this regard, especially because in it, he returns to the subject of death via its role in the Requiem Mass.[46]

A brief excerpt of Ligeti's *Aventures* plays as Dave arrives at the end of his journey, most clearly heard in the whispering voices on the shot of Dave standing in what appears to be a bright hotel room. Paul Griffiths notes that this highly experimental stage work for voices and small instrumental ensemble has "something of the character of strip cartoons—with all that that implies about the general character being ironic, the succession being one of sharply focused pictures of encounters and mental conditions, not those encounters and conditions themselves."[47] Griffiths's evocation of still frames and metaphysical experience manifests itself in the still frames that capture split-second moments in Dave's journey, and what may be a liminal, metaphysical process.

Aside from introducing Ligeti to a large audience, the appearance of Ligeti's music in *2001* eased the way for more experimental music in wide-release films. Soon turning to the avant-garde repertoire would become a viable choice for the horror and psychological thriller genres, especially following the success of William Friedkin's *The Exorcist* (1973) and Kubrick's own *The Shining*. Ligeti's music in *2001* left lasting impressions on attentive listeners who later created their own soundtracks. The clearest case of this influence may be in the soundtrack of Danny Boyle's *Sunshine* (2007), for which Karl Hyde wrote some of the music. Hyde has acknowledged the astonishing impact of hearing *Lux aeterna* in *2001*, which provided an obvious point of inspiration for the music—down to the choice of pitches—that plays in *Sunshine* as Capa (Cillian Murphy) first emerges into space to make repairs to the ship's shields.[48] This scene is one of many in *Sunshine* that refer to *2001*.

Ligeti's distinctive 1960s style also has more tonal relatives in film music (original and borrowed) by composers of the minimalist tradition, a style that uses meter in ways that approach the style of rock and other popular musics with repetitive dance beats. Godfrey Reggio's *Qatsi* trilogy (1982, 1988, 2002)—which itself owes to Kubrick's *2001* in its epic scope and its imaginative reliance on cinematography, editing, and prominent music—hinges on the unified sense of interlocking rhythm, speed, and intensity both in Philip Glass's music and in the genesis and acceleration of processes that constitute the film's visual aesthetic and subject matter.

The Sun Comes Up: Nietzschean Overtones

Richard Strauss's *Also sprach Zarathustra* demands to be considered in relation to Ligeti's music in *2001*; Strauss's music follows Ligeti's music to mark moments of transformative discovery, breakthrough, or realization. As a contrasting pair, these composers' works illuminate each other, particularly in light of Strauss's subject matter and the composers' respective musical styles. *Zarathustra* appears three times in *2001*: in the opening celestial imagery and credits following *Atmosphères*, in the scene of the apeman's epiphany shortly following the appearance of the monolith with Ligeti's "Kyrie," and following Ligeti's *Aventures* as Dave transforms into the Star Child. These moments posit Ligeti's music as the antecedent to the consequent of Strauss's; if Ligeti's music suggests a liminal culmination and formation of life forces and intelligence, we might then ask, what kind of rejoinder comes with Strauss?

Like the other works in the soundtrack, Strauss's music contrasts with Ligeti's for being tonal, but tonality is no mere happenstance in the opening measures of Strauss's piece; it is their subject and their raison d'être. The pitch material explicitly spells out the overtone or harmonic series in the opening moments and subsequent measures. The overtone series, an acoustic phenomenon here taken as a musical motive, accounts for naturally occurring frequencies that are part and parcel of the sounds one hears every day. It is furthermore connected to, and sometimes identified as a cause of, structures underlying a vast body of music: namely, that which uses fifths and fourths, and functional, triadic harmony. While a diverse array of approaches to melody and harmony exists in musical traditions around the world, weakening any claim that the series informs music universally, the beginning of the overtone series as measured from a fundamental pitch (octave, fifth, fourth, major third, minor third, and so on) outlines the harmonic building blocks of much Western music in recent centuries.

Though the discovery of the overtone series dates to the ancient Greeks and has long correlated to large- and small-scale design in Western composition and musicianship, it was revitalized as a topic of musical and scientific interest in Strauss's time, in part by Hermann von Helmholz's influential interdisciplinary findings, published in 1863, *On the Sensations of Tone as a Physiological Basis for the Theory of Music*. Strauss's contemporary Gustav Mahler had relied on the overtone series and wide spacing of orchestral ranges to evoke nature in his first symphony, premiered in 1889. Strauss combined notions of nature and fanfare in the opening of *Zarathustra* seven years later. Though only the first twenty-two measures of this symphonic poem appear in *2001*, its attendant programmatic and philosophical connotations have adhered to *2001* as well.

The history of Strauss's ideas about Nietzsche's *Also sprach Zarathustra* and his own work's status as program music are complex and inconclusive. On one hand, Strauss's subtitle, "frei nach Nietzsche" (freely after Nietzsche), invites the listener to hear manifestations of Nietzsche in the music. On the other hand, he stated that he "did not intend to write philosophical music or portray Nietzsche's great work musically."[49] Where, then, does the work lie between a loose sense of inspiration and a denial of philosophical portrayal? Strauss's contemporaries and more recent commentators have responded in a variety of ways, even supplying new guides to the work and its themes. These guides endeavor to connect the music with the headings in the score that Strauss borrowed from Nietzsche's work. The basic, elusive problem behind these efforts remains, as Strauss scholar John Williamson notes, "the degree to which [the headings] acted as incentives to Strauss's musical imagination."[50] One might likewise ask to what extent Strauss's music (with or without the headings) influenced Kubrick's imagination. While it seems as though Kubrick's need for a piece that ended quickly indicates that he had the opening credits in mind, it is not clear whether Kubrick also planned to use the winning piece in subsequent moments; the connotations of Strauss's work could have presented a good reason to do so.

Though the opening theme comes with many questions, there are useful clues in the literature; Strauss labeled the opening melody the *Sonnenthema* (sun theme), a label whose resonance with Kubrick's film is obvious. More intriguing is the title "The World Riddle," ascribed to the opening theme by Arthur Hahn in a guide Strauss himself approved, which might help discern the ideas behind this music and the mystery of the monolith. The World Riddle entails two reciprocal parts: "the world entering the individual" and "the individual entering the world," both of which relate to Kubrick's film. While it would be difficult to locate such metaphysical notions in the music, the broader concept of a riddle is an apt fit for the opening passage—one that illuminates the role of the music in Kubrick's film as well.

Strauss's opening melody, a slow giant of a fanfare, is intriguing from a musical point of view; its three identical, ascending statements of a brass melody end with three different harmonic cadences. The last seems to be the "right" way to end and seems to satisfy a question or solve a riddle, for it allows the music to move not only to a new key (from C to F) but also into a more fully developed and grand cadence that seems to energize the entire orchestra. As the last and most grandiose, this third statement carries connotations of progress or breakthrough by virtue of the musical topics it employs. The music finally modulates, though briefly, to a new tonal center that widens the harmonic ambitus of the work and thus its potential for further development. The forces of the orchestra are unified, and the melodic gestures drench the last cadence in a sense of purposeful finality (a surprising choice considering that Strauss's work has only just begun). The passage might, for Strauss, also speak to the enormity of—and ultimate triumph over—philosophical questions Friedrich Nietzsche poses in his eponymous writing.

In *2001*, the quiet, deep beginning of *Zarathustra* first appears on the heels of *Atmosphères*, reframing Ligeti's work as a sort of noise-killer opening that allows the audience to settle in order to better hear Strauss. Immediately after *Atmosphères* fades, an organ, a contrabassoon, and double basses, along with a bass drum roll played with timpani sticks, begin to rumble on the pitch C. The sound is not immediately recognizable as music, and its introduction by the avant-garde Ligeti gives the audience little to go on. Like the images of the monolith to come, the opening of *Zarathustra* stands out and invites scrutiny, while not yet divulging its origins in time or space or its significance.

As the first note of *Also sprach Zarathustra* rumbles, the blue and white MGM logo appears, then fades to black. The first iteration of the brass melody begins to rise, but the screen remains black until the explosive entrance of the ensemble, which conjures the appearance of the sun rising over the earth. The phrase lands on a minor chord, like a first attempt to answer the riddle, followed by thundering timpani strokes. Kubrick gives us cause to locate not a mere sense of connection between his film and Strauss's music, but a causal relationship. Here the alliance of the first big musical event with Kubrick's images of the sun and earth connects them, both thematically and temporally, and establishes music—which precedes the image—as the generative force in this combination. The opening melody begins a second time, continuing the sense of rising echoed in the image of the sun rising over the earth and fostering a sense of something momentous and awesome in its growing shape and striking cadence, but this time the cadence pushes upward instead of downward, landing on a major chord. The major chord, by virtue of associations accorded to it in Western music, may sound like an optimistic revision of the answer to the first phrase, yet the riddle remains unsolved.

The third time, the melody culminates in a cadence that dislodges the music from the tonality of C to an F major chord. This grand musical gesture finally sticks the landing and verily shouts, "Ta-daaaaa!" The small words onscreen, "A STANLEY KUBRICK PRODUCTION," understate Kubrick's presence, but the music insists the opposite. The joke in this moment comes from the tension between the humility of the little letters and the sweeping, expansive music they seem to unleash. A momentary ambiguity arises from the suggestion that Kubrick's "production" is not the film, but the sun and the earth, pictured. This would be one of several moments in *2001* in which music casts a dwarfing perspective on humans and their achievements. In addition to the precedence of music in the general order of things, Kubrick calls the audience's attention to the importance of momentary detail in synchronizing the appearance of his own name with the big cadence in this final iteration of the melody.

Strauss's music does more than simply make these images palpable in these opening moments; it helps convey some of the themes of interest both for Strauss and Kubrick. It is, for example, difficult to ignore the relevance of Strauss's comment that he wanted "to convey in music an idea of the evolution of the human race from its origin, through the various phases of development, religious as well as scientific, up to Nietzsche's idea of the Superman."[51] Such a description would handily account for the scene of the apeman's realization of the bone's usefulness, the scenes portraying relationships between humans and technology, and the nature of Dave's transformation at the end of the film.

Kubrick's film would appear to take on both halves of Nietzsche's riddle, which Strauss wrote in the margins of his score: the "world entering the individual," which corresponds to the overwhelming Star Gate sequence, and "the individual entering the world," which broadly describes the advents of human progress across the film and steadily broadens the concept of "world." The label "The World Riddle" also matches my proposal that the incipit and its three endings enact the working out of a problem, not unlike the structure and concept of another work dedicated to existential mystery: Charles Ives's *The Unanswered Question* (first version completed in 1908).[52]

By virtue of evoking the first part of the overtone series, whose complete range extends infinitely and beyond the capabilities of human hearing, *Zarathustra* points beyond its present moment and beyond the tones heard in these twenty-two measures. Its qualities as a musical beginning suggest continuation and perpetuity, even in light of the strong cadence that, for Kubrick's purposes, provided a convenient conclusion. At the same time, the excerpt's dazzling final cadence vanishes rapidly along with the impressive images, yielding to quiet, and to a diminished perspective on human triumphs on a canvas of universal proportions. The passage might be best understood as a model of negotiating challenges to win survival, both for Nietzsche's protagonist and for Kubrick's characters.

In considering the weight of Strauss's music in the soundtrack overall, one might be tempted to favor it as some kind of emblem, were it not for Kubrick's reprise of the *Blue Danube* right after Dave's transformation. At the end of the film, the appearance of the relatively humble, tractable *Danube* seems to offer a final word on the state of human progress. In answer to the question of how humans will measure up when encountering another form of intelligence, it seems to say we have a long way to go, in a last, swift stroke of musical relativism.

Side Effects and Repercussions

Debate over Kubrick's provisional treatment of North's music and its story as a cautionary tale for composers persist nearly half a century since the film's release, though findings in recent research have contributed to a more detailed and balanced account of the circumstances. North's disappointment reflected his belief that Kubrick failed to honor an unspoken code. Kubrick fulfilled his obligations to North in commissioning the music and paying him, but his more pressing obligation, to the film, meant choosing the music he thought was best for it. Fans of North and of newly written soundtracks worried over what seemed to threaten the role of the film composer, but Kubrick's approach proved to be a rare outcome rather than the new rule, much less the death knell for original scores.[53] Nevertheless, the turn of events has imbued much commentary on music in *2001* with an ethical charge, especially as the composer's difficulty in controlling the use (or nonuse) of his or her music in a film represents a perennial challenge and exemplifies the composer's vulnerability in the multimedia marketplace.

Kubrick's choices in *2001* also offered a model for creating film around existing music—either completely or in selected scenes—and, accordingly, new aesthetic possibilities. His feat may have been giving these concert works good homes—probably the best homes they could hope to have in 1968 and perhaps thereafter. *2001* displayed the unique qualities of these pieces to their greatest advantage by forging alliances between images, on one hand, with memories, connotations, histories, and musical elements, on the other.

The alliances between music and Kubrick's images have proven so strong that they have, for many, become difficult to forget; the works seem to belong to the film. Claudia Gorbman notes this special adhesion; the musical choices "become the music of the specific movie scene rather than the piece one may have known before."[54] Kubrick's images seem to have been created as visual manifestations of this music, but for listeners familiar with the works before seeing *2001*, there may be unwanted effects. One may imagine, for example, adding to Gorbman's formulation, "How annoying!" or "How delightful!" Michel Chion's inability to hear the *Blue Danube* "without thinking of spaceships" implies inconvenience at least.[55] K. J. Donnelly likewise registers the complicating factors of multimedia for existing music, and for *Also sprach Zarathustra* in particular when he wonders whether it is an outstanding work in its own right and whether we can ever know.[56] And regarding the audience of *2001* who does not know any of the music, will Kubrick's film rob them of a certain amount of freedom to form subjective responses to it?

In addition to the possibility that the use of existing music in multimedia may work preclusively against other meanings and, indeed, set expectations for visual and narrative accompaniments, there are even more destructive aesthetic implications, perhaps best illustrated in *A Clockwork Orange*, a film that might well "ruin" "Singin' in the Rain" or Beethoven's Ninth Symphony for an audience member. This is the iconoclastic aspect of Kubrick that brings destructive consequences.

Kubrick's choices in *2001* had remarkable sticking power in the popular imagination. While many believe they do indeed work well, Roger Ebert goes one step further in stating, "Kubrick's film is almost unique in *enhancing* the music by its association with his images."[57] The fusion of music and film that complicates musical evaluation in Donnelly's point of view does not seem to bother Ebert, who seems to have rediscovered a forgotten delight.

Kubrick's success with existing music took a decisive and prescient step toward the democratization of technology and media, now evidenced in a spate of user-generated content on the Internet whose success may involve the tension between originality and explicit imitation. Few of the creators of mash-ups and videos are film-school graduates, and their creative processes likely entail trial and error and experimentation. It is worth noting that Kubrick would fit this description as well, though he had the benefit of his years honing skills as a photographer before he began filmmaking, skills that translated saliently into his directorial work, as Vincent LoBrutto has shown.[58]

In a discussion of existing music in film, Royal Brown articulates the apparent quality of music as somehow separate from its film context; it is "an image in its own right."[59] This cross-sensory description of music in film helps evoke a sense of the audience's subjective assembly of the parts into meaning—meaning that often plays against the images' conventional associations. Some commentary persists that casts Kubrick's choices in *2001* as arbitrary or irreconcilable with the film, but one cannot stop an existing work from bringing its baggage any more than one can stop the connotations of an actor's previous roles from influencing the audience's understanding of a new one.[60] If one can hear references in the minuet in a Mozart symphony to the contexts of aristocratic custom, and meaningful rhetorical expression in its melodies and phrases, why should one do otherwise when that minuet appears in a film? On the other hand, commentary on interrelationships of music and images and drama has proliferated, showing that any signals of the a priori life of existing music is only one aspect of the composition. The frameworks of historical context and musical elements necessarily enter the discussion.

Tactics for addressing the epistemological issues of classical and other kinds of existing music in film seem appropriate and timely in light of the increasing frequency with which filmmakers and other creators of multimedia integrate existing music in contemporary art. The cycling and recycling of existing music in multimedia is not only a staple of twentieth- and twenty-first-century aesthetics; it defines the contemporary experience of classical music. First encounters with classical music tend to occur in the context of films, television programs, and advertisements rather than in the concert hall. Popular media is the only way many listeners interact with classical music. If this point seems exaggerated, it offers a clear explanation for positing the soundtrack of *2001*, as so many have, as a seminal moment in film music, one that has influenced subsequent creative uses and new conventions of existing music in films and media, far beyond the cinema.

Existing music demands a multivalent approach: the music and image must be taken together, and previous associations, whether historical and original or more recently formulated, necessarily become a part of meaning. Kubrick's film centrally participates in his generation's unique understanding of existing music; his inclusion of Khachaturian, Ligeti, Johann Strauss Jr., and Richard Strauss was not merely an act of exposing audiences to their music or integrating music that played against generic norms. The continued response to music in *2001* points to the curious durability of musical works and to the persistence of both cultural memory and a desire to reinvent it. Kubrick's film made these works vividly relevant by virtue of their virtuosic deployment in the cinematic whole even as the power of other venues to provide relevant encounters with music—such as the concert halls from which these works came—would seem to diminish. The shock of the initial mismatch between existing works and the visual and narrative content of *2001* was an indispensable catalyst to the mutual vitality that results, but it was only the beginning. It is not the mere act of borrowing but the active reimagining of musical works that has followed—on the part of Kubrick and of the audience—that earned the film its enduring place in popular culture.

7

MUSICAL DIALECTICS AND THE MORE TROUBLESOME

BEETHOVEN

UPON ITS RELEASE in 1971, *A Clockwork Orange* caused controversy for its pervasive violence, its cynical view of the nature of man, embodied in a cast of unredeeming characters, and its caricature and critique of a bumbling and ineffectual government that would condition its people. Some found the film's violence and rape objectionable, and others spoke out against the film as moral guardians, fearing it would incite violence in young viewers, despite the growing trend in film since the 1950s of gritty, graphic violence and unsavory main characters. About one year after the release of *A Clockwork Orange*, Kubrick withdrew the film in Britain because of the intensity of the response from a variety of sectors. That so many voiced concerns about the film's events (or something like them) coming to pass—a vague echo of the estimation of realism in the general scenario of *Dr. Strangelove*—indicates that Kubrick did more than repulse audiences with violence; he tapped into concerns over essential societal issues. The heated but temporary reactions against the film have since given way to more enduring discussions about Kubrick's use of violence in the service of dramatizing central questions of Anthony Burgess's novel, about free will, government control, and the consequences of one person's decisions for others; these topics remain touchstones in the discourse about the film.

Kubrick garnered acclaim for his bold realizations of many of Burgess's stylistic inventions and his futuristic-dystopic setting in the film's memorably strange-sounding dialogue and set designs. The drama turns around the problematic character of Alex, who resembles, in some ways, a "criminal hero": brutal, individualistic, ambitious, and doomed.[1] Alex's only ambition seems to be enjoying either listening to music or committing violent acts, and he eludes the ultimate condemnation that has resolved the fate of so many other film criminals, and absolved film audiences at the same time. Alex's antiheroic tendencies, including behaviors that do not neatly fit together or help the audience classify him or respond to him, consistently play into the film's interests in morality, humanity, taste, and even the conditioned response.

Kubrick seized upon the musical element in Burgess's novel, which plays a central role in conditioning in the story; Anthony Burgess explained, "As the novel is about brainwashing, so it is also a little device of brainwashing in itself—or at least a carefully programmed series of lessons on the Russian language. You learn the words without noticing, and a glossary is unnecessary."[2] The register of audible sound in film allowed Kubrick a venue for conditioning the audience through both language and music, whereas a reader of the novel would be conditioned by words alone.

Music stands out as a salient force in *A Clockwork Orange*, both in the plot itself and as the only element in the film with the potential to be recognized by the audience. Recognition of the music exists potentially at the general level—in other words, the listener registers the characteristics of classical music broadly—and at a specific level, when the listener can identify the specific composer or title, and possibly additional meanings or connotations of the music. Musical recognition plays a crucial role in the conditioning of Alex, the protagonist, of Mr. Alexander, the writer, and of the audience, but in the opening third of the film, it plays the much more basic role of calling attention to the music as such (via the familiar classical sound, at the very least), among an array of unfamiliar elements: the disjunct and alienating visual aesthetic, strange language, and inexplicably violent characters and events.

Kubrick took a broad and rich approach to the music for *A Clockwork Orange*, including a range of recognizable musical idioms (e.g., classical, popular) and a smaller subset of recognizable tunes (Beethoven's "Ode to Joy" melody from the Ninth Symphony; Arthur Freed and Herb Nacio Brown's "Singin' in the Rain"). Kubrick furthermore includes music that cannot be recognized because it is original (by Wendy Carlos), and there are even visual references—for example, on the printing on a tape cassette—to fictitious musicians. Kubrick thus follows in the spirit of Burgess whose array of figures includes Beethoven and Handel alongside fictitious ones like Adrian Schweigselber. Two undated screenplay drafts by Burgess attest to the fecundity of the author's imagination in this game of inventing and reinventing composers, such as "Benjy Britt," presumably based on Benjamin Britten, and others like "Denson" and "Hugelhoff."[3] While music plays a central role in Burgess's novel, the screenplays include many more references to music, and details as to how it is heard (for example, coming from an adjacent room)—details that clearly inspired Kubrick's screenplay and the story's realization in film.[4] Burgess's screenplays and novel and Kubrick's screenplay and film foster an awareness of subjective levels of familiarity with specific music and musicians.

The film's soundtrack exhibits an array of classical works and popular-style songs that often help gauge Alex's status in the story. On the one hand, it seems clear that popular music, represented by Erika Eigen's "I Wanna Marry a Lighthouse Keeper," fulfills its role as "inane music" (see chapter 1); it plays diegetically when Alex returns home to find he has been replaced by Joe, a lodger taken in by his parents while Alex was incarcerated. The facile song, in Alex's ears, set in stark opposition to the classical music he loves, comes across as an insult added to the injury of his disownment and as a reminder of the intellectual and cultural divide between Alex and nearly everyone else. The popular tune "Molly Malone" is also sung by the drunk vagrant, helping to round out the sense that it stands for all Alex derides, but if popular music represents all that is common and undiscerning, classical music requires finer distinctions.

Beethoven and Rossini: A Fight beyond the Death

While film's ability to forge new meanings or reshape old ones for musical works is well established and recognized, *A Clockwork Orange* is an assiduous essay, and one that adopts the peculiar strategy of creating meaning only to destroy or reconfigure it by means of a chain of dialectical oppositions. Formulations that posit existing music and its connotations and histories as an interdependent player in the cinematic whole are a necessity for discussions of Kubrick, but in *A Clockwork Orange*, Kubrick ups the ante. To develop Burgess's themes of musical value and liability Kubrick did not merely propose a complex dialectic of music and image; rather, his dialectic comprises the battle of musical works with each other. The resulting instability of musical meaning and value plays directly into the film's themes of moral, social, and aesthetic relativism.

Music plays in both diegetic and nondiegetic registers in *A Clockwork Orange* to animate Burgess's themes of conditioning, recognition, and the malleability of meaning; accordingly, Kubrick complicates and compromises these categories throughout the film, starting in the very first scene with Alex's voice-over narration clashing against the image of his still figure on the screen. Beethoven's music stands out for the amount of times it plays, for its roles in intense scenes, and its exclusively diegetic presence, in which it conspicuously contrasts with the nondiegetic Rossini. Beethoven's music is not background but belongs to and participates in Alex's story, and Alex is aware of it whenever it plays. In this way, Beethoven's music, and to some extent other works in the film, like "Singin' in the Rain," both act upon the characters and audience and take part in the film's patterns of shifting power. Each appearance of music recontextualizes the music that came before, and provides a point of comparison for the music to come.

Of the classical composers in the soundtrack, Rossini's and Beethoven's music plays the most. Kubrick borrows two overtures from Rossini, *La gazza ladra* and *William Tell*, the latter of which is broken up and distributed according to its contrasting moods. Its melancholy opening makes a plea for sympathy in the middle third of the film—Alex's capture, treatment, and then his dislocation in the world upon his release. The overture's better-known fast section, which enjoyed popularity as the theme song for *The Lone Ranger* radio and television shows from the 1930s and 1950s, respectively, lends its bracing evocation of speed to the comedic effect of the fast-motion bedroom scene of Alex and the two girls from the record shop. It is worth noting, however, that those who strongly recall the Lone Ranger on hearing this music and the strict moral code that defined his character—something of which Kubrick was undoubtedly aware—would read Alex's excesses and the frivolity of the action of this scene as an ironic disavowal.

One of the several ways in which Beethoven's music participates in dialectics in *A Clockwork Orange* is in its juxtaposition with Rossini, the other most-heard composer in the film. Aside from establishing contrast between the two by assigning Beethoven a strictly diegetic role, and Rossini a strictly nondiegetic role, the supposition of the pair as opposites has a basis in music reception history. In their time, Rossini was by far the more popular composer, though his detractors associated his music—mainly operas—with buffoonery and frivolity in comparison to the great and serious Beethoven. Beethoven represented (among other things) sophistication, sensitivity, and intellect. His music was (and still is) thought to be challenging and edifying for the assiduous listener. Raphael Georg Kiesewetter noted the polarity of the two composers in the 1830s, labeling it the "era of Beethoven and Rossini";[5] the learned and elevated music of Beethoven stood at odds with the sensual and superficial music of Rossini. This formulation suggests that Beethoven's pieces are texts to be struggled with, while Rossini's music provides simpler pleasures.[6] The film amplifies these connotations by pairing Rossini with the bodily and sensual—and violent—escapades undertaken with joy by Alex and his friends. Alex's joy in listening to Beethoven, on the other hand, represents a greater satisfaction, a private, noumenal reward. In giving the audience the music of Rossini (as nondiegetic music), and giving Beethoven to Alex (he appreciates and elects to listen to Beethoven's music in the diegesis), Kubrick reinvigorates and reinforces the Rossini-Beethoven dialectic and uses it to verify Alex's sophistication, intelligence, and power in the story.

While on the surface, the triumph and bombast of Rossini's music reflects Alex's pleasure in violence, the presence of Rossini, as the Italian upstart who would threaten Beethoven, also signifies the subtext of changing popular opinion and the dangers of the masses. These subtexts are sharply conveyed in the scene at the river, when Alex assaults his friends in an attempt to bring them back under his control.

The scene plays out in slow motion, but *La gazza ladra* plays in real time; the visuals and music are literally out of sync, a metaphor for the mounting discord between Alex and his gang. The music continues into the next scene, at normal speed, in which Alex reprimands his friends for having questioned his authority. His friends' growing ferment and their reluctance to forgive Alex for hurting them or to accept him as their leader is obvious. *La gazza ladra* continues to play up to the moment his gang betrays him and leaves him to be arrested outside the Cat Lady's house. In this way, *La gazza ladra* predicts Alex's fall from popularity, a pivotal point in the plot of *A Clockwork Orange*, and once it has served this purpose, it is not heard again. The real surprise is that Beethoven would soon assume the role of Alex's musical enemy in one of the film's dialectical shifts involving music that reorders its ideological landscape and hierarchies. This cinematic manifestation of a musicological trope (Beethoven versus Rossini) also prefigures the much more complex questions that the film, as a whole, poses about Beethoven's Ninth Symphony.

Agony, Ecstasy, and the Accidents of Taste

The forms of music (diegetic or nondiegetic, synthesized or acoustic, performed or listened to, popular or classical) and characters' responses to music reflect the film's more obviously shifting power dynamics. More important, they reveal the subjectivity, liability, and malleability of musical perception and taste. Kubrick employs diegetic music for the most important scenes across the film, each of which constitutes one part of a pair, according to the film's too-neat episodic structure in the first and last of its three parts—that is, the violent adventures of the film's opening, in which Alex attacks a series of people, have counterparts in the ending part of the film, in which Alex's victims exact their revenge upon him. The deployment and permutations of music highlight and animate this structure throughout.

Diegetic music—especially the Scherzo and Finale of Beethoven's Ninth Symphony and the song "Singin' in the Rain"—features prominently in the most viscerally engaging and, for many viewers, disturbing scenes in *A Clockwork Orange*. In nearly each scene with diegetic music, the music is also pointedly contentious along the lines of who is the player or performer and who is the listener; how the characters interact and, in some cases, whether they like the music; and how it is being used. These variables take part in marking differences between scenes in the first third of the film and their variants in the final third of the film.

The choice to present orchestral, acoustic versions of both of the symphony movements alongside electronic ones by Wendy Carlos and Rachel Elkind evokes the anxiety over the loss of the original the age of mechanical reproduction brought about and, like the idea of a clockwork orange, furnishes an apt metaphor for the loss of the individual in the name of progress and the safety of the state. The contrast of acoustic and synthetic also provides a dialectic pair in the soundscape.

Tension between the writer and his wife, on one hand, and Alex and his friends, on the other, defines the scene of the attack on the writer and his wife, which features Alex's rendition of "Singin' in the Rain." This attack seals a connection between the song and the violence itself in that Alex hits his victims in rhythm with his song. The attack and the song alike remain ingrained in the writer's memory in the final part of the film, in which Alex sings the song again. Hearing Alex sing the song confirms his identity for the writer and seems to send the writer into a traumatic memory of the attack via the conditioned response. The writer, who knows about Alex's conditioning against Beethoven, drugs Alex in a scene that has a conspicuously stagey quality: Alex awaits his host, seated at a table in the very room in which he once attacked the writer and his wife (see Figure 7.1). Kubrick's camera sits this time on the opposite side of the room, in contrast to the camera's position at the beginning of Alex's earlier attack, emphasizing the dialectical pairing. The writer later plays a recording of the Scherzo from the Ninth Symphony to a captive Alex to exact his revenge.

These pairings delineate a simple maxim: performers of live music and players of mediated music have great control and influence over their listeners and over the meaning of the music. In Alex's subjection to the Ludovico treatment in the middle portion of the film, which includes parts of Beethoven's Ninth Symphony, Alex protests desperately against the use of the music. Music notably attends upon the first signs of discord between Alex and his friends as well: when the singer in the milk

FIGURE 7.1 Alex waits, as though on a stage, for the comeuppance the film's patterns have conditioned the audience to expect. Inevitably, music will play a part. *A Clockwork Orange*, Warner Bros. Pictures, 1971.

bar sings part of Beethoven's Ninth, Alex is enraptured, but Dim interrupts with a disdainful noise and Alex hits him.

As disturbing as the scenes and their use of music may be, even more unsettling in the film and thereafter is the availability of music—any music—to violent uses, and the seeming failure of music to remain faithful to any of its original ideals—Gene Kelly's carefree, earnest "Singin' in the Rain" or the vaunted notions often attached to Beethoven and to his Ninth Symphony in particular. The audience is likely to respond to these scenes because of their visceral nature and compelling and prominent music, but also because strong opinions and emotional responses to music are a commonplace in contemporary Western civilization, one with which the audience can readily identify.

Alongside the arrays of violent scenes in the first and third parts of the film, Kubrick fashions two opposite scenes centering on Alex: the bedroom scherzo scene, which deploys diegetic music for Alex's musical pleasure, free of local conflict, and the scene of Alex's conditioning, in which the accidental inclusion of Beethoven's music pains him. Each case illustrates deeply effective ways of creating meaning, each highly dependent on the listener's (Alex's, in this case) knowledge, taste, and circumstances.

Alex's listening experience in his bedroom is completely under his control; he selects the music and volume, and his eye, then his mind's eye, select images to go with it. Kubrick's visual editing makes Alex's authorship of this fantasy clear. The scene is a powerful statement by the director concerning the level of engagement and imagination he expects from his audience. The scene also posits film spectatorship as a private utopia that each audience member crafts for him- or herself. Notable here is the difficulty of maintaining a clear grip on the music's status; it begins as diegetic music in Alex's bedroom, and remains at least that, but does the music also become native to Alex's fantasy, and therefore become its nondiegetic music? Is "nondiegetic" sufficient to describe music that animates and informs the very substance of Alex's fantasy? Kubrick challenges the categories here to display not merely music's great importance, but its precedence in creative listening experiences, including cinematic ones.

At the other end of the spectrum is the conditioning scene. During the Ludovico treatment, Alex is drugged so that the elements of his multimedia experience are forced into disharmony. Alex made the single choice to accept the Ludovico treatment, but was unprepared for the appearance of Beethoven's music with violence, and his subsequent conditioning against both of these. Again, the element of control is framed as the key to aesthetic experience.

As Alex is made to watch the Nazi propaganda film, immobilized and with his eyes clamped open, a synthesized version of the Turkish march passage from the finale of the Ninth Symphony accompanies on the soundtrack (see Figure 7.2).[7] He protests the use of Beethoven's music, shouting, "It's a sin—using Ludwig van like

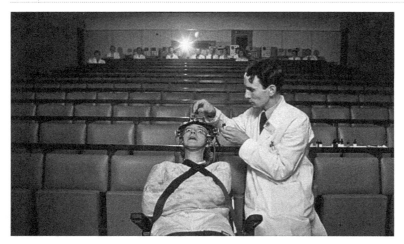

FIGURE 7.2 Alex undergoes the Ludovico treatment in the central act of
A Clockwork Orange. The manner in which Beethoven's music appears throughout the
film raises questions about the conditioned response, taste formation, and the nature
of musical aesthetics. *A Clockwork Orange*, Warner Bros. Pictures, 1971.

that! He did no harm to anyone! Beethoven just wrote music!" The head scientist
remarks to the nurse, "It can't be helped. It's the punishment element, perhaps. The
governor ought to be pleased," and "I'm sorry, Alex. This is for your own good," and
"You must take your chance, boy. The choice has been all yours." The scene dramatizes the extreme unpleasantness that music can represent, as a result of association
or other factors, but the accidental (and coincidental) nature of the inclusion of
Beethoven's music suggests that musical taste itself is not perhaps only a product
of factors by which listeners are conditioned, but *conditional* as well. In this pair of
scenes, Alex's deep sensitivity to Beethoven cuts both ways.

Kubrick's tactics in pairing scenes across the film raise questions with implications
about the nature of musical experience, perhaps most important: What is the difference between taste and conditioning? To what extent might the nature of aesthetics
be habitual and automatic rather than a product of study, reflection, and judgment?
Might Burgess and Kubrick be wondering whether the conditions of modern life
threaten musical understanding, whether the postmodern ubiquity of music precludes us from truly hearing it?

The More Troublesome Beethoven

Most commentary on music is inspired by a desire to extol its good qualities, yet
music research since the late twentieth century, and Beethoven scholarship in particular, has increasingly addressed the dark side of music—its irreconcilable and

troubling elements, and the implementation of music in torture. Robynn Stilwell has identified the trope of film villains associated with Beethoven and the ways in which it reflects the darker aspects of the Beethoven myth: "While the more emotional, irrational, and even violent elements have tended to be neatened away, out of sight, or at times even forcibly removed by musicologists, popular culture has retained, revitalized, and recirculated the more troublesome Beethoven."[8]

Even the earliest writings on the symphony's power identify something "terrifying" and "fiery," and a "quality of antagonism."[9] Certainly, Alex is an emblem if not the modern progenitor of the criminal Beethoven fan type. Beethoven scholar Scott Burnham calls the treatment of the troublesome Beethoven "a subtradition detailing the dangerous effects of listening to Beethoven's music," an activity that seems to push the act of listening to music out of aesthetics and into public welfare.[10] To the extent that popular notions gain credibility over time and feed back into scholarship, one must wonder to what extent the images and ideas associated with Beethoven in *A Clockwork Orange* created a place for Susan McClary's work on masculine violence in Beethoven's music, to take one example, and what role the film may have had, even if tangential, in inspiring her scholarship.[11] In summarizing the paradoxes of the piece, McClary offers, "The Ninth Symphony is probably our most compelling articulation in music of the contradictory impulses that have organized patriarchal culture since the Enlightenment."[12] Paradox defines Beethoven scholarship and even inspires some of the final words Scott Burnham offers in the "Beethoven" entry in the *New Grove Dictionary of Music and Musicians*: "It is indeed difficult, if not impossible, to imagine a time when Beethoven's music will not continue to exercise its paradoxically confounding and foundational force."[13]

The engagement of the senses by a film, including an illuminated screen that precludes other visual stimuli, and high volume levels for sound, leaves the audience in a difficult position from which to cope with unwanted sights and sounds. Randy Rasmussen points out, "In the context of Ludovico conditioning, that combination [of the Nazi film with Beethoven's Ninth] is a threat to Alex's very capacity for creative association."[14] In this moment in *A Clockwork Orange*, Alex is forced into the horror of passive receptivity. In precluding creative response—incapacitating Alex and the film audience—Kubrick exacts his greatest violence in virtuosically realizing one of the story's central themes. Rasmussen's description resonates with descriptions by detainees of their experiences during torture in their common identification of a threat to one's subjectivity, in which creativity—including the creation and maintenance of personal belief—is a crucial part.

Those who classify the music and torture scenes in *A Clockwork Orange* as a nightmarish vision of the worst-case scenario might be surprised to learn that the mechanisms it displays resemble real ones that have been used for decades by the US government.[15] As Suzanne Cusick's studies suggest, it is neither ideas of violence nor incongruity in themselves that have the greatest impact when music and methods of torture are combined; rather, the predisposition of the subject and his or her subjective associations and perceptions regarding recognizable components of the stimuli will be the greatest factors.

An Antihero's Symphony

The ambitious design of Beethoven's Ninth Symphony contains a collection of recognizable forms, gestures, topics, sounds, and even a text in its final movement, yet it has puzzled as many listeners as it has impressed since its premiere in the 1820s. No single analytical apparatus or interpretive strategy has proven to be "the key" to the symphony, and commentators furthermore seem to disagree about its overall success. Nicholas Cook observes, "Every interpretation of it is contradicted by the work itself,"[16] and James Webster's rather more extreme estimation is that " 'the' form of the finale of Beethoven's Ninth does not exist."[17] These epistemological problems resonate with Alex's refusal to fit in; the symphony might stand shoulder to shoulder with others of its kind, but there are no others of its kind.

The eclectic symphony has invited a variety of strategies, each of which emphasizes selected aspects of the composer's craft or elucidates a particular interpretation, often in relation to the poetic text Beethoven includes in the final movement. The symphony also comes in Beethoven's late period, but differs from most of his other late-period works by simply being in the public genre of the symphony and by what many believe to be its optimistic message. The Ninth Symphony also refuses to conform to traits of Beethoven's middle, "heroic" period, the period in which he wrote the Fifth Symphony and other works in which commentators hear clear narratives of struggle and eventual triumph.

For those seeking meaning via the text, I propose that Beethoven's particular take on Friedrich von Schiller's poem "Ode to Joy" (1803 version) speaks through the verses he selected, but perhaps even more loudly in terms of those he did *not* select. That Beethoven set only about one-third of these verses was likely a factor of the length of the work, but questions remain about how he chose them. Aside from quite a few lines exalting drinking, Beethoven seems to have avoided verses that would have raised ideological if not logistical problems for a cohesive message and that concern topics at the heart of *A Clockwork Orange*. Beethoven omitted lines that call for forgiveness and for conformity in joyfulness: "Sorrow and want should enlist, / With the happy to be joyful. / Let anger and vengeance be forgotten, / Our deadly enemy forgiven, / No tears shall oppress him, / No regrets torment the soul. / Let our book of sin be negated! / Atonement for the entire world!"[18] Beethoven's vision of the Ode seems tempered by cautious realism; forgiveness, punishment, and brotherhood are not clearly addressed.

Though it is not certain what Beethoven's motivation may have been for falling shy of adopting text with such promises, the government officials in *A Clockwork Orange* would evade accountability and therefore avoid making specific promises about their plans to deal with matters of equality, fair treatment, and the treatment of criminals. They will likely return to conventional methods of punishment now that the effects of the Ludovico treatment have drawn public censure.

Notable about the texts Beethoven chooses for the Ninth are their antiheroic flavor. Scott Burnham has described the heroic in Beethoven as "the necessity of struggle and eventual triumph as an index of man's greatness,"[19] but in the lines Beethoven set, the unity of men would erase individual achievement: "All who can call at least one soul theirs / Join in our song of praise / But any who cannot must creep tearfully / Away from our circle." In fact, these lines would seem to exclude anyone for singularity—heroic or otherwise. There seems to be no way to reconcile the ideals in Schiller's text about brotherhood with Beethovenian notions of individuality and the heroic that so often accord to the composer and his mythology. Likewise, Alex certainly struggles and suffers, but he never undergoes the hero's requisite transformation as a result of self-realization; instead, he is restored to his original, criminal state because the government wishes to avoid criticism.

Beethoven leaves out text that describes joy achieved through suffering and struggle. This omission amounts to what Esteban Buch has called "the Utopia of a Joy where Sorrow had left no trace."[20] This phrase might seem to imply that the means justifies the end, an apt paradigm for describing the government's willingness to condition its criminals against violent behavior as long as it can keep its methods secret.

Beethoven's choices of text would jettison the struggles of heroic narratives—the stuff by which societies measure individual greatness. But a world with no criminals is also a world with no heroes; it is homogeneous and undifferentiated. It is difficult to imagine that Beethoven was sincere in eschewing heroic ideals in favor of the contentment and gratitude of Schiller's poem, and indeed his excerption leaves unanswered questions.

Musical style in the symphony does not help reveal Beethoven's perspective on these matters. The array of styles in the final movement makes for a patchwork with no clear foundation. Nicholas Cook notices that Beethoven seems to exaggerate juxtapositions of style at the expense of establishing a cohesive tone, describing it as the ultraserious and slapstick, a phrase that well suits Kubrick's aesthetic in *A Clockwork Orange* as well. What Cook identifies as the point of greatest contrast is amplified in *A Clockwork Orange* during the scene in which Alex is at his most vulnerable; Alex is immobilized in the chair of torture as a verse is sung that translates as "Joyful, like a hero flying to victory." The scenes of inspections and signatures in the prison, and preparations for the Ludovico treatment, are full of absurd elements that highlight the satirical aspects of the film, yet Kubrick's intention could not be more serious.

A Clockwork Orange echoes the difficult questions raised by Schiller's idea "All men become brothers." Considering the nature of Alex and his gang, and the authority figures alike, would we really want to be brothers with *all* men? Cook points to a shift in musical style that indicates Beethoven's distance from the message by taking it out of his contemporary moment: "Perhaps the most explicit technique of Beethoven's irony is anachronism." Cook's description of Beethoven's digression into a Mozartean idiom has grim implications:

> As the verbal expression reaches maximum intensity, the music goes into quotation marks. Nothing could more clearly express Beethoven's detachment from his own message; nothing could more clearly indicate the retrospective, and therefore ultimately futile, nature of the Enlightenment ideals that Schiller's words proclaim.[21]

Fanny Mendelssohn wrote in a particularly perceptive contemporary response to the symphony and its stylistic confusion that it "fall[s] from its height into the opposite extreme—into burlesque."[22] Schiller's text does not allow for individuality under the banner of brotherhood, and Beethoven perpetuates this insolubility in his symphony. This very paradox fuels the moral issues of *A Clockwork Orange*, which, like Beethoven's Symphony, does not offer answers as to how an omelet can be made without breaking any eggs: "magic" (*Zauber*) is the closest Schiller gets to illuminating the way to this utopia.

The Ninth's mysterious silence on practical matters of attaining the ideal state contributes to its great availability. The Ninth served as a sort of stamp of German celebrity endorsement of tactics whose ends are believed to justify the means, such as those of the Nazi regime. Superficially, then, the Ninth seems tailor-made for occasions of government cover-up such as the one at the end of *A Clockwork Orange*, but at the same time, it conveys unresolved problems and empty reassurance. The "Ode to Joy" melody, as arranged by Herbert von Karajan for orchestra, without text or singers, avoids favoring Germany with a German text, and at the same time it buries the possible meanings and problems of the words far from the surface. In this form, the tune has served as the official anthem of the European Union since 1972. Stripped of its words, the melody is rendered harmless, inoffensive, and generic, like Muzak.

Of all the problem areas in the Ninth Symphony, it is the very end—the finale of the finale—that may be most ambivalent of all. In the final passages, Beethoven puts on a spectacular show of ending gestures, as though to distract us from the issues in the text he has left unresolved, and without ever coming out from behind the many stylistic masks he has flaunted throughout. The part of the coda heard in *A Clockwork Orange* (from measure 851 to the end) pulls out all the stops—a climactic aggregation of the instrumental and vocal forces, crescendo and accelerando, and a final cadence with the force of an exclamation mark—yet the more emphatic and macho Beethoven's display of finality, the more impotent the final bars become. Rather than triumph, the gestural and stylistic excesses of the symphony's final bars suggest instead a frantic, flagging performer who forces a conclusion and beats a hasty retreat off the stage.

The sung text in this final scene merely advises, "Seek [your Creator] beyond the starry canopy! / Beyond the stars he must surely dwell,"[23] words that have a hollow ring in the post-Enlightenment age, especially where workable solutions are sorely needed. The government figures in the final scene of the film, too, bring forth a flurry of gestures of resolution that are empty: handshakes, promises, and conciliatory gifts.

Both the symphony and the film fail to deliver the proper endings their respective audiences have been led to expect. That Beethoven would sacrifice a well-wrought ending when he surely could have supplied one underlines the degree of what seems to be a crisis of faith in humanity expressed in the language of musical stylistic iconoclasm.

Alex's Legacy: Where Is He Now?

Ambiguous, aberrant, classical-music-loving misfits of cinema, criminal though they may be, continue to build on Alex's legacy as intelligent, clever, and aesthetically discerning. Robynn Stilwell has studied three action villains associated with Beethoven: Emil Fouchon of *Hard Target* (John Woo, 1992); Stansfield in *Leon, the Professional* (Luc Besson, 1994); and Hans Gruber of *Die Hard* (John McTiernan, 1998).[24] Danijela Kulezic-Wilson notes that the character of Alex from Gus van Sant's *Elephant* (2003) is modeled on Kubrick's Alex; he is violent, drinks milk, and plays Beethoven's *Moonlight Sonata* on the piano. She also detects a debt to *A Clockwork Orange* in the piece's crossing of the diegetic-nondiegetic border and in the complex and ambiguous disposition of the soundtrack throughout.[25]

In *V for Vendetta* (James McTeigue, 2005), the title character (Hugo Weaving) lives in a dystopian London that suffers at the hands of its fascist government, though it persecutes its people more aggressively than in Alex's world. Music is a contested and repressed commodity in the film and invariably plays a role in scenes of justice and revolution, such as the playing of Beethoven's Fifth Symphony in one confrontation. The same symphony's signature tune rings out in wan, domesticated tones as the doorbell at the home of the writer and his wife in *A Clockwork Orange*, an ironically placid harbinger of their demise.

Another recent addition to this group is Andrew Scott's compelling portrayal of James Moriarty in Stephen Moffat's *Sherlock* series for BBC television. Another charismatic, bright, crime-for-the-sake-of-it antihero, Moriarty pulls off an elaborate and balletic theft of the crown jewels in "The Reichenbach Fall" (series 2, episode 3) while listening to Rossini's *La gazza ladra* overture on his headphones. In addition to the direct connection to *A Clockwork Orange* by way of Rossini's music, the scene's sync points and aestheticization of violence pay clear homage to Alex. In addition to keeping the world entertained from the safety of theater seats or sofas at home, these fictional figures continue to mark the problem of both the artist and the criminal in society and serve as a reminder of their roles in contemporary life.

Kubrick's recontextualization of Beethoven is, in a sense, also a reproduction of Beethoven that, like Alex's row of Christ figurines, necessitates some loss of the original. Beethoven's visual and aural presence in *A Clockwork Orange* gives him practically as much substance as (if not more than) most of the film's living characters. The violence done to Beethoven by way of transformation, careless inclusion in the conditioning process, and repurposing as a weapon symbolizes the greater violence done in a society that would endeavor to erase its transgressors, embodied in the troublesome character of Alex. Kubrick concludes, as he hopes his audience will, that accepting "all the good and all the wicked" is a small price to pay for a culture of free will and artistic vitality.

8

KUBRICK'S SPIN ON MAX OPHÜLS AND THE

INELUCTABLE WALTZ

THOUGH IT IS TEMPTING to approach Kubrick as a solitary and original director who worked against traditions more than within them, situating him in the context of the wider world of filmmaking and film-music practices yields a deeper and more salient portrait of his style, particularly in relation to Max Ophüls, an important and acknowledged influence on Kubrick. By examining how the directors treated common topics and aesthetics, and their shared fascination with the waltz, each can be better understood in his own terms; a host of Ophüls's felicitous devices and techniques greatly illuminate Kubrick's work and deserve more discussion in their own right.[1] Throughout this chapter, Ophüls serves as a valuable sounding board for understanding Kubrick, especially *Eyes Wide Shut*. What Kubrick shares with Ophüls is not merely a taste for waltzes, or the visual or narrative patterns they seem to inspire and guarantee, but a whole network of interrelated themes and stylistic elements that are especially evident in *Eyes Wide Shut*. But Kubrick's divergences from Ophüls in this last and ambiguously received film point to his interest in the ambiguous surfaces of the narrative that outline the ineffectual, empty lives and interactions of the characters more than in the clear plot development or consequences such as those of Ophüls's teleologic and tragic works.

Superficially, the directors have much in common. Both were Jewish and traversed the Atlantic in the course of their careers. Both were subject to a similar dynamic of critical response: initial resistance at best, followed by gradual acceptance and adulation.[2] Both were averse to traveling by airplane.

The films of Ophüls and Kubrick share a wealth of intertwined themes, topics, and subject matter, despite eclecticism of genre—Ophüls even specified as his

177

ambitions to change from one vein to another and not be defined by one style or specialty.³ The two directors are well known for celebrating mise en scène and cinematography, particularly with intrepid, moving cameras, and—most important for this study—they creatively privilege and draw upon music and dance. Like Kubrick, Ophüls has been treated as an auteur, and the films of Kubrick and Ophüls have been described, though usually separately, in highly similar terms. Kubrick's own admission and anecdotes of cast and crew members speak to Ophüls's influence, particularly in relation to *Paths of Glory*. In a letter to critic Alexander Walker, Kubrick takes pains to describe what he admired in Ophüls, including music and its balletlike qualities:

> I did very much like Max Ophüls's work. I loved his extravagant camera moves which seemed to go on and on forever in labyrinthine sets. The staging of these great camera moves appeared more like a beautifully choreographed ballet than anything else: a spindly waiter hurrying along with a tray of drinks over his head, leading the camera to a couple dancing, who, in turn, whirled the camera to a hussar climbing the stairs, and on and on the camera would go, all to beautiful music. I don't think that Ophüls ever received the critical appreciation he deserved for films like *Le Plaisir*, *The Earrings of Madame de*... and *La Ronde*.⁴

Kubrick was aware that he even shared a studio with Ophüls when he made *Paths of Glory*, and he may have chosen it for that very reason: "When I went to Munich in 1957 to make *Paths of Glory*, at the Geiselgasteig Studios, I found the last sad remnants of a great filmmaker—the dilapidated, cracked, and peeling sets that Ophüls had used on what would prove to be his last film, *Lola Montès*."⁵ Kubrick was more forthcoming in an interview with Michel Ciment: "Highest of all I would rate Max Ophüls, who for me possessed every possible quality. He has an exceptional flair for sniffing out good subjects, and he got the most out of them."⁶ The connection between the two directors has steadily gained validity in Kubrick commentary since the release of *Eyes Wide Shut*, a film seen by some as proof of Ophüls's influence and as Kubrick's homage to him.

The Unseen and Uncanny, and Trapped Characters

The distinctive sense of fate that permeates the work of Ophüls and Kubrick is rooted in the directors' keen preoccupation with unbending social structures—for example, the bourgeoisie and aristocracy, and the military—and the failure of characters to break out of these systems despite their desires. Characters' options are predetermined by their respective social classes, each of which accord to a clearly delineated hierarchy. Fritz (Wolfgang Liebeneiner), a low-ranking officer in Ophüls's *Liebelei*, cannot transcend his socially imposed limitations, and his attempts to do so are punished with death. Alan Williams sums up these circumstances: " 'Personality' is replaced by social stereotype and…nothing can truly 'happen' because it has all happened before."[7] This bleak but apt remark applies equally, and broadly, to Ophüls and Kubrick, whose characters are rendered as types rather than as individuals. Though Ophüls centralizes women whereas Kubrick tends to marginalize them, the narrator's proclamation at the end of *Barry Lyndon* seems a fitting final word on most of their characters: "They are all equal now."

Ophüls and Kubrick make sure the systems that trap their characters are discernible in multiple ways. Their characters bear uniforms, signs of material wealth, foreign accents, and other traits. Both directors emphasize clothing, dressing and undressing, and costumes, for example in the many rituals of dressing and undressing throughout *Eyes Wide Shut*, and the dressing up of female characters in many of Ophüls's films, especially Lisa (Joan Fontaine) in *Letter from an Unknown Woman* and Lola in *Lola Montès*.

Both directors drew from Arthur Schnitzler—Ophüls for *Liebelei* (1933) and *La Ronde* (1950), and Kubrick for *Eyes Wide Shut* (1999).[8] These and other stories Ophüls adapted for the screen, such as Stefan Zweig's *Letter from an Unknown Woman* (1948), all take place in fin-de-siècle or early twentieth-century Vienna.[9] Schnitzler's stories maintain some remove from their characters, and often deal with sex and death. Kubrick also spoke about his fascination with Schnitzler in unpublished sections of a wide-ranging, lengthy interview with the *New York Times*'s William Kloman:

> I saw a letter in *Psychological Quarterly* that Freud wrote to Schnitzler where he said that Freud had always avoided meeting Schnitzler socially…because he said he had always regarded Schnitzler as his doppelganger, and there's supposed to be some superstition that if you ever meet your doppelganger, you'll die.[10]

Kubrick has clearly attended to some basic psychological tenets that would find form in *Eyes Wide Shut*, and he summarizes the author's dramatic achievements thus: "Schnitzler's plays are absolute gems of buried psychological motivation."[11]

Despite this interest in psychology, characters are less important than the types they represent, and the larger events and themes of the story. Both directors, however, knew the voice was an important key for conveying drama. Ophüls, perhaps owing to his background in theater and radio drama, felt the voice outweighed the words spoken, and chapter 1 of this study presents evidence of Kubrick's similar viewpoint.[12]

To allow important plot events to go unwitnessed by the audience is a decided alternative to the Hollywood directive to show everything, and one that amplifies the paranoia surrounding the themes of the narrative. In Kubrick and Ophüls, what goes unseen (whether invisible or simply withheld from our view) but gets discovered later is usually something awful and irreversible. Both directors are interested in moments that clearly highlight what has transpired "when we weren't looking" or could not see. Wendy's discovery of pages upon pages of Jack's "All work and no play" manuscript in *The Shining* is a memorable case in point. Far more than tastefully averting the camera's eye, Ophüls leaves blanks for the audience to fill in during duels and suicides, knowing that what the audience imagines is worse than any image he can show. In Kubrick's *2001*, HAL murders the hibernating astronauts, an act the audience understands but cannot see or even truly locate (see chapter 1 for a discussion of visible words in Kubrick's films).

Even when the audience does witness what seems to be important dialogue in a Kubrick or Ophüls film, however, clarity and understanding do not necessarily follow. A detractor of Ophüls characterizes this particular quality:

> If someone opens his mouth in a film, you expect rightly that he will say something. You are naïve enough to want to understand what he says. Ophüls constantly teases us with his method of obfuscation, as profound and exact as it may be. And one does not want to remain teased, uninformed, and left hungry. Also, this stylish device is irritating. The film becomes ever more unsettling.[13]

This criticism hits upon qualities Kubrick would take to a stylized extreme in the empty repeated phrases in *Eyes Wide Shut*.

Ill luck and death dog the characters of *Eyes Wide Shut*. These unseen deaths contribute to a sense of forces beyond the control of the characters, and beyond the limits of spectators' knowledge; death is invisible and intrepid, controlled, it is implied, by the wealthiest men. The forces at play in *Eyes Wide Shut* seem all the more sinister and obscure for going unwitnessed, and the nature of Mandy's death and Nick's disappearance remain mysterious. All of this contributes to a nightmarish paranoia that reflects the story's source, Schnitzler's *Traumnovelle*. The price for social freedom, Schnitzler knew, was an infringement of privacy and a compromised control over one's personal relationships.[14] Bill gains freedom, and the audience gets to follow him. Bill loses control of the situation, however, and the spectator accordingly gives up knowledge. By denying the camera omniscience, Kubrick and Ophüls create the unsettling and compelling illusion of an absent director, as a ghost ship with no one at the helm.

While Kubrick did not make a spectacle of baring the device to the extent Ophüls did, both directors foster ambiguity regarding music's status as diegetic or nondiegetic (see chapter 2). This technique leads the audience to feelings of uncertainty, of uncanny closeness with the characters, and even the illusion of sharing a space with them—all of which point to the privilege of music in the cinematic palette. Ophüls crafts several prolonged instances in which music's status as diegetic or nondiegetic is unclear. Louise's (Danielle Darrieux) humming and singing at the beginning of *Madame de...*, for example, is finally revealed to be diegetic, but for the duration of the opening scene, she is accompanied by, and even in clear, phrase-by-phrase dialogue with, a nondiegetic orchestra. Ophüls sets up aural ambiguities and impossible-to-anticipate moments regarding the status of sound for his spectators to discover and be surprised, disarmed, and delighted by. Kubrick's technique of delaying the audience's discovery of music's source in the diegesis, for example at the beginning of *Eyes Wide Shut*, or coming from Lolita's radio, owes squarely to Ophüls, whose surprises about the diegesis extend beyond music and drama.

Music as Master

The amount and manner of presentation of music in Ophüls is remarkable considering that his source materials are spare in terms of music (one waltz each is mentioned in Schnitzler's *Liebelei* and *Traumnovelle*). It was doubtless Ophüls's background as a director of variety theater that inspired him to infuse his films with music. Ophüls adds a lot of music to *Liebelei* that is elaborately designed in terms of diegetic or nondiegetic status, and deliberate in style, so that contrasting musical styles emerge to help delineate interclass relationships throughout the film.

Ophüls usually frames his drama with a scrap of a musical performance that is in progress, or going on in the background. This overheard or backstage music often gives the impression that, somehow, music is the generating force behind the drama. In trademark fashion, Ophüls begins *Liebelei* backstage at a production of Mozart's *Die Entführung aus dem Serail*. The camera alights on a poster advertising the production, calling the spectator's attention to it, and music plays from the finale of the second act. During the intermission, the emperor arrives at the theater and the crowd rises to the pit orchestra's rendition of the Emperor's Hymn. It is during this otherwise visually and narratively static moment that Mizzi (Luise Ullrich) drops her opera glasses from the balcony, the act that will cause her and Christine (Magda Schneider) to meet Theo (Carl Esmond) and Fritz, the two young soldiers.

Ophüls constructs a romantic situation in which the characters meet by chance at the opera, in contrast to Schnitzler's version, where there is no mention of the opera and the characters are already acquainted at the start of the play. In Ophüls's version, music is a clear impetus; it is a force at once within and beyond the immediate moment of the drama that binds the characters via a common rhythmic, enveloping experience as though casting a spell. As a force that structures and stands for time, music becomes the symbol and locus of plot and destiny.

Diegetic Song as Commentary

The drama within the drama is an old conceit but one that is musically rendered by both Ophüls and Kubrick in two very similar scenes. The last music in *Liebelei* is Christine's own tender singing of Brahms's song "Schwesterlein" near the end of the film. During her audition, she sings on the stage for the directors of the opera, who are seated in the house. She is surrounded by a disorganized array of props befitting Ophüls's taste for Baroque clutter in the mise en scène. Ophüls's scene resonates with the vulnerable image and tentative singing of "Der treue Husar" ("The Faithful Hussar") by the German woman (Christiane Kubrick) at the conclusion of Kubrick's *Paths of Glory*. The two women appear modest in dress and demeanor, and both undergo an emotional change. Christine knows she is being judged by the directors, but the words she sings prompt her to reflect on Fritz and worry about the fate of their love. The German woman in *Paths of Glory* is displayed for the French soldiers who initially mock and harangue her; she begins to encourage them and connect with them with her eyes as they become moved by her song.

In both *Paths of Glory* and *Liebelei*, both the act of performance and the songs themselves inform and motivate the larger dramas in progress. Both songs evoke childlike qualities; Brahms's is melancholy and lullabye-like, and "The Faithful Hussar" has simple melodies and a repeating rhythmic motif. Both songs describe family, the deaths of young people, and the ends of romances. Both are in triple meter and therefore evoke the waltz, though neither would be mistaken for one.

In both cases, the performance of the song effects changes in character emotions, and a shift in character perspectives that, in turn, mirrors a parallel shift in focus from the medium (the singing or the song itself) to the content (the words, or the sentiment suggested by the melody). Christine begins her singing rather happily, swinging her arms gently in time with the meter. As the song progresses and she attends to the words, she becomes pensive. In the lyrics, framed as a conversation between a brother and sister, the sister speaks about her approaching death. Christine's voice falters as the lyrics become ever more grim.

FIGURE 8.1 In *Paths of Glory*, the woman's singing in the tavern transforms her listeners even though they do not understand the words. United Artists, 1957.

Kubrick, on the other hand, steers the power of sung music to a different end in *Paths of Glory*; the soldiers who mock the German woman at first revel in the very spectacle of a woman. As the sound of her singing emerges through the hoots and whistles in the tavern, the soldiers slowly become captivated and greatly moved, though they do not understand what she sings (see Figure 8.1). Jan Harlan comments on the familiarity of "Der treue Husar" among Germans, and the song's function in the film:

> Everybody knows this song—it is an old "soldiers tune"—it is a song the girl would have ready under the circumstances and under pressure... The song is a wonderful tool to show the de-masking of these not so tough guys who live under these terrible circumstances. The view of a singing pretty girl only points out the misery and loneliness and being home-sick.[15]

Most important in these related scenes is that the act of singing effects significant emotional changes and realizations. In *Paths of Glory*, the soldiers are emotionally transformed and experience a moment of respite from the horrors of war. Christine in *Liebelei* learns of—but also invokes and guarantees—her fate in the form of song; Ophüls endows music with an uncanny power that Kubrick would embrace in his later films.

Letting Music Have the Last Word

Both Kubrick and Ophüls are keenly aware of the power of the music in final scenes and over ending credits to keep open and raw any emotional wounds or moral outrage the audience might feel. Ophüls and Kubrick create films full of beautiful images, to be sure, but they also confront the audience with ugly realities and aspects of humanity. For ending credits, these directors call on music to perpetuate a bad taste in the mouth, an uneasiness over injustice and disaster that could have been averted—feelings meant to linger with the audience.

Lest the audience be too optimistic after the heartwarming tavern song at the end of *Paths of Glory*, Gerald Fried supplies a nondiegetic, orchestral rendition of "Der treue Husar" but one that is military in instrumentation and character.[16] Kubrick cruelly deflates the hope of the moment in this mean commandeering of the folk tune by the military, as it were. This moment, which obliterates the song's tenderness with bombast, is a reminder of other such moments, for example in the history of Beethoven's Ninth Symphony and its adoption and adaptation by a variety of campaigns and causes,[17] as Kubrick acknowledges and practices himself in *A Clockwork Orange*. The irony in the bright, militaristic version of "Der treue Husar" at the end of *Paths of Glory* ends the film with a note of bleak reality meant to stoke the audience's resistance and outrage.

Ophüls too practices irony through music, most clearly in the final scene of *Madame de...*, where the theme for the earrings, part of the original score by Oscar Straus, is subject to a final, sour variation that preserves the integrity of the melody and harmony, but death-knell chords in the trombones in a clashing key rudely intrude. Irony results from the juxtaposition of musical elements here, as in Fried's militarized version of "Der treue Husar." Ophüls's camera comes to rest on the earrings, a gift from Madame de... to the church, while the music blares the horror of her vanity and ultimate sacrifice of her life to it. These final musical moments provoke an immediate response but also point back to music as the force propelling the drama.

Dances and Dance Music: The Special Powers of the Waltz

Waltzes—whether newly written or taken from the existing repertoire—boast a number of assets that make them particularly available to cinema. Waltzes, such as those by Johann Strauss Jr., a popular choice of both Ophüls and Kubrick, are characterized by gracious, fluid, simple melodies, and phrases parsed into regular chunks of measures according to the dance and always respecting the triple meter. More broadly, the waltz can be a potent symbol or connote numerous things that owe either to the waltz's social history, its choreography, or other meanings it has picked up along the way.

The association between rounded objects and circular motion with waltzes and other triple meter music goes back at least as far as 1774, when Goethe made an explicit connection between celestial motion and waltzing dancers in *The Sorrows of Young Werther*; Lotte and Werther "soon took to waltzing and circled round each other like the spheres"[18] Chapter 6 discusses other manifestations of circularity and waltzes in connection with Strauss's waltzes in *2001*.

The spread of the waltz's popularity in the late 1700s met with extreme enthusiasm and censure; it was the first dance that allowed for exclusivity of each couple from other dancers, and furthermore in an embracing position that was deemed "indecent." Some voiced concern that the health and moral state of the dancers were in jeopardy, and it was deemed especially risky and detrimental to women. Never had dancers danced so close to each other or so fast.[19] Unlike other dances like quadrilles and contredanses, the waltz did not require a viewing audience (though it often had a rapt one), no doubt further disarming dancers of their inhibitions.[20] By the beginning of the eighteenth century, pamphlets were published with titles like "Proof that waltzing is a main source of the weakness of the body and mind of our generation."[21] Sevin Yaraman observes that in the context of operas—even those written more than a century after the waltz's appearance—waltzes were still used to mark women: "Women who waltzed were unabashedly sexual and seductive."[22] She lists *La bohème*'s Musetta and *Wozzeck*'s Marie among the offenders. Ophüls's women inherit this vulnerability to the dance and its music.

The popularity of the waltz grew over the nineteenth century and reached its zenith in the hands of Johann Strauss Jr. and his contemporaries. The rage for the waltz, spurred by Strauss's tours in the 1830s of Germany, France, Britain, and Russia, threatened the popularity of other genres, which apparently troubled Chopin as well as Wagner, who called Strauss "this demon of the Viennese popular spirit."[23] Demon is an apt word here, considering the spell-like power the waltz seems to exert upon the dancers.

Though it may be difficult to see the waltz as dangerous, considering that the waltz has been long and far out-scandaled by other dances, a wide variety of films engage the popular elegance of the waltz and its dark shadow. In the 1940s the waltz was often ambiguous or even sinister because of a vague association with the Nazi threat. Alfred Hitchcock mined waltzes by Johann Strauss Jr. and Franz Lehár for their ambiguity, and attached the music to dubious characters.[24] Nino Rota's waltz for *The Godfather* (1972) is perhaps cinema's most famous fateful waltz.

Twirling at the crossroads of the visual and thematic, the waltz animates scenes with double intensity. This special quality of the waltz, of which cinema takes great advantage, attended the waltz in its heyday. Eric McKee has supported his rich description of the waltz as a multimedia event with a study of nineteenth-century visual art and written descriptions. The visual depictions show an enraptured, gazing male audience, and evidence of energetic synergy between the musicians (some of whom look at the dancers as they play or lead the band) and the dancers. McKee notes:

> Such prominent depictions of an orchestral leader, which become increasingly common in the early nineteenth century, not only foreground the presence of music in this scene but also draw attention to the creative connections between the dance and music: the musicians' music inspires the dancers, and the spectacle of the dancers inspires the musicians.[25]

Ophüls's films, and moments in Kubrick's, would capitalize on this concept of the charged interdependence of dancers and the waltz.

Ophüls privileges the waltz among musical genres; it is perfect accompaniment for his circular images and turning camera and for symbolizing the closed and ineluctable paths his characters must take. The very premise and eponymous central motif of Ophüls's *La Ronde* is exemplary. The characters cannot quit their compulsive, seemingly mindless coupling and recoupling throughout the story, as dictated by the merry-go-round and its waltz, complete with lyrics *about* the turning of the characters. The visible merry-go-round in *La Ronde* is an obvious circular, turning apparatus, as described in the lyrics of Oscar Straus's recurring title song, "La ronde de l'amour," sung by Anton Walbrook, the story's raconteur and *meneur de jeu*. Susan White deems the circle the perfect symbol of movement and stasis in Ophüls, describing it as "the dialectical synthesis of the moving and the fixed," and the locus of exchange—for better or worse—of anything and everything, by the characters.[26] For many of his other films, the waltz would pose a clear threat to female protagonists. The permissive ambiguity of the waltz even makes it into the dialogue of *Liebelei* when Theodore observes that waltzes are "a bit risqué, but exciting."

For Ophüls, the romance of characters who dance or listen to waltzes together is typically destined to tragic failure. Waltzing provides an opportunity for Ophüls's characters to escape the constraints of the social situations that prohibit their love and creates a temporary postponement of their separation or demise. The waltz, in particular, provides an opportunity for a man and woman to dance in public, yet to the exclusion of those around them. The exclusivity of the waltz is what makes the affair between Louise and Baron Donati (Vittorio De Sica) in *Madame de...* possible in the first place. Louise entertains another dance partner to the strains of unremarkable, duple-meter tunes, but the sweeping waltz accompanies her dancing with the baron. In a sense, the waltz *is* the true domain of their relationship; it is where the characters truly live as they wish. Eric McKee points to responses to the waltz in the nineteenth century that speak to this sense of space and permissiveness: "Waltz music in these accounts both unconsciously triggers pleasurable emotions and sensations and activates a mental space in which to construct and contemplate thoughts and images—real or imaginary—drawn from the domain of the ballroom."[27] Again, the qualities accorded to the waltz in its time vividly come to life in Ophüls's and Kubrick's films, for fantasizing dancing characters as for those who watch them, including the film audience.

That waltzes can generate the sense of a particular place echoes in descriptions by Piers Bizony and others that register a sense of place in response to the spaceship scenes with the *Blue Danube* waltzes in *2001* (see chapter 6). An original, tender waltz by Gustavo Santaolalla likewise marks an emotional and physical location in Ang Lee's *Brokeback Mountain* (2005). Lee gets great mileage out of this musical safe haven and uses it to frame the characters' love as a social impossibility and to emphasize the characters' need for a private place in which it can exist.

The seemingly magical powers of the waltz to allow relationships that could not occur in the "real life" of the drama seems to fit into Michel Chion's concept of the "keep singing" effect: "when a piece of diegetic music—often a song—seems to have the power to momentarily hold evil or chaos at bay, as a kind of spell or charm."[28] For Ophüls and Kubrick, there's a "keep dancing" effect too. Dance music enables the couple's fantasy of perpetuating their courtship and distracts from everyday obstacles.

Eric McKee makes another valuable observation in his study of waltzes that the dancers lose sight of the world in a literal, physiological sense.[29] The dancers focus on each other's eyes to mitigate any dizziness and disorientation caused by spinning. As a result, their surroundings appear as an indistinct blur, and they cannot see where they are going. This is an apt analogy for Ophüls's and other cinematic couples caught up in their infatuations and the excitement of the moment.

The dialogue between Louise and the baron conforms to obvious, repetitive patterns, just as their dancing does. The repetition in the waltz—both music and steps—circumscribes the couple and their behavior, conferring a sense of scriptedness to their interaction in the most literal way, and creating the impression that they are in the waltz's power and have no choice in the path they will take, as dancers or as lovers.

FIGURE 8.2 The bandleader, prominent in this revolving mise en
scène, calls attention to the power of music—in this case a waltz by
Oscar Straus—in Ophüls's *The Earrings of Madame de...* Franco London
Films, 1953.

Ophüls squeezes all he can out of circles, even evoking images of a carousel, in the
form of a band on a central stage (and led by a conductor who spins with respect to
the camera), around which the dancers spin (see Figure 8.2).

The waltz plays before the shot of Louise and the baron dancing together. When
the camera finds them, they are already dancing, and at the end of this long scene,
the camera abandons the couple before they finish dancing. This editing helps cast
the waltz as an uncontainable, even eternal force; the waltz dominates this portion
of the film in every way, yet the cinematic apparati seem unable to capture its enormity. As the sequence progresses, the two look into each other's eyes more and more.

Seemingly at the waltz's mercy, the characters repeat their steps and their words.
But the path of the waltz does not quite remain static; rather, variations in the dialogue indicate ever smaller intervals of time between their meetings, and a gradual,
mutual forgetting of Louise's husband. Changes and locale and clothing, and their
evidently changing emotions mark the passage of time in this hypnotic montage. It
is as though the gravitational force of the waltz were pulling them ever closer to a
dangerous epicenter. The characters begin this scene with casual flirtation and a light
mood, and end up smitten and hypnotized. And in the story as in the dance itself,
there is no turning back.

As a highly repetitive, circular dance, the waltz serves as another manifestation of
the image of the circle, so important to Ophüls's films. Alan Williams points out,
"The circle is never a superfluous, 'decorative' entity in the film; it always signifies
real or frozen movement, a movement which, far from being 'free,' constantly repeats

itself."[30] His comment, in reference to *Lola Montès*, equally applies to *La Ronde* and *Madame de...* This points up a crucial paradox of the waltz. Its socially permissive nature is an opportunity for a particular kind of escape, yet at the same time one cannot break free of its prescribed patterns. It is an escape from one kind of circumscription into another, and the cost can be high.

Circles, and the circular patterns comprising the dancing of the waltz—and, by association, suggested simply by the sound of waltzes—stand for the patterns and forces controlling characters' lives, as manifest in the carousel in *La Ronde*. The waltz often carries a sense of foregone conclusion (typically an ill-fated one, for Ophüls). The steps of the waltz are, after all, rigidly prescribed and predictable in their repetition.

Ophüls and Kubrick both draw a fine line between choreographed dance and military maneuvers; these become manifestations of systems that oppress the characters.[31] In *Madame de...* Ophüls juxtaposes shots of dancers with shots of military activity to invite the comparison, while Kubrick's use of the waltz in *Paths of Glory* is more prolonged and metaphorical. Colonel Dax visits General Broulard (Adolphe Menjou) while the general is throwing a party. First, the guests at the party are seen waltzing in their finery to Strauss's *Artist's Life* waltzes. The waltzes continue to be heard outside the door for the duration of Dax's and Broulard's conversation in the adjacent room. The music is ironic and particularly irritating to Dax—and perhaps to the audience—for being lighthearted, relentlessly congenial, and oblivious to the grave sentence that is to be passed on Dax and his men.

For the majority of this scene, music is unmoored from its function as dance music (the party where the dancing occurs is offscreen after the camera's initial glide through the room), but the ever present music wafting in casts their dialogue as a rhetorical skirmish that yet has a civil veneer and takes pains to follow protocol (see Figure 8.3). In relation to this scene, Vincent LoBrutto identifies Ophüls's influence: "Kubrick inherited the mantle of the moving camera from Ophüls, but when combined with his own bleak vision the dance became not Ophüls's dance of elegance and humanity but a Kubrick dance of doom."[32] LoBrutto's characterization of elegance and humanity is apt, but Ophüls's dances most certainly entail doom as well. In light of Ophüls and other waltz-as-doom precursors, the music handily portends the futility of Dax's attempts to make one final plea for his unfairly condemned soldiers.

Remarkably, though Kubrick is fond of waltzes, his dancing characters never dance to them.[33] Rather, Kubrick occasionally extracts the waltz from its function as dance music so it acts on a purely symbolic level. Another striking example of dance music without dancing is Handel's Sarabande in D minor, variously orchestrated by Leonard Rosenman, throughout *Barry Lyndon* (see chapter 4). The Sarabande

1211

FIGURE 8.3 Colonel Dax tries to negotiate with General Broulard for the lives of his wrongly condemned men in *Paths of Glory* while Strauss's *Artist's Life* waltz spills in from the other room. United Artists, 1957.

haunts scenes connected to duels and death, and particularly the duel Redmond will ultimately have with his stepson. Though there is a scene of Irish folk dancing in the early scenes, no one dances to the Sarabande—its monumental presence over the opening titles would seem to forbid it—and in fact it never becomes diegetic, though it presides over young Bryan's funeral procession.

Eyes Wide Shut as Ophüls Homage and Revision

Ophüls's influence is most obvious in Kubrick's final film, yet Kubrick draws a distinctly non-Ophülsian conclusion. Michel Chion briefly connects the two directors in his monograph on *2001: A Space Odyssey*, throughout which music figures strongly in his analysis. Chion claims *Eyes Wide Shut* "can be seen as Kubrick's final homage to the film-maker he admired most of all, Max Ophüls, and especially to the waltz of *The Earrings of Madame de…*" but uses the connections to support his theory that *Eyes Wide Shut* fulfills the promise, made in *2001*, of the birth of a baby boy.[34] Considering the Freudian underpinnings of *Eyes Wide Shut*, the advent of a baby boy would be a tenable psychosexual threat, perhaps the next one awaiting Bill in the course of his attempts to negotiate the anxieties of married life. But whereas Chion deems the end of *Eyes Wide Shut* to be "both a codicil to Kubrick's oeuvre and an answer to *2001*,"[35] it is more correctly conceived as a revision of Ophüls and a final fantasia on major themes with which both directors grappled. Kubrick never showed interest in revising his work wholesale, or remaking his films, though he addresses certain subjects and ideas time and again. Chion's formulation of a *2001—Eyes Wide Shut* pair, conceived as such, seems unlikely considering that this director was ever moving on to new projects and made his important themes plain.

Eyes Wide Shut, containing Kubrick's most overt and sustained references to Ophüls, is resplendent with fluid camerawork. Many scenes are set in spacious, ornate, decadent interiors such as those in *Madame de...*, yet in rich color. The exposition of *Madame de...* boasts the film's most balletic camerawork, and the most dancing. The camera style of *Eyes Wide Shut* is mainly uninterrupted by fore- or middle-ground objects, departing from Ophüls's approach. Kubrick's camera's continuous, "unblinking" contact with the narrative contributes to the film's static, hypnotic quality and gives the impression of a continuous, dreamlike gaze. Kubrick remarks on the similarity between watching a film and dreaming:

> I think an audience watching a film or a play is in a state very similar to dreaming, and that the dramatic experience becomes a kind of controlled dream...The important point here is that the film communicates on a subconscious level, and the audience responds to the basic shape of the story on a subconscious level, as it responds to a dream.[36]

These musings on the nature of the spectator's experience also speak to Kubrick's interest in adapting a story that reflects on dreams and fantasies, and how they shape conscious thoughts and daily life.

In *Madame de...* and *Eyes Wide Shut*, both of which lack a narrator, a series of related events throw the films' respective marriages into crisis. *Madame de...* concerns André, a general (Charles Boyer); his wife, Louise (Darrieux); and Baron Donati (de Sica), the Italian diplomat with whom she has an affair. Louise secretly sells the earrings André had given her as a wedding present, because she is in debt. Unbeknownst to Louise, the jeweler tells André about the transaction, and André buys them back again. He gives the earrings to his mistress, who in turn loses them at the gambling tables in Constantinople. Baron Donati buys the earrings from a shop in Constantinople and later, when he has fallen in love with Louise, presents them to her. Louise tells André that she has found the earrings she supposedly lost, but he knows this to be impossible. He confronts Donati, so often seen with his wife, and challenges him to a duel. Donati is killed. Louise's death follows.

Eyes Wide Shut revolves around the relationships of Bill Harford, a doctor, with his wife, Alice, and with a number of other characters that articulate the film's central interests in wealth, commerce, and sex. The centrality of Alice as an important female character with significant agency in the drama is unusual in Kubrick, and the film's preoccupation with the representation of women are two clues that point to Ophüls's influence.[37]

When the couple attends an opulent Christmas party, both are approached by attractive members of the opposite sex who engage them with flirtation. This provides the impetus for a conversation Bill and Alice have the following night in which Alice questions Bill's motivation to be faithful to her, and relates her own past desire for another man. Troubled by Alice's capacity to want someone else, though she did not act on it, Bill stumbles into a series of increasingly dark adventures that bring him into the orbit of prostitutes and masked characters at an orgy at a Long Island mansion. Ultimately, Bill tells Alice of his night out and the two to remain together, apparently having decided to keep their respective anxieties and fantasies in check. The film explores the forces of desire, intention, jealousy, and anxiety, more as functions of economics and society than as individual experience. It is this interest of the film that Tim Kreider believes has been largely lost in the initial critical response to the film, a response colored perhaps by media hype about its sexual aspects.[38]

Affinities between *Madame de...* and *Eyes Wide Shut* are evident from the very first scenes. Both films show a woman preparing to go out, and both establish her centrality in shaping the narrative of the film. Music is crucial in announcing the power of Louise's character in *Madame de...*, and in contributing to a particular mode of storytelling and spectator receptivity in *Eyes Wide Shut* (see chapter 2).

Madame de... features original music by Oscar Straus. Straus changed his name from Strauss to Straus to distinguish himself from other musical Strausses, including those whose music Kubrick would famously borrow. Straus, popular in his time as a writer of operettas and cabaret songs, also wrote the song for *La Ronde* and other waltzes. The main title presents the film's two recurring musical themes: a sweeping waltz featuring brass in the melody, and a subdued, intimate, duple-metered theme in the strings. The former is the waltz that always accompanies dance scenes involving the baron and Louise, though it also appears in other scenes, and the latter is a theme representing the earrings. The opening scene shows Louise contemplating her jewelry and furs in an effort to choose something to pawn. She sings some of her passing thoughts (about the fur coats in her closet, for example) in a rather unlikely way, and hums other lines of Straus's "earrings" theme. Her musical interaction with the nondiegetic orchestra is uncanny and shows her to be in a position of agency.

For *Eyes Wide Shut*, Kubrick selects the second waltz from Shostakovich's *Suite for Variety Stage Orchestra*. The revelation that the music is issuing—and has been issuing since the very first title—from the radio in the Harfords' bedroom, does not so much establish agency as foster a receptive state in which the audience should be suspicious that things may not be what they seem.[39] There is a flat matter-of-factness with which Bill's adventures unfold, as salient as the impression that the bulk of the film, not just the ceremonial scenes at the orgy, is staged to feature Bill as an unknowing player, a classic dream scenario.

Madame de... sets up repetitive visual patterns by placing characters time and again within frames in the mise en scène. The spectator views characters reflected in mirrors, or through windows or screens. The Baroque clutter of the opulent, urban interiors contains its own motifs; a painting of a woman appears in two different locales in the film—first in the jeweler's upstairs office, and later seen through a door into a hallway in the general's house (approximately forty-five minutes into the film, after Louise tells André she wants to go away).

The excessive and thematically worked-out visual style of *Madame de...* is echoed in *Eyes Wide Shut* in the plethora of Christmas lights that decorate all manner of interiors. Masks on the wall in Domino's apartment foreshadow masks at the orgy. Like the recurring painting of the woman in *Earrings*, there is also a Christmas decoration in two scenes in *Eyes Wide Shut*. The decoration, in the shape of two red candles on an arch measuring at least six feet across, first appears in a hallway in the Zieglers' house; it also hangs above the steps in the foyer of the café that Bill visits later.

In the case of Ophüls, it is likely that the recognition of the painting is intended. Of all the objects in the film, it stands out in the mise en scène in both of its appearances, and therefore symbolizes circularity, recurrence, and fate. For Kubrick, whose attention to even the most mundane details was well known, the reappearance of the Christmas decoration cannot have been a matter of simply reusing a prop. For Kubrick too, its reappearance manifests the uncanny, dreamlike interrelatedness of the film's events.

Eyes Wide Shut presents other parallels and doubles: Victor's brightly lit, opulent home in the city as a contrast to the dark mansion in Long Island; Domino, the prostitute Bill meets on the street, who the audience later learns is HIV positive, and Mandy, the prostitute who dies under mysterious circumstances after the orgy; Bill receives a slow, deliberate kiss from Domino, and later, Mandy and Bill, both wearing masks covering their entire faces, share a similarly slow kiss at the orgy, mask to mask; Bill saves Mandy's life in the beginning of the film, at Ziegler's Christmas party, and a masked Mandy offers herself in exchange for Bill's release when he is discovered at the orgy; the parties, at Ziegler's and at the mansion, are doubles. In both party scenes, there are references to, or scenes in, private spaces away from the party, characters save each other's lives, and seduction, or the prospect of seduction, manifests in varying ways.

A mask plays an important role too in Ophüls's short film "The Mask," from *Le Plaisir*, in which a masked man dances the quadrille and other numbers with dancers in a tavern. In his excitement, the man faints and is taken to an upstairs room, where a doctor arrives to treat him. The mask is removed to reveal a joyfully smiling, elderly face. The scene has clear affinities with the house call Bill makes at Ziegler's party, yet in this case Mandy is masked in unconsciousness, and the audience has not seen the events just before. The scene in *Eyes Wide Shut* seems to give "The Mask" a dreamlike reshuffling of character types and movements in and out of public and private spaces.

At the orgy in *Eyes Wide Shut*, Kubrick substitutes one woman for another in the same mask, a point elaborated by Chion as an illustration of the audience's failure to truly look at what is shown—particularly if the object is a naked female body.[40] The unexplained, somewhat dreamlike switch of the women plays into the film's preoccupation with interchangeability and doubtful identity. In *Madame de…* Nanny, Louise's servant and confidante, dresses ever more like Louise throughout the story—one of the factors at work dissolving Louise's identity.

The incessant pairings of parallel scenes across *Madame de…* and its rigidly structured feel circumscribe the characters, and drain them of their individuality. Williams observes that the film is "*over*-patterned to such an extent that the narrative itself and the characters it sets in motion seem to become the justification of the work's systems of development,"[41] and he likens the characters to "prisoners in a grid of patterns of which they are unaware."[42] Despite the Baroque surface of many of Ophüls's images, and a feeling that his visual cup runneth over, Ophüls yet cultivates a feeling of emptiness. A persistent incompletion lies at the heart of both *Madame de…* and *La Ronde* that plays against Ophüls's celebrated, opulent mises en scène— a combination that contributes to his films' distinctive melancholy. In one way or another, both directors take pains to leave blanks.

Narrative parallels and doubles speak to Kubrick's taste for unlikely congruity, taken to its greatest extreme in the symmetrical narrative structure of *A Clockwork Orange*, and these extensively inspire the design and feel of *Eyes Wide Shut*. The story is haunted by unlikely coincidences, like Mandy's death following her theatrical "sacrifice" at the orgy, and Alice describing a dream she had that reflects what Bill saw hours earlier. There are also recurring images, and persistent interruptions to Bill's adventures that set the story in a world whose seams are almost visible.

Madame de… maintains a certain detachment and cynicism that hides inner emotional and psychological workings. *Eyes Wide Shut*'s characters are similarly opaque, as a result of the narrative flow and the content of their dialogue, though vestiges of class distinctions haunt the drama as well. The limits of Bill's understanding of the events in the drama are ultimately drawn along economic borders, for example between him and Ziegler, his ultrawealthy patient. An unexpected lower limit also emerges when Bill is unable to get a clear answer about what happened to Nick—a pianist, among the "lower" working-class characters—even after he attempts to get information from the hotel desk clerk and a waitress at a coffee shop, other working-class characters. Ophüls's irony and ambivalence about the middle class translates to a similar ambivalence in Kubrick about the upper-middle class, of which Bill is a part. As Susan White puts it, Ophüls depicts the middle class "as both the only place where social freedom can abide and as the final link in a chain of social hypocrisy."[43] This formulation captures Bill's entrapment, like an Ophüls character, in his station in life, and in between the special privileges and knowledge of both Ziegler's class and of Nick's. The waltz, heard at the beginning and end of the film, perfectly symbolizes the pretense of class intermingling and its limitation to the particular act of scripted rituals—dancing, and professional and social encounters. The waltz too points to its own cruel, original double standards and ironies; women and men were free to waltz, but only the women were judged. *bias on female* .

The dialogue and its manner of delivery in *Eyes Wide Shut* also serves to obscure and empty out the characters' thoughts and feelings. A great deal of repetition of phrases by one person and then another permeates the film and dialogue, which unfolds at a languid pace. Nowhere is the gulf between words and understanding so well displayed as in the scene in Ziegler's billiards room. Here, much is said, but little is revealed in Ziegler's halting and blunt conversation with Bill. Bill and Alice's dialogue throughout the film tends toward the mundane. Though it ranges from the fantastic to the real, the dialogue is most important for stirring up desire and jealousy, which seems to brew within or come from beyond these characters as individuals; their feelings are hard to guess or locate. These feelings are most important as markers of their respective limits of control in society; Bill runs up against these limits in his adventures, and Alice in turn is even more circumscribed.

The character of Sandor Szavost (Sky Dumont), the handsome Hungarian who flirts with Alice at the Christmas party, seems to have stepped right out of an Ophüls film, with his distinguished, somewhat timeless appearance, his suave, European manner of flirtation, and his single-mindedness in pursuing Alice. He even resembles Baron Donati from *Madame de…* and Alice's and Louise's dresses and hairstyles are similar (see Figures 8.4 and 8.5). The dialogue between Alice and Sandor, in light of Ophüls, is some of the most interesting in the film. "Old Fashioned Way," plays as he asks her what she does. The music might be a reminder of the legacy typified in *Madame de…* of adultery that grows out of dance-floor small talk. When Sandor asks Alice why she would want to be married, the audience is reminded that in the New York of the late 1990s, marriage was more a choice than a foregone conclusion for many women. Sandor tries to tempt Alice with a rather anachronistic explanation for why women would choose to marry: so they could lose their virginity and then be with the men they truly wanted. If pressed for proof for this theory, Sandor might point to an Ophüls film.

FIGURE 8.4 Louise and the baron dance in belle-époque finery in
The Earrings of Madame de… Franco London Films, 1953.

FIGURE 8.5 Alice dances with Sandor Savost, the intriguing European, recalling the style and
dress of Louise in *Madame de…* as well as its theme of infidelity. *Eyes Wide Shut*, Warner Bros.
Pictures, 1999.

The dissolve that initiates Alice and Sandor's dancing reflects the memorable dissolves that stitch together a series of dance scenes across a period of weeks in the first third of *Madame de...* That Alice resists Sandor's advances, despite the glowing lights, the many glasses of champagne she has had, the dance after dance in his arms, signals that this film will *not* follow Ophülsian rules of romantic relationships: in this case, Alice will not succumb, and her marriage with Bill will remain intact. The sticky slowness of Alice's speech when she rejects Sandor's invitation to see the sculpture garden underlines that she is pushing against decades of convention in not allowing even the notion of indiscretion—here, permitted by the surroundings, especially the music, the dancing, and the absence of her husband—to sway her from fidelity.

There are several reasons Kubrick may not have wanted a waltz for this scene. First, it may have seemed anachronistic for even the most upscale party in New York in the 1990s, or created too great of a set piece that it might detract from the real set piece of the film's exposition, Alice's monologue the following night. At the party, the source of Alice's susceptibility is transferred from music to alcohol—an immediate, clear, and widely relatable symbol of disinhibition and, potentially, indiscretion for contemporary audiences who may not recognize the dangers of the waltz. In light of Ophüls, however, the moderate-tempo duple-meter music in this scene renders Sandor unthreatening and inconsequential—he is simply a type—while the waltz would have it another way.

Significantly, Alice's eyes are closed by the end of her dancing with Sandor. Surely, she is drunk, but in a film ostensibly about seeing and knowing—so readily represented with gazing and eyes—her closed lids seem to stave off the threat Sandor poses to her marriage, and the reality of her own subjugation to men. As a song ends, she is jostled from her reverie and opens her eyes. This moment reinforces the association of tipsiness with the spell of music. She becomes once more aware of her surroundings and her tipsy condition, but also of her marriage and her control of herself. She rejects Sandor's last entreaties to see her again as the strains of "I Only Have Eyes for You" begins—another reminder that eyes and seeing play important parts in the story and that she is in a monogamous relationship (she only has eyes for Bill).

In this potentially plot-advancing scene, Alice rejects an Ophülsian course of events. That Alice makes such a choice—precluding the obvious option of a romance with Sandor when all conventional signs point to it, and when the legacy of Ophüls virtually guarantees it—displays the centrality and agency of her character in the narrative. The story is purportedly about Bill, but his adventures are touched off by his torment over Alice's passing, unfulfilled infatuation with another man she encountered months earlier.

The waltz has proven so momentous in cinema that the fact that Kubrick uses it as the frame rather than in crucial scenes proves that what ultimately happens in *Eyes Wide Shut* amounts to trivia in comparison to the larger story of the couple's marriage. The only visual reference to spinning in the imagery seems to be the large, gliding revolving door by which Bill enters the hospital; it recalls both Edmund Goulding's revolving door in *Grand Hotel* and Ophüls's turning machines and their significance of the interchangeability and the coming and going of characters. In this case, Mandy's exit is permanent.

The waltz assures the audience that the story of Bill and Alice *is* a love story, though much of what qualifies it as such is kept hidden from our view—even their love scene is cut short. What the waltz leaves in doubt is the fate of the Harfords' marriage after the final cut to black. Like Alice, who is afraid of the word "forever," Kubrick falls short of making a promise.

Those in the audience looking and listening even more closely, however, will be rewarded by finding another waltz nearly hidden in the film. The song "Wien, Du Stadt meiner Träume" ("Vienna, City of my Dreams") plays on the small television in the Harfords' kitchen as part of the film *Blume in Love*. Alice watches and snacks absentmindedly as she waits for Bill to return home, late at night. The film, directed by Paul Mazursky (who acted in Kubrick's *Fear and Desire*) is set in Venice, a seeming link to the masks of *Eyes Wide Shut*. In the story, the main character, a divorce lawyer, discovers he still loves his former wife, whom he drove away with an indiscretion with another woman. Its subject of the consequences of recklessly endangering a marriage with infidelity has clear resonance with *Eyes Wide Shut*.

"Baron or no Baron, I'm Going Home," or, How the Story Ends

Music inspires Kubrick's and Ophüls's narrative and audiovisual designs, constituting a critical component of their styles. The directors' interest in predetermined, musically analogous patterns that characters are powerless to alter, and narrative patterns at large, ally their styles strongly. The irreversible course of events set in motion and beyond character control in *Madame de…*, *Liebelei*, and *La Ronde* is readily evident in almost all of Kubrick's other films, notably *The Killing*, *Dr. Strangelove*, *2001: A Space Odyssey*, *A Clockwork Orange*, *The Shining*, and *Full Metal Jacket*. Remarkably, *Eyes Wide Shut* ultimately escapes this category because of its conclusion; Bill and Alice reconcile.[44] Kubrick has assumed many aspects of Ophüls's style, but avoided the Ophülsian conclusion of ruined relationships and death for the central characters. Alice's resistance to Sandor at the Christmas party is a clue that foreshadows the elusion of an Ophülsian demise; Kubrick mitigates the decadent somewhat by allowing his characters to live with it, but only because the characters seem ignorant to it. As at the end of *A Clockwork Orange*, Kubrick leaves the films weightiest issues unresolved.

If the verdict on Bill and Alice's relationship is a more optimistic one than Ophüls would supply, it is still ambiguous. Most unsettling is the residue of impotence and ignorance left by Bill's failure to break the chains of hypocrisy, and the repressive machinations of capitalism that bind the lower class to the upper class. Bill and Alice's persistence to make their marriage work seems to come as a mindless distraction from any real confrontation of the wealthy corrupt and the various systems that support it. The dualities of the film persist through the final word, "Fuck," spoken by Alice, which describes sexual union for the couple but is at the same time a shrugging dismissal of the unresolved issues that trouble their world. Like a waltz, the sexual act is repetitive and compulsive, and maintains what Kubrick shows to be a bifurcated, repressive, and even deadly status quo.

The final sounding of Shostakovich's waltz maintains Kubrick's taste for closing irony—it is elegant, beautiful, and even celebratory in parts. It evokes the Viennese waltz tradition in no uncertain terms, though in a more recent Soviet flavor. It does its job of reminding us, via the waltz's history, of its cycle of permission and punishment, its incitement to fantasy, and its strict choreography, themes that multiply inform *Eyes Wide Shut*. For the visual salinity, glimpses of sumptuous beauty, and problematic themes of Kubrick's films on the whole, the waltz is a fitting analogue and apt point of arrival, and departure, for his final work.

CODA

A MAJOR DIRECTOR of the latter twentieth century, Stanley Kubrick challenges his audience with searing portrayals of social and political themes; delights with visual spectacle, craft, and originality; and surprises with a diverse array of genres. The musical designs and techniques of Kubrick's filmmaking comprise a remarkably vast palette—one that the films seem to practically exhaust. In employing music, Kubrick is characteristically selective in terms of when, what, and how, and at times audacious for making his designs plain—influencing many to note the irony in his choices—and inventing something astonishingly new out of old parts.

Though Kubrick has been famous for choosing existing works, especially classical pieces, I hope I have shown the depth of nuance in these choices and, beyond that, the importance of the manner in which music is implemented—whether newly written or existing. Kubrick engineers cinematic conditions and coincidences in which the music will thrive and have potent leverage to generate and shape interpretation, effect and affect emotional response, and convey other less quantifiable aspects of the films' nonvisual, nonverbal elements. These conditions help broadcast the importance of music: it plays in the absence or near absence of other sound; it refers to something in the diegesis through synchronization; it is diegetic or described by characters; it demands attention because it is familiar or creates marked contrast; it recurs. Once one can understand the musical elements in detail and how they operate in the cinematic whole, it does appear that Kubrick lays bare the device, yet the effects are difficult to resist.

Musical effects range from the local and immediate, such as the swift, decisive opening of *2001* with *Also sprach Zarathustra*, to the overarching and recurrent, like the trail of breadcrumbs Ligeti leaves in *Eyes Wide Shut*. Often the films rely on combinations of large and small-scale musical effect. Music "out in the open," as much music in Kubrick is, begs for closer scrutiny, revealing that the films wring out music's inherent features—harmonies, melodies, rhythms, timbres and dynamics— to animate and make palpable the images and drama and to effect particular perceptions of time or agency. A multivalent approach to music in the films shows the music to be an interdependent element in postmodern, multimedial compositions; though Kubrick largely operates within generic expectation, music often works against it. If Kubrick grabs attention with choices of music that seem odd, fitting, or ironic, it is not an avant-garde end in itself but a signal and entry point into the sensibilities and concerns that drive the film. In each sonic surprise is an invitation to look and listen again and see and hear more each time; Kubrick remarked, "A good film, like a piece of music...should be able to be seen more than once,"[1] and he believed watching a good movie repeatedly was similar to the way "you re-read a book or hear a piece of music."[2]

Following in the spirit of Max Ophüls, music assumes the uncanny qualities of authorship and fate, exaggerating the dwarfing perspective on characters in favor of a focus on the larger societal and political forces they must negotiate. In Kubrick's work the waltz in particular evokes deep layers of social permission and punishment, not to mention its plain choreographic elements. As a ubiquitous dance, the waltz was highly available to cinematic purpose for both Kubrick and Ophüls, as for many others. A particular mode of memory Eric McKee observes in nineteenth-century accounts of the waltz has a distinctively protocinematic ring to it: "Waltz music...both unconsciously triggers pleasurable emotions and sensations and activates a mental space in which to construct and contemplate thoughts and images—real or imaginary—drawn from the domain of the ballroom."[3] The visual nature of memories associated with waltzes, and the invocation of space in contemporary accounts, certainly resonates with responses to Kubrick's use of the waltz in *2001* but also well describes the connections between musical sound and physicality, physiology, psychology, image, and emotion that Kubrick's filmmaking would more broadly exploit, not to mention the creativity he wanted from his audience.

Kubrick presents music as an item of daily life for the characters (dancing and performing characters appear in *The Killing, Paths of Glory, Lolita, A Clockwork Orange, The Shining*, and *Eyes Wide Shut*) and allows it to appear like a found object for the drama at hand, much in the way Ophüls did. Ophüls took advantage of diegetic music from an adjacent room, or even across distances, such as in the climactic scene in *Liebelei* that posits the rehearsal of Beethoven's Fifth Symphony in one location as the accompaniment to a suicide in another. Like Ophüls, Kubrick prizes those areas just offstage, or in the next room, for these fleeting, composite atmospheres that signal unseen forces and important moments. Such a conception also contributes to a sense of the music, and the forces of the drama, extending invisibly beyond the frame, and beyond the film itself. *The Shining* exemplifies Kubrick's efforts to realize the extensive qualities of sound and music—qualities that seem to hover in a region somewhere between the components of cinema and the imagination of the audience.

In addition to tapping into the listener's memory "jukebox," and the facts and beliefs surrounding a work's history, Kubrick's use of existing music, especially classical music, both situates the film in terms of the music it uses and in turn recasts the music and its previous meanings along the lines of the film. Kubrick created what would now appear to be the most ready reference for the waltz with the pairing of the *Blue Danube* and his spaceships in *2001*; countless anecdotes describe listeners who know the *Blue Danube* only as the music of Kubrick's film. The staying power of Kubrick's choices have proven remarkable, and some audience members would likely prefer to forget the musical recasting of Beethoven's Ninth Symphony and "Singin' in the Rain" in *A Clockwork Orange*. In this film, Kubrick shows the potential for musical familiarity to be a pleasure as well as a liability; threats and anxieties are the hidden freight of knowledge and memory. Music is more than a signpost for something from the real world; it is a time traveler. Existing music infuses film with tension by opening wormholes, to borrow K. J. Donnelly's term, whose time and logic pull against the narrative grain. Anyone can plunk an existing piece of music into a film, but not just anyone can make it work; Kubrick put music and other elements together in a way that seemed, as Roger Ebert put it, logical[4] and used music to achieve sharp, convergent focus via acute placement, alignment, and historical resonance.

Dialectics along the lines of musical diegesis versus nondiegesis, performed versus listened to, loved versus loathed, and other juxtapositions deepen the force of Kubrick's dramas and articulate his characters and their relationships. Musical style itself is a meaningful register; it not only refers to its own cultural connotations but also helps Kubrick instantly and directly map out dramatic territory, such as those that sort into two contrasting types, for example, inane music versus dramatic original underscore in *Full Metal Jacket*. Kubrick dips into repertoires of existing music that generate an experience of recognition that evokes at the least a sense of era, such as songs from the time of the Vietnam War, and at most, the engagement of highly detailed caches of musical history and meaning, such as the complexities of Beethoven's multilayered public image and the thorny problems of his Ninth Symphony.

The alteration of music in Kubrick's work far outreaches the practical need to make it fit the length of a scene; the excision of entire themes from an existing movement, as in the case of Schubert's trio in *Barry Lyndon* and the transformation of classical works in arresting renditions by Wendy Carlos and Rachel Elkind in *A*

Clockwork Orange and *The Shining*, answer to pointed dramatic and thematic needs. Virtuosic tailoring also exists in the amply evident variations of Nelson Riddle's original "Lolita Ya Ya" and other cues throughout *Lolita*. Here the music politely persists in sounding Humbert's desire—all the more for its contrast against characters oblivious to it, or events and moods for which it is purposefully inappropriate: Charlotte's sudden death, and the concern of others that follows.

These alterations tinker with the mechanics of form and function, highlighting and manipulating their syntactic and expressive features. This degree of change of the familiar musical object signals Kubrick's directorial hand (like Ophüls's visible bandleader or *jeu de meneur*) and affords music an enormous measure of control and influence, while the dialogue, action and visuals so often pull in the opposite direction toward ambiguity and even nondisclosure. Kubrick nearly forces music to the center by decentering and defusing these elements of conventional efficacy and directness. Music is then free to shrink or amplify emotional distances between characters, or between the characters and the audience, and to sound the themes that ultimately control the characters and contextualize their actions.

Many filmmakers have followed Kubrick in asking the audience to play games of recognition—in and across films and other media—a tactic that proliferates on the Internet in user-uploaded homages to audiovisual art of all kinds. This experimental thread in Kubrick's work offers the fun of a puzzle to the audience even as it serves other purposes, such as revealing the ugliness of the moral landscape; music elides and collides.

Kubrick's overall style may best register in terms of how the films *feel*; *New York Times* film critic A. O. Scott makes the apt claim that Kubrick's films feel "a little bit off" and that "our disorientation is the strongest evidence of the filmmaker's mastery."[5] Music, and perhaps existing music especially, with its sticky tentacles grabbing listener's memories and pointing to former contexts, is well disposed to affect in this way and contribute to Kubrick's goal of an experience for his audience beyond verbal and other expository conventions.

Kubrick married into a musical family, and his own fascination with music and musicians contributed to his unique musical-cinematic signature. Though Kubrick made the final decisions, his brother-in-law and producer of many of the films, Jan Harlan, made many suggestions and inventive solutions Kubrick used, for example the opening of *Also sprach Zarathustra* for *2001* and the clever alterations to Schubert's trio for *Barry Lyndon*. Dominic Harlan, Jan's son and Kubrick's nephew, supplied fine performances of the piano works by Ligeti and Liszt for *Eyes Wide Shut*. Kubrick constantly brought home new CDs, and his pursuit of music extended well beyond his filmmaking. He enjoyed music from a variety of genres and selected recordings of classical music to send to his father.[6] Jan Harlan recalls that toward the end of his life, Kubrick's favorite pieces of music included Schubert's C major String Quintet and Brahms's *Ein deutsches Requiem*. Music was more than an occupational pursuit, an insight that casts Kubrick's selection process of music for the films as a labor of love. His soundtracks become exhibits of his favorite performances of his favorite works (he considered no less than three recordings of Mozart's *Requiem* for *Eyes Wide Shut*).

Kubrick seems to have had a secret wish to be a *jeu de meneur* or conductor figure, and even mused about the conductor's life. Michael Herr recalls Kubrick's charming remarks: "He once told me that if he hadn't become a director he might have liked being a conductor. 'They get to play the whole orchestra, and they get plenty of exercise,' he said, waving his arms a bit, 'and most of them live to be really old.' "[7]

Kubrick imagines himself in the musical world on another occasion: "If you are going to compare [directors] to composers, I would say that Coppola would be like Wagner and I would like to think of myself as Mozart. I like to have that precision and the correctness—classical rather than romantic."[8] In the sense that Kubrick well understands the impact familiar music can make, and his sensitive deployment of music in the drama, "classical" fits. As Mozart did before him, Kubrick relied on the social meanings of dance music and made decisions about music always with aesthetics in mind. While Mozart kept music beautiful, even for the most raging operatic characters, Kubrick rejected at least one work he loved because it was *too* beautiful for the occasion: Wagner's song "Im Triebhaus" (In the Greenhouse) from his *Wesendonck Lieder* would have helped evoke the late nineteenth century and, as a work inspired by Wagner's extramarital desires for Matthilde Wesendonck, was highly relevant to *Eyes Wide Shut*. Kubrick opted for Ligeti's piercing *Musica ricercata* instead.

Kubrick's ear for tone, musical and verbal, animates the spoken words of the films as well. Documents attest to adjustments needed for take after take of James Mason's voice-over narration for *Lolita*, a process that likely occurred again during the two weeks it took Malcolm McDowell to record his voice-over for *A Clockwork Orange*. Kubrick knew that voice would determine the audience's response to HAL; his detailed descriptions and list of actors considered led to the memorable choice of Douglas Rain. Kubrick listened and responded too at recording sessions throughout his career. His input at the sessions for *Lolita* helped create a sympathetic Humbert and a theme for his desire that still sounds like a tongue-in-cheek parody of pop music ("polite—not raucous").

Kubrick's aspirations—however fanciful—to the musician's life were honored in a concert in his memory at the Barbican Centre on April 16, 2000, "By Means of Music: A Concert for Stanley Kubrick." The concert poster reads, "To mark the first anniversary of Stanley Kubrick's death, his family present this musical retrospective of his films. The concert celebrates the renowned director's love of music, which further expresses 'by means of music' [Richard Strauss] Kubrick's ideas and feelings, in such classics of the cinema as *2001—a Space Odyssey*, *A Clockwork Orange* and his final work, *Eyes Wide Shut*."[9] These words reflect the view I hope to have expressed that many of Kubrick's ideas are born in music and are most effective when music-borne; when we hear the music he has used in his films again, we meet Kubrick again too.

The concert featured director Tony Palmer as a speaker, family members as speakers and performers, and the London Concertante under the baton of Jonathan Finney. The program of works, made famous or more famous in Kubrick's films, included a selection of existing works as well as Jocelyn Pook's original cues, "Naval Officer" and "The Dream."

The family's choice to honor the director in this way speaks to his love of music, a love he shared with his family in and beyond his professional life, and seems an especially fitting tribute and endpoint; the pieces, like borrowed toys, were put back where they came from, undeniably changed by their famous turns in Kubrick's films. Though the famous images were not visible, they continued to flicker and flash in the private cinema of each listener's imagination, ignited by the music that became much more than part and parcel to his art.

Notes

CHAPTER 1

1. Stanley Kubrick, interview by William Kloman (New York, NY, April 1968), unpublished transcript, Stanley Kubrick Archive, University of the Arts, London.

2. Michel Ciment, *Kubrick: The Definitive Edition*, trans. Gilbert Adair, additional material trans. Robert Bononno (New York: Faber and Faber, 2001), 41.

3. Michel Chion has provided detailed studies of relevant scenes from *2001: A Space Odyssey* and *Eyes Wide Shut*. See Michel Chion, *Eyes Wide Shut*, trans. Trista Selous (London: BFI, 2002), and *Kubrick's Cinema Odyssey*, trans. Claudia Gorbman (London: BFI, 2001).

4. Stanley Kubrick, "Words and Movies," *Sight and Sound* (1960–61), cited in Ciment, *Kubrick*, 38.

5. Sidney Pollack, "The Haven/Mission Control," *Eyes Wide Shut* bonus disc, Warner Brothers, 2007.

6. Michel Chion writes glowingly and at length about the hypnotically repeated words in this "big male duet," while Andrew Sarris finds that Ziegler "takes forever to make the plot more confused than it was before he started to explain it in the most tedious manner imaginable." Indeed, it is a set piece deliberately devoid of sparkle, an anticlimactic denouement with no momentum or purpose other than to perpetuate the frustrating barriers around Bill. Chion, *Kubrick's Cinema Odyssey*, 27, 76–78; Andrew Sarris, "Eyes Don't Have It: Kubrick's Turgid Finale," *New York Observer,* July 25, 1999, http://observer.com/1999/07/26/eyes-dont-have-it-kubricks-turgid-finale/ (accessed May 15, 2012).

7. Stanley Kubrick, interview with Françoise Maupin, English transcript, October 8, 1987, Stanley Kubrick Archive.

8. François Truffaut, letter to Stanley Kubrick, undated, Stanley Kubrick Archive.

9. Notes relating to *Lolita*, Stanley Kubrick Archive.

10. Stanley Kubrick, letter to Benn Reyes, July 17, 1967, Stanley Kubrick Archive. Winston Hibler, a prolific producer for Disney, was best known for narrating Disney films.

11. Louis Blau, telex to Stanley Kubrick August 22, 1967, Stanley Kubrick Archive.

12. Stanley Kubrick, letter to Floyd Peterson, September 25, 1967, Stanley Kubrick Archive.

13. I was reminded anew of the quiet horror of this moment at screening of this film in 2001 in midtown Manhattan. As HAL's denials began, the theater was conspicuously quiet except for one young man who was evidently seeing the film for the first time, outed by his whispered expletive.

14. Michel Chion discusses the uncanny and charged power of the telephone in cinema in *Film, a Sound Art*, trans. Claudia Gorbman (New York: Columbia University Press, 2009).

15. A rare exception comes in *The Simpsons*: Bart complains of "a pain in me gulliver" in the episode "A Streetcar Named Marge," season 4 (8F18), aired October 1, 1992.

16. *The Simpsons* has referenced Kubrick's work no fewer than a dozen times, including references in episode titles, images, dialogue, and other forms of semblance to Kubrick's characters and scenes.

17. Among the many documents in the Kubrick Archive, I came across a leaf of unlined paper on which Kubrick had written, several times, "It is a pleasure to write with this pen," evidencing his connoisseur-like enthusiasm for office supplies.

18. Chion, *Kubrick's Cinema Odyssey*, 123.

19. Chion, *Film*, 173.

20. Greg Jenkins, *Stanley Kubrick and the Art of Adaptation: Three Novels, Three Films* (Jefferson, NC: McFarland, 1997), 81.

21. Edwin H. Morris & Company, Inc., unsigned letter to Stanley Kubrick, undated, Stanley Kubrick Archive. Under the sentimental lyrics, the letter implores Kubrick, "Do your best to have the lyrics used. It will enhance the possibilities of a major recording."

22. Davey's survey of Gloria's apartment as she sleeps, including touching her stockings and smelling perfume from a bottle on the dresser, is an unusually strong moment of homage in Kubrick.

23. Stanley Kubrick, letter to Robert Ferguson, September 23, 1963, Stanley Kubrick Archive.

24. Chion, *Kubrick's Cinema Odyssey*, 28.

25. Stanley Kubrick, letter to Robert Ferguson, September 23, 1963, Stanley Kubrick Archive.

26. James Naremore, *On Kubrick* (London: BFI, 2007), 102.

27. Vera Nabokov, letter to Stanley Kubrick, December 4, 1960, Stanley Kubrick Archive.

28. James B. Harris, letter to Vera Nabokov, December 21, 1960, Stanley Kubrick Archive.

29. Stanley Kubrick, letter to James B. Harris, November 8, 1963, Stanley Kubrick Archive.

30. The tune enjoyed some popularity following the release of the film. A version of it was recorded as a B-side for the single "Lucille" by the surf guitar group The Ventures on Dolton Records in 1962.

31. Vincent LoBrutto does not specify which cue is in question here. In a discussion of what seems to be the same incident, Peter J. Levinson identifies the music in question as Riddle's main title. LoBrutto, *Stanley Kubrick: A Biography* (New York: Donald I. Fine, 1997), 214. Peter J. Levinson, *September in the Rain: The Life of Nelson Riddle* (New York: Watson-Guptill, 2001), 206.

32. This scene, which Kubrick invented, struck Nabokov as "appropriate and delightful," though Nabokov's overall reaction to Kubrick's film was complex and ambivalent, as the introduction to

his screenplay shows. Vladimir Nabokov, *Lolita: A Screenplay* (New York: Random House, 1961). See preface to the 1974 edition, xii–xiii.

33. Stanley Kubrick, letter to Robert Ferguson, September 23, 1963, Stanley Kubrick Archive.

34. Stephen King, *The Shining*, double-spaced copy, undated, 393, Stanley Kubrick Archive.

35. Stanley Kubrick, interview with Danièle Heymann, English transcript, October 8, 1987, 10, Stanley Kubrick Archive.

36. It is not clear what the contents of this record were, or how it related to the contents of the soundtrack album.

37. Stanley Kubrick, letter to the projectionist, December 8, 1975, Stanley Kubrick Archive.

38. Ray Lovejoy memo to Stanley Kubrick, "Barry Lyndon—Investigation and checkout 'Look' Theater, Stockholm, complaint," September 7, 1977, Stanley Kubrick Archive.

39. Stanley Kubrick, telex to Dick Lederer, July 8, 1975.

40. Stanley Kubrick Archive.

41. Gordon Stainforth, who masterfully blended sound and music in *The Shining*, came to work on the film in early April, just over a month before the film opened.

42. Jenkins, *Stanley Kubrick and the Art of Adaptation*, 82.

CHAPTER 2

1. Handwritten note dated April 15 (probably 1987), Stanley Kubrick Archive.

2. Though Hallorann's telepathic voice comes through in the pantry scene in *The Shining* as a sort of voice-over, it is rather a special case, and difficult to classify according to the terms in this discussion. A similar moment occurs in *Eyes Wide Shut* when Bill looks at Alice in the kitchen and recalls her voice as she spoke about her dream.

3. Nelson Riddle, *Lolita*, piano reduction manuscript, undated, Nelson Riddle Collection at the University of Arizona.

4. Nelson Riddle, *Lolita*, piano reduction manuscript, Nelson Riddle Collection.

5. Nicole Rafter, *Shots in the Mirror: Crime Films and Society* (New York: Oxford University Press, 2000), 57.

6. Randolph Jordan has traced a correlation across the film between sonic and marital fidelity in "The Mask That Conceals Nothing: On the Concepts of Marital Fidelity and the Lo-Fi Soundscape in *Eyes Wide Shut*," in *Stanley Kubrick: Essays on His Films and Legacy*, ed. Gary D. Rhodes (Jefferson, NC: McFarland, 2008), 157–69.

7. Michel Chion, *Eyes Wide Shut*, trans. Trista Selous (London: BFI, 2002), 8–9.

8. John Caldwell, "Ricercare," in *Grove Music Online, Oxford Music Online*, http://www.oxfordmusiconline.com.eres.library.manoa.hawaii.edu/subscriber/article/grove/music/23373 (accessed July 18, 2012).

9. Claudia Gorbman has also noted these similarities. See Gorbman, "Ears Wide Open: Kubrick's Music," in *Changing Tunes: The Use of Preexisting Music in Fllm*, ed. Phil Powrie and Robynn Stilwell (Aldershot, UK: Ashgate, 2006), 15.

10. The mystique of unfinished masterworks also extends to *Eyes Wide Shut*. Michel Ciment describes Kubrick's uncharacteristic decision to send an unmixed version of the film, four and a half months before its scheduled release, to Tom Cruise, Nicole Kidman, and Warner heads Terry Semel and Bob Daley as "something of a mystery." It is unclear why Kubrick solicited feedback so far in advance of the release. Michel Ciment, *Kubrick: The Definitive Edition*, trans. Gilbert Adair, with additional material trans. Robert Bononno (New York: Faber and Faber, 2001), 311.

CHAPTER 3

1. Heinrich Schenker, "Der Geist der musikalischen Technik," *Musikalischen Wochenblatt* 26 (1895); translated by William Pastille as "The Spirit of Musical Technique," *Theoria* 3 (1988): 86.

2. There has been a recent flowering of literature on the nature of listener anticipation, notably David Huron's *Sweet Anticipation: Music and the Psychology of Expectation* (Cambridge, MA: MIT Press, 2006).

3. "Vectorized" is Chion's term for music's apparent ability to imbue a realistic sense of time in cinema.

4. Numerous films employ the ticking of a clock, as in the famous example of *High Noon*. A steady pulse associated with time ticking away, and with various images of clocks, dictates the rhythm and tempo of Dimitri Tiomkin's music in a climactic scene leading to the startling sound of the train whistle that announces Frank Miller's arrival in town.

5. Edward T. Cone, "Three Ways of Reading a Mystery—or a Brahms Intermezzo," in *Music: A View from Delft: Selected Essays*, ed. Robert P. Morgan (Chicago: University of Chicago Press, 1989), 77–93.

6. Stanley Kubrick, interview with Danièle Heymann, English transcript, October 8, 1987, 15, Stanley Kubrick Archive.

7. Interestingly, these two scenes are in fact not identical, but two very similar takes.

8. David Code describes the remarkable breakdown of narrative logic in this scene as a "momentary lapse into temporal incoherence." David Code, "Rehearing *The Shining*: Musical Undercurrents in the Overlook Hotel," in *Music in the Horror Film: Listening to Fear*, ed. Neil Lerner (New York: Routledge, 2010), 145.

9. The existing concert works in the film include Bartók's *Music for Strings, Percussion and Celesta*, III; Ligeti's *Lontano*; Penderecki's *The Awakening of Jacob, De Natura Sonoris no. 1, De Natura Sonoris no. 2, Polymorphia, Canon for Tape and Orchestra*, and Passover Canon song 8 and Ewangelia from *Utrenja*.

10. Rick Altman, *Sound Theory Sound Practice* (New York: Routledge, 1992).

11. K. J. Donnelly, *The Spectre of Sound: Music in Film and Television* (London: BFI, 2005), 37.

12. Ibid., 37.

13. Wendy Carlos, notes on *Rediscovering Lost Scores*, http://www.wendycarlos.com/+rls1.html (accessed July 10, 2010).

14. Greg Jenkins, *Stanley Kubrick and the Art of Adaptation: Three Novels, Three Films* (Jefferson, NC: McFarland, 1997), 81.

15. Ibid., 82.

16. Leonard Lionnet, "Point Counter Point: Interactions between Pre-existing Music and Narrative Structure in Stanley Kubrick's *The Shining*" (DMA diss., City University of New York, 2003); Jeremy Barham, "Incorporating Monsters: Music as Context, Character and Construction in *The Shining*," University of Surrey, Publications from the Department of Music, 2007; Julia Heimerdinger, *Neue Musik in Spielfilm* (Saarbreucken: Pfau Verlag, 2007).

17. Heimerdinger, *Neue Musik in Spielfilm*, 63, n. 132.

18. Elizabeth Mullen, "Do You Speak Kubrick?: Orchestrating Transgression and Mastering Malaise in *The Shining*," *Image [&] Narrative* (e-journal) 10, issue 2 (2009), http://www.imageandnarrative.be/l_auteur_et_son_imaginaire/mullen.htm (accessed May 26, 2012).

19. The reintroduction of material from previous movements is an old practice, perhaps most effectively animated in the Fifth and Ninth Symphonies of Beethoven, whose final movements

very conspicuously reprise material from previous movements. Bartók, however, sneaks his first-movement melody into the third movement, with no particular fanfare. Its identity therefore dawns on listeners more gradually.

20. Stephen King, *The Shining*, double-spaced copy, undated, 393, Stanley Kubrick Archive.

21. Stephen King, *The Shining*, double-spaced copy, undated, 393, Stanley Kubrick Archive.

22. Stephen King, *The Shining*, double-spaced copy, undated, 373, Stanley Kubrick Archive.

23. Stanley Kubrick, interview by William Kloman (New York, NY, April 1968), unpublished transcript, Stanley Kubrick Archive, University of the Arts, London, 15.

24. See Wolfram Schwinger, *Krzysztof Penderecki: His Life and Work*, trans. William Mann (London: Schott & Co., 1989), 220–23.

CHAPTER 4

1. Dominic Harlan, the producer's son, would later create recordings of Franz Liszt's *Nuages gris* and György Ligeti's *Musica ricercata* for *Eyes Wide Shut*, but his performances stay true to the letter of these scores.

2. Of all the musical materials at the Stanley Kubrick Archive, those relating to *Barry Lyndon* are the most copious, organized, and complete. It is not clear whether more musical documentation (beyond the archive's holdings) existed for the other films, but *Barry Lyndon*'s music seems to have exacted an unusual amount of work.

3. Correspondence and other documents in the Kubrick Archive suggest that Previn was too busy to reach, let alone take on a project of this scale in a short time. Though a letter dated August 12, 1975, from Jan Harlan to Mr. Hibbert of the musicians' union names Rota as musical director, Rota bowed out by August 26 due to his misgivings about being associated with pieces Kubrick had become attached to, about doing the work of arranging and orchestrating, and about the fact that Kubrick would retain the right to choose music he wanted, regardless of what Rota contributed. A letter from Rota's assistant, Riccardo Aragno, suggests that Kubrick adopted the same approach with Rota as he had with North on *2001*, including disclosing the possibility that no original music would end up in the film. Riccardo Aragno, letter to Stanley Kubrick, August 26, 1975, Stanley Kubrick Archive.

4. Jan Harlan, letter to Mr. Eggers at Deutsche Grammophon, August 29, 1973, Stanley Kubrick Archive.

5. Music notes relating to *Barry Lyndon*, Stanley Kubrick Archive.

6. Notes from recording sessions for *Barry Lyndon*, Stanley Kubrick Archive.

7. Kubrick explored the possibility of using Schubert's Arpeggione Sonata (written in 1824), and a particular recording at that. Rosamunde Strode writes Kubrick's secretary on Benjamin Britten's behalf, naming a price of 100 pounds per minute for use of "an excerpt from Schubert's Sonata for Arpeggione in A Min., which he recorded with Mstislav Rostropovich for Decca," a price that was probably dissuasive. Rosamunde Strode, Letter to Margaret Adams, Kubrick's secretary, October 21, 1975, Stanley Kubrick Archive. Kubrick may also have discounted the piece for aesthetic reasons; the first movement, while pensive, is melodically very active and demanding of the ear, in contrast to the trio movement's melody. The slow movement of the sonata is pleasant, peaceful, and in a major key. The last movement is nearly in the spirit of a concerto finale, far from the feeling Kubrick accomplishes with the other works in *Barry Lyndon*.

8. Thomas Allen Nelson, "Barry Lyndon: Kubrick's Cinema of Disparity," *Rocky Mountain Review of Language and Literature* 33, no. 1 (Winter 1979): 39.

9. András Schiff, "Schubert's Piano Sonatas: Thoughts about Interpretation and Performance," in *Schubert Studies*, ed. Brian Newbould (Aldershot, UK: Ashgate, 1998), 197.

10. Walter Frisch, *Schubert: Critical and Analytical Studies*, ed. Walter Frisch (Lincoln: University of Nebraska Press, 1986), x.

11. Charles Rosen, "Schubert and the Example of Mozart," in *Schubert the Progressive: History, Performance Practice, Analysis*, ed. Brian Newbould (Aldershot, UK: Ashgate, 2003), 2.

12. Ibid., 19.

13. Theodor W. Adorno, "Schubert" (1928), trans. Jonathan Dunsby and Beate Perrey, *19th-Century Music* 29, no. 1 (2005): 14.

14. Edward Said, *On Late Style: Music and Literature against the Grain* (New York: Pantheon, 2006).

15. Joseph Straus collects and synthesizes a large amount of critical writings on late style in "Disability and 'Late Style' in Music," *Journal of Musicology* 25, no. 1 (Winter 2008): 3–45.

16. Ibid., 6.

17. Jan Harlan, letter to Ralph Holmes, October 2, 1975, Stanley Kubrick Archive.

CHAPTER 5

1. *Lolita*, manuscript score, Nelson Riddle Archive.

2. Nelson Riddle, piano reduction for *Lolita*, Nelson Riddle Archive.

3. Claudia Gorbman has described the opening scene of *Eyes Wide Shut* in similar terms, hearing Shostakovich's waltz as the orchestral accompaniment to the actors' operatic deliveries of the lines. Claudia Gorbman, "Ears Wide Open: Kubrick's Music," in *Changing Tunes: The Use of Pre-Existing Music in Film*, ed. Phil Powrie and Robynn Jeananne Stilwell (Aldershot, UK: Ashgate, 2006), 8–9.

4. The eleven-movement work, of which only one movement appears in *Eyes Wide Shut*, proceeds in short, eclectic movements whose gestures include but range beyond Baroque imitative techniques into other time periods and styles, leaving Ligeti's motivation to evoke the ricercar something of a mystery, as opposed to, say, the much more flexible "fantasia," for example.

5. This system is described in my own work that serves as a foundation for this discussion, and later in Claudia Gorbman's. Katherine McQuiston, "Recognizing Music in the Films of Stanley Kubrick" (PhD diss., Columbia University, 2005), 141–55. Gorbman, "Ears Wide Open," 9–15.

6. For the sake of navigating this discussion, I adopt the chapter labels on the DVD release.

7. In the movie theater, Ligeti's music in the film is considerably more riveting than in the context of home viewing.

CHAPTER 6

1. Annette Michelson's response to Kubrick's film especially shows the impact of *2001* in affecting new ways of thinking and writing about audience experience. Annette Michelson, "Bodies in Space: Film as 'Carnal Knowledge,'" *Artforum* 7, no. 6 (February 1969): 53–63.

2. *Sight and Sound* 22, no. 9 (September 2012), 39–56.

3. Stanley Kubrick, interview with Eric Norden, *Stanley Kubrick: Interviews*, ed. Gene Phillips, Conversations with Filmmakers Series (Jackson: University Press of Mississippi, 2001), 47–48.

4. Roger Ebert, "2001: A Space Odyssey," *Chicago Sun-Times*, March 27, 1997, http://rogerebert.suntimes.com/apps/pbcs.dll/article?AID=/19970327/REVIEWS08/401010362/1023 (accessed June 9, 2012).

5. Paul Merkley established in his fine research on *2001* many foundational facts regarding music in the film. See Paul Merkley, "'Stanley Hates This but I Like It!': North vs. Kubrick on the Music for *2001: A Space Odyssey*," *Journal of Film Music* 2, no. 1 (Fall 2007): 1–34. Two additional articles clarify some of Merkley's points and add detail, from the Stanley Kubrick Archive, and the Paul Sacher Archive, respectively: Kate McQuiston, "'An Effort to Decide': More Research into Kubrick's Music Choices for *2001: A Space Odyssey*," *Journal of Film Music* 3, no. 2 (2011): 145–54; and Julia Heimerdinger, "'I have been compromised. I am now fighting against it': Ligeti vs. Kubrick and the music for *2001: A Space Odyssey*," *Journal of Film Music* 3, no. 2 (2011): 127–43. Heimerdinger's work brings forth details relating to Ligeti's case and illuminates ethical issues surrounding the director, performers, and publishers.

6. Stanley Kubrick. "Profile: Stanley Kubrick," interview by Jeremy Bernstein, November 27, 1966, *Stanley Kubrick: Interviews*, ed. Gene Philips (Jackson: University of Mississippi Press, 2001), 38.

7. For more details of this correspondence, see McQuiston, "'An Effort to Decide,'" 148–49.

8. Merkley quotes Harlan's interview from the radio series *Silverscreen Beats*, produced by Fiona Croall. Merkley, "'Stanley Hates This but I Like It!'" 8, n. 25.

9. A letter from North to Kubrick dated December 7 expresses his concerns about the size and recording capabilities of the recording studio. The archive also houses a signed copy of North's contract, specifying North's fee of $25,000, dated December 14. Stanley Kubrick Archive.

10. David Cloud and Leslie Zador, "The Missing Score for '2001,'" Alex North interview in *Los Angeles Free Press*, November 27, 1970.

11. Merkley, "'Stanley Hates This but I Like It!'" 4.

12. Roger Caras, letter to Stanley Kubrick, September 7, 1966, Stanley Kubrick Archive.

13. Julie Hubbert devotes detailed attention to this subject in her well-researched study of music in film with respect to a variety of industry forces, *Celluloid Symphonies: Texts and Contexts in Film Music History* (Berkeley: University of California Press, 2011).

14. Robynn Stilwell, "Music in Films: A Critical Review of Literature, 1980–1996," *Journal of Film Music* 1, no. 1 (2002): 46–47.

15. Editors' introduction, *Celluloid Jukebox: Popular Music and the Movies since the 50s*, ed. Jonathan Romney and Adrian Wootton (London: BFI, 1995), 2.

16. See Piers Bizony's detailed documentary study on the making of the film, *2001: Filming the Future* (London: Aurum, 1994), 118–24, for description of how the film's visual effects were achieved.

17. Eric McKee, *Decorum of the Minuet, Delirium of the Waltz: A Study of Dance-Music Relations in ¾ Time* (Bloomington: Indiana University Press, 2011).

18. The waltzes are the most written-about pieces in any Kubrick film. Interpretations of the tone of the waltzes in this context, let alone anything more detailed, are wildly divergent. For a survey of responses to the waltzes in the film, see David W. Patterson, "Music, Structure and Metaphor in Stanley Kubrick's *2001: A Space Odyssey*," *American Music* 22, no. 3 (2004): 444–71.

19. On the subject of von Karajan's surprise upon discovering the use of the recording in the film, see Julia Heimerdinger, "'I have been compromised. I am now fighting against it': Ligeti vs.

Kubrick and the music for *2001: A Space Odyssey,*" *Journal of Film Music* 3, no. 2 (2011): 127–43. See especially 141–42.

20. Von Karajan takes the customary liberty of disregarding some of the repeats in the score.

21. Bizony, *2001: Filming the Future*, 8–9.

22. The *Blue Danube*'s lesser-known origins as a choral work are discussed by Stephen Sano in "The 'Chorwaltzer' of Johann Strauss, Jr.: 'An der schonen blauen Donau' revisited" (DMA thesis, Stanford University, 1994).

23. The disconnect between the advanced state of technology and the business of attending to age-old human necessities is a running thread—even a running joke—in the film, but summarized in the poignant shot of Dr. Floyd reading (apprehensively?) the elaborate instructions for the antigravity toilet.

24. Sevin Yaraman, *Revolving Embrace: The Waltz as Sex, Steps, and Sound*, Monographs in Musicology No. 12 (Hillsdale, NY: Pendragon, 2002), 142.

25. James Naremore, *On Kubrick* (London: BFI, 2007), 4.

26. For a discussion of triple-meter music's association in staged works and cinema with circular objects and motion, see chapter 8.

27. David W. Patterson, "Music, Structure and Metaphor in Stanley Kubrick's '2001: A Space Odyssey,'" *American Music* 22, no. 3 (2004): 454.

28. For more symbolic uses of the waltz, particularly its dooming effect, see chapter 8.

29. The population of Vienna grew by 259 percent between 1860 and 1890. See Sano, "The 'Chorwalzer' of Johann Strauss, Jr.," 17.

30. Joseph Wechsberg, *The Waltz Emperors* (New York: G. P. Putnam's Sons, 1973), 236.

31. Piers Bizony, *2001: Filming the Future*, 8–9. Bizony's book is an invaluable documentary account of the production of the film.

32. Chion, *Kubrick's Cinema Odyssey*, 108.

33. Ciment, *Kubrick*, 131.

34. Tanya Brown, "The Music of 2001," *Vector* 215 (2001): 13.

35. Gorbman, "Ears Wide Open: Kubrick's Music," 4.

36. Irwin Bazelon, *Knowing the Score: Notes on Film Music* (New York: Arco, 1981), 200.

37. Ibid., 201.

38. Ebert, "2001: A Space Odyssey."

39. Eduard Hanslick, *Vienna's Golden Years of Music: 1850–1900*, translated and edited by Henry Pleasants (New York: Simon and Schuster, 1950), 326.

40. Patterson's multifaceted study includes anything in the film that could be categorized as music including the classical works, BBC News show music, the singing of Frank's parents, and the rhythmic sounds of computerized systems, and reveals a close relationship between the initial pitches of each of the main musical works across the film.

41. For an account of Khachaturian's film scoring activities, see Victor Yuzefovich, *Aram Khachaturyan*, trans. Nicholas Kournokoff and Vladimir Bobrov (New York: Sphinx, 1985), 73–93.

42. Julia Heimerdinger follows the details of Ligeti's experiences relating to the use of his music in *2001* in "'I have been compromised. I am now fighting against it.'"

43. Jane Piper Clendinning, "The Pattern-Meccanico Compositions of György Ligeti," *Perspectives of New Music* 31, no. 1 (Winter 1993): 195.

44. Paul Griffiths, *György Ligeti* (London: Robson, 1983), 31–32.

45. Richard Steinitz, *György Ligeti: Music of the Imagination* (London: Faber, 2003), 150.

46. In addition to the discussion of late style in chapter 4, Joseph N. Straus provides compelling case studies of late style works in relation to composers' bodily lives, in "Disability and 'Late Style' in Music," *Journal of Musicology* 25, no. 1 (Winter 2008): 3–45.

47. Griffiths, *György Ligeti*, 44.

48. Mark Kermode, "2007: A Scorching New Space Odyssey," *Observer*, March 24, 2007, (accessed December 15, 2012).

49. Henry T. Finck, *Richard Strauss: The Man and His Works* (Boston: Little, Brown and Company, 1917), 181, as cited in Charles Youmans, "The Private Intellectual Context of Richard Strauss's *Also sprach Zarathustra*," *19th-Century Music* 22, no. 2 (1998): 102.

50. John Williamson, *Strauss: Also sprach Zarathustra* (Cambridge: Cambridge University Press, 1993), 8.

51. Ibid., 28.

52. Ives's piece has been used in film, perhaps most creatively and with strategic integration to articulate different possible realities in Tom Tykwer's 1998 *Lola Rennt* (*Run, Lola, Run*).

53. Julie Hubbert has shown that rather than pushing orchestral scores out of the market, new paradigms for scores in the 1960s put pressure on composers using orchestras to do so in new and inventive ways, often with unconventional approaches to instruments and by blending contemporary styles with traditional ones. Julie Hubbert, *Celluloid Symphonies: Texts and Contexts in Film Music History* (Berkeley: University of California Press, 2011), 301–3.

54. Gorbman, "Ears Wide Open," 4.

55. Chion, *Kubrick's Cinema Odyssey*, 91.

56. Donnelly, *The Spectre of Sound*, 14.

57. Ebert, "2001: A Space Odyssey."

58. Vincent LoBrutto, *Stanley Kubrick: A Biography* (New York: Penguin, 1997).

59. Royal S. Brown, *Overtones and Undertones: Reading Film Music* (Berkeley: University of California Press, 1994), 240.

60. It was for this very reason that Robert Wise cast British actor Michael Rennie, then unknown in the United States, as the alien Klaatu in *The Day the Earth Stood Still* (1951) instead of Spencer Tracy, a familiar and trusted face. Lucille Ball makes a comment on the adherence of actors to particular roles in an episode of *The Lucy-Desi Comedy Hour* featuring Fred MacMurray when she whispers to Ricky, "I haven't trusted him since I saw him in *Double Indemnity*." "Lucy Hunts Uranium," episode 1, season 3, *The Lucy-Desi Comedy Hour*, aired January 3, 1958.

CHAPTER 7

1. Nicole Rafter, *Shots in the Mirror: Crime Films and Society* (New York: Oxford University Press, 2000), 150.

2. Anthony Burgess, "Juice from a Clockwork Orange," in *Perspectives on Stanley Kubrick*, ed. Mario Falsetto (London: G. K. Hall, 1996), 188 (first printed in *Rolling Stone*, June 8, 1972).

3. James Wierzbicki notes differences between Burgess's novel and Kubrick's film regarding references to music and musicians in "Banality Triumphant: Iconographic Use of Beethoven's Ninth Symphony in Recent Films," *Beethoven Forum* 10, no. 2 (Fall 2003): 113–38.

4. Anthony Burgess, *A Clockwork Orange*, First Draft Screenplay, undated, and *A Clockwork Orange*, Screenplay Draft 1, undated, Stanley Kubrick Archive.

5. Raphael Georg Kiesewetter puts this concept forth in his *Geschichte der europäisch-abendländischen oder unserer heutigen Musik* of 1834, as discussed by Carl Dahlhaus in *Nineteenth-Century Music*, trans. J. Bradford Robinson (Berkeley: University of California Press, 1989), 8.

6. Carl Dahlhaus describes an essential difference in experiencing the two composers' styles; "There was nothing to 'understand' about the magic that emanated from Rossini's music; the emotions that Beethoven's work engendered, however, were mingled with a challenge to decipher, in patient exertion, the meaning of what had taken place in the music."

7. It is not clear whether the synthesized version is a reflection of how Alex perceives it, distorted by the drugs in his system. If we were able to hear the music objectively, however (as, for example, the scientists in the room hear it), it may very well be an orchestral, non-electronic recording.

8. Robynn Stilwell, "Hysterical Beethoven," *Beethoven Forum* 10, no. 2 (2003): 163.

9. Nicholas Cook, *Beethoven Symphony No. 9* (Cambridge: Cambridge University Press, 1993), 27.

10. Joseph Kerman et al., "Beethoven, Ludwig van," in *Grove Music Online, Oxford Music Online*, http://www.oxfordmusiconline.com.eres.library.manoa.hawaii.edu/subscriber/article/grove/music/40026pg19 (accessed June 6, 2012).

11. Susan McClary, "Getting Down Off the Beanstalk: The Presence of a Woman's Voice in Janika Vandervelde's *Genesis II*," in *Feminine Endings*, 2nd ed. (Minneapolis: University of Minnesota Press, 2002), 112–31.

12. Ibid., 129.

13. Joseph Kerman et al., "Beethoven, Ludwig van," in *Grove Music Online, Oxford Music Online*, http://www.oxfordmusiconline.com.eres.library.manoa.hawaii.edu/subscriber/article/grove/music/40026pg19 (accessed June 6, 2012).

14. Randy Rasmussen, *Stanley Kubrick: Seven Films Analyzed.* (London: McFarland & Company, 2001), 151.

15. Suzanne Cusick presents research on the use of music in the interrogation of detainees in US facilities in "'You are in a place that is out of the world…': Music in the Détention Camps of the 'Global War on Terror,'" *Journal of the Society for American Music* 2, no. 2 (2008): 1–26.

16. Cook, *Beethoven Symphony No. 9*, 100.

17. James Webster, "The Form of the Finale of Beethoven's Ninth Symphony," *Beethoven Forum* 1 (1992): 36.

18. Translation by David Benjamin Levy, *Beethoven: The Ninth Symphony* (New Haven, CT: Yale University Press, 2003), 13. Translation reproduced with permission of Yale University Press, all rights reserved.

19. Scott Burnham, *Beethoven Hero* (Princeton, NJ: Princeton University Press, 1995), xiv.

20. Esteban Buch, *Beethoven's Ninth: A Political History*, trans. Richard Miller (Chicago: University of Chicago Press, 1999).

21. Cook, *Beethoven's Ninth Symphony*, 103–4.

22. George Grove, *Beethoven and His Nine Symphonies*, 3rd ed. (New York: Dover, 1962), 392.

23. Levy, *Beethoven: The Ninth Symphony*, 12.

24. Stilwell, "Hysterical Beethoven," 163.

25. Danijela Kulezic-Wilson, "Gus Van Sant's Soundwalks and Audio-Visual *Musique concrète*," in *Music, Sound and Filmmakers*, ed. James Wierzbicki (New York: Routledge, 2012), 83.

CHAPTER 8

1. See Susan White, *The Cinema of Max Ophüls: Magisterial Vision and the Figure of Woman* (New York: Columbia University Press, 1995), and Alan Larson Williams, *Max Ophüls and the Cinema of Desire: Style and Spectacle in Four Films, 1948–1955* (New York: Arno, 1980), for two illuminating studies of the director.

2. Anthony Lane illuminates some challenges to Ophüls's reception in the United States in "Master of Ceremonies: The Films of Max Ophüls," *New Yorker*, July 8, 2002, http://www.newyorker.com/archive/2002/07/08/020708crat_atlarge (accessed June 29, 2010).

3. Martina Müller, "Vom Souffleurkasten über das Mikro auf die Leinwand: Max Ophüls," *Frauen und Film* 42 (August 1987): 62. Translation mine.

4. Alexander Walker, Sybil Taylor, and Ulrich Ruchti, *Stanley Kubrick, Director*, rev. and exp. ed. (New York: Norton, 1999), 14.

5. Ibid., 14.

6. Michel Ciment, *Kubrick: The Definitive Edition*, translated by Gilbert Adair, 1980; reprinted with additional material translated by Roberto Bononno (New York: Faber & Faber, 2001), 34.

7. Williams, *Max Ophüls and the Cinema of Desire*, 85.

8. The dates and titles of the works by Schnitzler that inspired these films are *Liebelei* (1896), *Reigen* (1912), and *Traumnovelle* (1926), respectively.

9. These films, along with the French-language *Le Plaisir, Madame de…* and *Lola Montès*, represent the most celebrated by the director. Ophüls's films characteristically cross national borders and languages, and they mix characters of different nationalities with cosmopolitan panache. Only the couple of "American" films (*Caught* and *Reckless Moment*) stand apart from this trend.

10. Stanley Kubrick, interview by William Kloman, April 4, 1968, transcript, 62, Stanley Kubrick Archive.

11. Ibid., 63. Kubrick met Peter Schnitzler, the author's grandson, on at least one occasion. An admiring letter of May 27, 1959, to Kubrick from the young Schnitzler, at the time an aspiring filmmaker, thanks Kubrick for allowing him to visit the set of *Spartacus* and describes efforts under way to obtain copies of his grandfather's notebooks, and information from the agent who handles them "in regard to motion picture rights, etc." Peter says he plans to take Kubrick up on his offer to visit his set again and is hopeful that he will by then have the notebooks to share with him. The paper trail ends there, however, and it is not clear whether the two did indeed meet again. Peter Schnitzler, letter to Stanley Kubrick, May 27, 1959, Stanley Kubrick Archive.

12. See Müller, "Vom Souffleurkasten über das Mikro auf die Leinwand," particularly 68.

13. *Süddeutsche Zeitung*, January 15, 1956, quoted in Müller, "Vom Souffleurkasten über das Mikro auf die Leinwand," 63, translation mine.

14. Peter Gay explores this theme in depth in *Schnitzler's Century: The Making of Middle Class Culture, 1815–1914* (New York: W. W. Norton, 2002), taking the invasion of Schnitzler's privacy (he discovered his father reading his diary) as a point of departure. In this biographical anecdote, the act of reading constitutes a deep and formative sense of violation in the young Schnitzler that would color his dramatic writings.

15. Email from Jan Harlan to the author, June 7, 2010.

16. Krin Gabbard locates this music and the Strauss waltz during Dax's visit to Broulard as the first of Kubrick's ironic pairings of music and drama. "Redeemed by Ludwig Van: Kubrick's

Musical Strategy in *A Clockwork Orange*," *Cinesonic: Experiencing the Soundtrack*, ed. Philip Brophy (North Ryde, Australia: Australian Film Television and Radio School, 2001), 149–67.

17. This subject is explored at length in Esteban Buch, *Beethoven's Ninth: A Political History*, trans. Richard Miller (Chicago: University of Chicago Press, 1999).

18. Andrew Lamb, "Waltz (i)," in *Grove Music Online, Oxford Music Online*, http://www.oxfordmusiconline.com.eres.library.manoa.hawaii.edu/subscriber/article/grove/music/29881 (accessed July 7, 2010).

19. See Sevin Yaraman, *Revolving Embrace: The Waltz as Sex, Steps, and Sound*, Monographs in Musicology 12 (Hillsdale, NY: Pendragon, 2002), particularly 1–16, for a vivid picture of the waltz's reception history and moral and physical issues. For detailed discussion of nuances of the waltz in different regions during the eighteenth and nineteenth centuries, see Elizabeth Aldrich, *From the Ballroom to Hell: Grace and Folly in Nineteenth-Century Dance* (Evanston, IL: Northwestern University Press, 1991).

20. Ibid., 19. Eric McKee illuminates the connection of the waltz to its antecedent, the minuet, noting that both of these dances were meant to display an individual's attributes to onlookers. Eric McKee, *Decorum of the Minuet, Delirium of the Waltz: A Study of Dance-Music Relations in ¾ Time* (Bloomington: Indiana University Press, 2011).

21. Lamb, "Waltz (i)."

22. Yaraman, *Revolving Embrace*, 53.

23. Lamb, "Waltz (i)."

24. Jack Sullivan discusses the deployment of the composers' versions of Strauss and Lehár in *Hitchcock's Music* (New Haven, CT: Yale University Press, 2006), 84–95. Tiomkin quipped about his take on Lehár, "I gave 'The Merry Widow' the atonal treatment and worse" (92).

25. McKee, *Decorum of the Minuet*, 98.

26. White, *The Cinema of Max Ophüls*, 24.

27. McKee, *Decorum of the Minuet*, 118.

28. Michel Chion, *Film: A Sound Art*, trans. Claudia Gorbman (New York: Columbia University Press, 2009), 479. Chion's concept of music's special power to perpetuate circumstances can equally apply to unfavorable and violent events—Alex's own singing during the attack on the writer and his wife in *A Clockwork Orange* and his later retribution are ready examples, and there are numerous other cases of music holding ill effects in place in the films of Sam Peckinpah, David Lynch, and Quentin Tarantino. Hitchcock's remake of his own *The Man Who Knew Too Much* (1956) offers a musical score and its execution as a blueprint for murder, surely a dark shadow of the "keep singing" effect.

29. McKee, *Decorum of the Minuet*, 91–92.

30. Williams, *Max Ophüls and the Cinema of Desire*, 145.

31. Julie Taymor explores dance as a metaphor for the suppressive military draft in an intense and richly imagined set piece featuring the song, "I Want You (She's So Heavy)" in her fantasia on songs by The Beatles, *Across the Universe* (2007). The recruiters wear identical masks with exaggerated features and engage in a cha-cha with the stripped recruits, who flop like dolls in their arms, and at the whims of the military machine. The scene emphasizes the feminizing effects of submitting to the military, an anxiety that pervades military culture as rendered in many war movies, including Kubrick's own *Full Metal Jacket*.

32. Vincent LoBrutto, *Stanley Kubrick: A Biography* (New York: Donald I. Fine, 1997), 138.

33. Production notes for *Lolita* describe a scene in which the title character hums an unnamed Strauss waltz. Stanley Kubrick Archive.

34. Michel Chion, *Kubrick's Cinema Odyssey*, trans. Claudia Gorbman (London: BFI, 2001), 165.

35. Ibid., vi.

36. Stanley Kubrick, "Kubrick Tells What Makes *Clockwork* Tick," interview by Bernard Weinraub, *New York Times*, January 4, 1972.

37. The female sniper in *Full Metal Jacket* is the only other complex and problematic female character in Kubrick.

38. Tim Kreider, review of *Eyes Wide Shut*, Warner Bros., *Film Quarterly* 53, no. 3 (Spring 2000): 41–48.

39. In a reading of the scene that implies a more specific and local affinity between the film and its music, Claudia Gorbman hears the Shostakovich as an opera-style accompaniment that renders Tom Cruise's speech as a recitative. Claudia Gorbman, "Ears Wide Open: Kubrick's Music," in *Changing Tunes: The Use of Pre-Existing Music in Film*, ed. Phil Powrie and Robynn Jeananne Stilwell (Aldershot, UK: Ashgate, 2006), 3–18.

40. Michel Chion, *Eyes Wide Shut*, trans. Trista Selous (London: BFI, 2002), 8–9.

41. Williams, *Max Ophüls and the Cinema of Desire*, 124–25.

42. Ibid., 127.

43. White, *The Cinema of Max Ophüls*, 46.

44. While working on the screenplay for Eyes Wide Shut, Kubrick was once again in touch with Peter Schnitzler and was particularly interested in finding out whether anything in his grandfather's papers suggested he had considered any alternative endings for Traumnovelle. This line of inquiry suggests Kubrick may have struggled with the ending, so different from those in Schnitzler's stories set by Ophuls.

Shortly after Kubrick bought the rights to make a film of the story, Federico Fellini approached Peter Schnitzler with the same request. I am grateful to Susan Ingram for sharing this information following her conversation with Peter Schnitzler in June 2013.

CODA

1. Stanley Kubrick, interview by Françoise Maupin, October 8, 1987, unpublished transcript, Stanley Kubrick Archive.

2. Stanley Kubrick, interview by Danièle Heymann, "Un entretien avec le réalisteur de 'Full Metal Jacket': Le Vietnam de Stanley Kubrick," October 20, 1987, unpublished transcript, Stanley Kubrick Archive.

3. Eric McKee, *Decorum of the Minuet, Delirium of the Waltz: A Study of Dance-Music Relations in ¾ Time* (Bloomington: Indiana University Press, 2011), 118.

4. Roger Ebert, "2001: A Space Odyssey," *Chicago Sun-Times*, March 27, 1997, http://rogerebert.suntimes.com/apps/pbcs.dll/article?AID=/19970327/REVIEWS08/401010362/1023 (accessed June 9, 2012).

5. A. O. Scott, "Critics' Picks: 'Lolita,'" *New York Times* online, July 26, 2010, http://video.nytimes.com/video/2010/07/26/movies/1247468048570/critics-picks-lolita.html?ref=movies (accessed July 13, 2012).

6. Stanley Kubrick, undated telex requesting Deutsche Grammophon records to be sent to his father. The telex was in a box of miscellaneous paperwork dated 1975. Stanley Kubrick Archive.

7. Michael Herr, *Kubrick* (New York: Grove, 2000), 65.

8. Kubrick, interview by Danièle Heymann, 34. In the Kubrick Archive, an entire notebook, undated, was devoted to Richard Wagner's *Ring* cycle; it detailed main characters and plot elements, but the purpose of these notes is unknown.

9. "By Means of Music," concert poster, April 16, 2000, Stanley Kubrick Archive.

Select Bibliography

Abrams, Jerold J. *The Philosophy of Stanley Kubrick*. Lexington: University Press of Kentucky, 2007.

Adorno, Theodor W. "Schubert" (1928). Translated by Jonathan Dunsby and Beate Perrey. *19th-Century Music* 29, no. 1 (Summer 2005): 1–14.

Agel, Jerome. *The Making of Kubrick's 2001*. New York: New American Library, 1970.

Aldrich, Elizabeth. *From the Ballroom to Hell: Grace and Folly in Nineteenth-Century Dance*. Evanston, IL: Northwestern University Press, 1991.

Altman, Rick. *Sound Theory, Sound Practice*. New York: Routledge, 1992.

Bacher, Lutz. *Max Ophüls in the Hollywood Studios*. New Brunswick, NJ: Rutgers University Press, 1996.

Barham, Jeremy. "Incorporating Monsters: Music as Context, Character and Construction in *The Shining*." Publications from the Department of Music, University of Surrey, 2007.

Baxter, John. *Stanley Kubrick: A Biography*. London: HarperCollins, 1997.

Bazelon, Irwin. *Knowing the Score: Notes on Film Music*. New York: Arco, 1981.

Bizony, Piers. *2001: Filming the Future*. London: Aurum, 1994.

Brown, Royal S. "Film and Classical Music." In *Film and the Arts in Symbiosis: A Resource Guide*, edited by Gary R. Edgerton, 165–215. New York: Greenwood, 1988.

———. *Overtones and Undertones: Reading Film Music*. Berkeley: University of California Press, 1994.

Brown, Tanya. "The Music of 2001." *Vector* 215 (2001): 12–14.

Buch, Esteban. *Beethoven's Ninth: A Political History*. Translated by Richard Miller. Chicago: University of Chicago Press, 1999.

Burgess, Anthony. "Juice from a Clockwork Orange." In *Perspectives on Stanley Kubrick*, edited by Mario Falsetto, 187–90. London: G. K. Hall and Co., 1996.

Burnham, Scott. *Beethoven Hero*. Princeton, NJ: Princeton University Press, 1995.

Carlos, Wendy. *Rediscovering Lost Scores*. http://www.wendycarlos.com/+rls1.html (accessed July 10, 2010).

Castle, Alion. *The Stanley Kubrick Archives*. Cologne: Taschen, 2005.

Chion, Michel. *Audio-vision: Sound on Screen*. Edited and translated by Claudia Gorbman. New York: Columbia University Press, 1994.

——. *Eyes Wide Shut*. Translated by Trista Selous. London: BFI, 2002.

——. *Film, a Sound Art*. Translated by Claudia Gorbman. New York: Columbia University Press, 2009.

——. *Kubrick's Cinema Odyssey*. Translated by Claudia Gorbman. London: BFI, 2001.

Ciment, Michel. *Kubrick: The Definitive Edition*. Translated by Gilbert Adair. Additional material translated by Robert Bononno. New York: Faber and Faber, 2001.

Clendinning, Jane Piper. "The Pattern-Meccanico Compositions of György Ligeti." *Perspectives of New Music* 31, no. 1 (Winter 1993): 192–234.

Cloud, David, and Leslie Zador. "The Missing Score for '2001.'" *Los Angeles Free Press*, November 27, 1970.

Cocks, Geoffrey. *The Wolf at the Door: Kubrick, History, and the Holocaust*. New York: P. Lang, 2004.

Cocks, Geoffrey, James Diedrick, and Glenn Petrusk. *Depth of Field: Stanley Kubrick, Film, and the Uses of History*. Madison: University of Wisconsin Press, 2006.

Code, David. "Rehearing *The Shining*: Musical Undercurrents in the Overlook Hotel." In *Music in the Horror Film: Listening to Fear*, edited by Neil Lerner, 133–51. New York: Routledge, 2010.

Cook, Nicholas. *Analysing Musical Multimedia*. New York: Oxford University Press, 1998.

——. *Beethoven Symphony No. 9*. Cambridge: Cambridge University Press, 1993.

Cusick, Suzanne. "'You are in a place that is out of the world...': Music in the Detention Camps of the 'Global War on Terror.'" *Journal of the Society for American Music* 2, no. 2 (2008): 1–26.

Donnelly, K. J. *Film Music: Critical Approaches*. Edinburgh: Edinburgh University Press, 2001.

——. *The Spectre of Sound: Music in Film and Television*. London: BFI, 2005.

Ebert, Roger. "2001: A Space Odyssey." *Chicago Sun-Times*, March 27, 1997. (accessed June 9, 2012).

Falsetto, Mario. *Stanley Kubrick: A Narrative and Stylistic Analysis*. Westport, CT: Greenwood, 1994.

——. *Perspectives on Stanley Kubrick*. Perspectives on Film. New York: G. K. Hall, 1996.

Frisch, Walter. *Schubert: Critical and Analytical Studies*. Lincoln: University of Nebraska Press, 1986.

Gabbard, Krin. "Redeemed by Ludwig Van: Kubrick's Musical Strategy in *A Clockwork Orange*." In *Cinesonic: Experiencing the Soundtrack*, edited by Philip Brophy, 149–67. North Ryde, Australia: Australian Film Television and Radio School, 2001.

García Mainar, Luis M. *Narrative and Stylistic Patterns in the Films of Stanley Kubrick*. European Studies in American Literature and Culture. Rochester, NY: Camden House, 1999.

Gay, Peter. *Schnitzler's Century: The Making of Middle Class Culture, 1815–1914*. New York: W. W. Norton, 2002.

Gorbman, Claudia. "Ears Wide Open: Kubrick's Music." In *Changing Tunes: The Use of Pre-Existing Music in Film*, edited by Phil Powrie and Robynn Jeananne Stilwell, 3–18. Aldershot, UK: Ashgate, 2006.

——. *Unheard Melodies: Narrative Film Music*. Bloomington: Indiana University Press, 1987.

Griffiths, Paul. *György Ligeti*. London: Robson, 1983.

Hanslick, Eduard. *Vienna's Golden Years of Music: 1850–1900*. Translated and edited by Henry Pleasants. New York: Simon and Schuster, 1950.

Heimerdinger, Julia. *Neue Musik im Spielfilm*. Saarbrücken: Pfau, 2007.

———. " 'I have been compromised. I am now fighting against it': Ligeti vs. Kubrick and the Music for *2001: A Space Odyssey*." *Journal of Film Music* 3, no. 2 (2011): 127–43.

Herr, Michael. *Kubrick*. New York: Grove, 2000.

Hoch, David G. "Mythic Patterns in 2001: A Space Odyssey." *Journal of Popular Culture* 4, no. 4 (Spring 1971): 961–65.

Hubbert, Julie. *Celluloid Symphonies: Texts and Contexts in Film Music History*. Berkeley: University of California Press, 2011.

Huron, David. *Sweet Anticipation: Music and the Psychology of Expectation*. Cambridge, MA: MIT Press, 2006.

Jenkins, Greg. *Stanley Kubrick and the Art of Adaptation: Three Novels, Three Films*. Jefferson, NC: McFarland, 1997.

Jordan, Randolph. "The Mask That Conceals Nothing: On the Concepts of Marital Fidelity and the Lo-Fi Soundscape in *Eyes Wide Shut*." In *Stanley Kubrick: Essays on His Films and Legacy*, edited by Gary D. Rhodes, 159–69. Jefferson, NC: McFarland, 2008.

Kerman, Joseph, et al. "Beethoven, Ludwig van." In *Grove Music Online. Oxford Music Online*, http://www.oxfordmusiconline.com.eres.library.manoa.hawaii.edu/subscriber/article/grove/music/40026pg19 (accessed June 6, 2012).

Kolker, Robert Phillip. *Stanley Kubrick's 2001: A Space Odyssey: New Essays*. New York: Oxford University Press, 2006.

Kreider, Tim. Review of *Eyes Wide Shut*. *Film Quarterly* 53, no. 3 (Spring, 2000): 41–48.

Kubrick, Stanley. "Kubrick Tells What Makes *Clockwork* Tick." Interview by Bernard Weinraub. *New York Times,* January 4, 1972.

Kubrick, Stanley, and Gene D. Phillips. *Stanley Kubrick: Interviews*. Conversations with Filmmakers Series. Jackson: University Press of Mississippi, 2001.

Kulezic-Wilson, Danijela. "Gus Van Sant's Soundwalks and Audio-visual *Musique concrète*." In *Music, Sound and Filmmakers*, edited by James Wierzbicki, 76–88. New York: Routledge, 2012.

Lane, Anthony. "Master of Ceremonies: The Films of Max Ophüls. *New Yorker*, July 8, 2002, http://www.newyorker.com/archive/2002/07/08/020708crat_atlarge (accessed June 29, 2010).

Leppert, Richard. "On Reading Adorno Hearing Schubert." *19th-Century Music* 29, no. 1 (Summer 2005): 56–63.

Levinson, Peter J. *September in the Rain: The Life of Nelson Riddle*. New York: Watson-Guptill, 2001.

Levy, David Benjamin. *Beethoven: The Ninth Symphony*. New Haven, CT: Yale University Press, 2003.

Ligeti, György, Péter Várnai, Josef Hausler, and Claude Samuel. *György Ligeti in Conversation with Péter Várnai, Josef Hausler, Claude Samuel and Himself*. London: Ernst Eulenberg, 1983.

Lionnet, Leonard. "Point Counter Point: Interactions between Pre-existing Music and Narrative Structure in Stanley Kubrick's *The Shining*." DMA diss., City University of New York, 2003.

LoBrutto, Vincent. *Stanley Kubrick: A Biography*. New York: Donald I. Fine, 1997.

McClary, Susan. "Getting Down Off the Beanstalk: The Presence of a Woman's Voice in Janika Vandervelde's *Genesis II*." In *Feminine Endings*, 2nd ed., 112–31. Minneapolis: University of Minnesota Press, 2002.

McDougal, Stuart Y. *Stanley Kubrick's "A Clockwork Orange."* Cambridge: Cambridge University Press, 2003.

McKee, Eric. *Decorum of the Minuet, Delirium of the Waltz: A Study of Dance-Music Relations in ¾ Time*. Bloomington: Indiana University Press, 2011.

McQuiston, Kate. "'An Effort to Decide': More Research into Kubrick's Music Choices for *2001: A Space Odyssey*." *Journal of Film Music* 3, no. 2 (2011): 145–54.

———. "Recognizing Music in the Films of Stanley Kubrick." PhD diss., Columbia University, 2005.

———. "The Stanley Kubrick Experience: Music, Nuclear Bombs, Disorientation and You." In *Music, Sound and Filmmakers: Sonic Style in Cinema*, edited by James Wierzbicki, 138–50. New York: Routledge, 2012.

Merkley, Paul. "'Stanley Hates This But I Like It!': North vs. Kubrick on the Music for *2001: A Space Odyssey*." *Journal of Film Music* 2, no. 1 (Fall 2007): 1–34.

Michelson, Annette. "Bodies in Space: Film as 'Carnal Knowledge,'" *Artforum* 7, no. 6 (February 1969): 53–63.

Mullen, Elizabeth. "Do You Speak Kubrick?: Orchestrating Transgression and Mastering Malaise in *The Shining*." *Image [&] Narrative* (e-journal) 10, issue 2 (2009): (accessed May 26, 2012).

Müller, Martina. "Vom Souffleurkasten uber das Mikro auf die Leinwand: Max *Ophüls* ." *Frauen und Film* 42 (August 1987): 60–71.

Nabokov, Vladimir. *Lolita: A Screenplay*. New York: Random House, 1974.

Naremore, James. *On Kubrick*. London: BFI, 2007.

Nelson, Thomas Allen. "Barry Lyndon: Kubrick's Cinema of Disparity." *Rocky Mountain Review of Language and Literature* 33, no. 1 (Winter 1979): 39–51.

———. *Kubrick: Inside a Film Artist's Maze*. New and expanded ed. Bloomington: Indiana University Press, 2000.

Patterson, David W. "Music, Structure and Metaphor in Stanley Kubrick's '2001: A Space Odyssey.'" *American Music* 22, no. 3 (2004): 444–71.

Phillips, Gene. *Stanley Kubrick: Interviews*. Conversations with Filmmakers Series. Jackson: University Press of Mississippi, 2001.

Powrie, Phil, and Robynn Jeananne Stilwell. *Changing Tunes: The Use of Pre-Existing Music in Film*. Aldershot, UK: Ashgate, 2006.

Rabinowitz, Peter J. "'A Bird of Like Rarest Spun Heavenmetal': Music in 'A Clockwork Orange.'" In *Stanley Kubrick's "A Clockwork Orange,"* edited by Stuart McDougal, 109–30. Cambridge: Cambridge University Press, 2003.

Rafter, Nicole. *Shots in the Mirror: Crime Films and Society*. New York: Oxford University Press, 2000.

Rasmussen, Randy. *Stanley Kubrick: Seven Films Analyzed* Jefferson, NC: McFarland, 2001.

Rhodes, Gary D. *Stanley Kubrick: Essays on His Films and Legacy*. Jefferson, NC: McFarland, 2008.

Romney, Jonathan, and Adrian Wootton. *Celluloid Jukebox: Popular Music and the Movies since the 50s*. London: BFI, 1995.

Rosen, Charles. "Schubert and the Example of Mozart." In *Schubert the Progressive: History, Performance Practice, Analysis*, edited by Brian Newbould, 1–20. Aldershot, UK: Ashgate, 2003.

Said, Edward. *On Late Style: Music and Literature against the Grain*. New York: Pantheon, 2006.

Sano, Stephen. "The *'Chorwalzer'* of Johann Strauss, Jr.: *'An der schonen blauen Donau'* Revisited." DMA thesis, Stanford University, 1994.

Sarris, Andrew. "Eyes Don't Have it: Kubrick's Turgid Finale." *New York Observer* online, July 25, 1999, http://observer.com/1999/07/26/eyes-dont-have-it-kubricks-turgid-finale/ (accessed May 15, 2012).

Scheurer, Timothy. "The Score for 2001: A Space Odyssey." *Journal of Popular Film and Television* 5, no. 4 (1998): 172–83.

Schwinger, Wolfram. *Krzysztof Penderecki: His Life and Work*. Translated by William Mann. London: Schott & Co., 1989.

Scott, A. O. "Critics' Picks: 'Lolita.' " *New York Times* online, July 26, 2010, (accessed July 13, 2012).

Steinitz, Richard. *György Ligeti: Music of the Imagination*. London: Faber, 2003.

Stilwell, Robynn J. "Hysterical Beethoven." *Beethoven Forum* 10, no. 2 (2003): 162–82.

———. "Music in Films: A Critical Review of Literature, 1980–1996." *Journal of Film Music* 1, no. 1 (2002): 46–47.

Straus, Joseph N. "Disability and 'Late Style' in Music." *Journal of Musicology* 25, no. 1 (Winter 2008): 3–45.

Sullivan, Jack. *Hitchcock's Music*. New Haven, CT: Yale University Press, 2006.

Walker, Alexander. *Stanley Kubrick: Director*. Visual analysis by Sybil Taylor and Ulrich Ruchti. Revised and expanded. New York: W. W. Norton and Co., 1999.

Webster, James. "The Form of the Finale of Beethoven's Ninth Symphony." *Beethoven Forum* 1 (1992): 25–62.

Wechsberg, Joseph. *The Waltz Emperors*. New York: G. P. Putnam's Sons, 1973.

White, Susan. *The Cinema of Max Ophuls: Magisterial Vision and the Figure of Woman*. New York: Columbia University Press, 1995.

———. "Male Bonding, Hollywood Orientalism, and the Repression of the Feminine in Kubrick's *Full Metal Jacket*." In *Inventing Vietnam: The War in Film and Television*, edited by Michael Anderegg, 204–30. Culture and the Moving Image series. Philadelphia: Temple University Press, 1991.

Wierzbicki, James. "Banality Triumphant: Iconographic Use of Beethoven's Ninth Symphony in Recent Films." *Beethoven Forum* 10, no. 2 (2003): 113–38.

Williams, Alan Larson. *Max Ophuls and the Cinema of Desire: Style and Spectacle in Four Films, 1948–1955*. Dissertations on Film. New York: Arno, 1980.

Williamson, John. *Strauss: Also sprach Zarathustra*. Cambridge: Cambridge University Press, 1993.

Yaraman, Sevin. *Revolving Embrace: The Waltz as Sex, Steps, and Sound*. Monographs in Musicology 12. Hillsdale, NY: Pendragon, 2002.

Youmans, Charles. "The Private Intellectual Context of Richard Strauss's *Also sprach Zarathustra*." *19th-Century Music* 22, no. 2 (1998): 101–26.

Yuzefovich, Victor. *Aram Khachaturyan*. Translated by Nicholas Kournokoff and Vladimir Bobrov. New York: Sphinx, 1985.

Index